Astrology Yoga

Astrology Yoga

Cosmic Cycles of Transformation

Mehtab Benton

Bookshelf Press

Astrology Yoga: Cosmic Cycles of Transformation
Copyright © 2013 by Michael Benton

All rights reserved. No part of this book may be used or reproduced by any means, graphic, electronic, or mechanical, including photocopying, recording, taping or by any information storage system without the written permission of the publisher except in the case of brief quotations embodied in critical articles and reviews.

Foreign publication rights available from the publisher.

Bookshelf Press books may be ordered through booksellers or by contacting:

Bookshelf Press
PO Box 50028
Austin, TX 78763
www.bookshelfpress.com
orders@bookshelfpress.com

You should not undertake any exercise or therapeutic regimen recommended in this book before consulting your personal physician. Neither the author nor the publisher shall be responsible or liable for any loss or damage allegedly arising as a consequence of your use or application of any information or suggestions contained in this book.

The author gratefully acknowledges the guidance and teachings of Yogi Bhajan and the faculty of the American College of Vedic Astrology. Cover and interior art by Brandi November Lyons (Hari Avtar at JupDesigns.com). Thanks also to MaryBeth Kenis (editorial assistance), Liz Nichols (web design), and Lori Satter (Cosmic Assistant).

ISBN: 978-1-939239-08-2 (hc)

Library of Congress Control Number: 2013909056

CONTENTS

Preface
    What Is Astrology Yoga? • i
    How to Use This Book • ii

1 The Relationship Between Yoga and Astrology • 1
    Misunderstandings About Astrology • 3
    Eastern Astrology Versus Western Astrology • 5
    The Language of Vedic Astrology • 7
    The Nine Planets (Grahas) of Astrology Yoga • 8
        The Sun (Surya): Light of the Soul
        The Moon (Chandra): Light of the Mind
        Mars (Mangala): The Spiritual Warrior
        Mercury (Budha): The Scholar
        Jupiter (Guru): The Teacher
        Venus (Shukra): The Divine Lover
        Saturn (Shani): The Yogi
        Rahu: The Doer and Future Karma
        Ketu: The Renunciate and Past Karma
    The Twelve Signs (Rashis) of Astrology Yoga • 28
        Aries (Mesha): Initiating Energy and Being
        Taurus (Vrishabha): Creative Potential and Manifestation
        Gemini (Mithuna): Changing Polarity and Duality
        Cancer (Kattaka): Reflective Expansion and Sensitivity
        Leo (Simha): Radiant Being and Self
        Virgo (Kanya): Divine Discontent and Integration
        Libra (Tula): Harmonious Equilibrium and Balance
        Scorpio (Vrishchika): Mystical Knowledge and Secrets
        Sagittarius (Dhanus): Purposeful Living and Knowledge
        Capricorn (Makara): Material Spiritualism and Structure
        Aquarius (Kumbha): Group Consciousness and Service
        Pisces (Meena): Universal Consciousness and Merger

The Twelve Houses (Bhavas) of Astrology Yoga • 38
>
> First House (Thanu Bhava): Incarnated Self
> Second House (Dhana Bhava): Innate Gifts
> Third House (Sahaja Bhava): Courageous Expression
> Fourth House (Sukha Bhava): Foundations of Consciousness
> Fifth House (Putra Bhava): Creative Consciousness
> Sixth House (Roga Bhava): Unlimited Spirit
> Seventh House (Kalatra Bhava): Self and Soul Mate
> Eighth House (Mrityu Bhava): Transformation and Rebirth
> Ninth House (Dharma Bhava): Truth and Purpose
> Tenth House (Karma Bhava): Self-Manifestation
> Eleventh House (Labha Bhava): Spiritual Fulfillment
> Twelfth House (Vyaya Bhava): Meditation and Liberation

2 Astrology, Yogic Anatomy, and Philosophy • 45

The Three Gunas • 45

The Five Bhutas • 46

The Eight Limbs of Yoga • 47
> Yamas – The Restrictions of Saturn
> Niyamas – The Dharma of Jupiter
> Asana – The Physicality of Mars
> Pranayama – The Movement of Mercury
> Pratyahara – The Negation of Ketu
> Dharana – The Focus of the Sun
> Dhyana – The Reflection of the Moon
> Samadhi – The Union of Venus

The Three Bodies of Yoga • 51
> Physical Body (Sthula Shaira)
> Subtle Body (Sukshma Shaira)
> Causal Body (Karana Shaira)

The Three Major Nadis • 53

The Five Sheaths of Existence • 54

The Seven Chakras • 56

3 Your Astrology Yoga Profile • 63

The Birth Chart: Signs, Planets and Houses • 63
Your Yoga Sun Sign • 64
The Aries Yogi
The Taurus Yogi
The Gemini Yogi
The Cancer Yogi
The Leo Yogi
The Virgo Yogi
The Libra Yogi
The Scorpio Yogi
The Sagittarius Yogi
The Capricorn Yogi
The Aquarius Yogi
The Pisces Yogi

Your Yoga Moon Sign • 77
Your Rising Sign • 81
Your Birth Day Planet • 86
Your Yoga Star Sign • 90
Your Karmic Planets: Rahu and Ketu • 107

4 Astrology Yoga Techniques • 123

Planetary Postures: Asanas of Astrology Yoga • 124
Planetary Pranayamas: Breathwork and the Planets • 139
Planetary Mudras: Astrology Yoga in Your Hands • 145
Planetary Mantras: Celestial Sounds of Power • 155
Planetary Meditations: Mastering Time and Space • 162
Sun Meditations
Moon Meditations
Mars Meditations
Mercury Meditations
Jupiter Meditations
Venus Meditations
Saturn Meditations
Rahu Meditations
Ketu Meditations

5 Your Astrological Life Cycles and Periods • 185

Your Planetary Periods (Dasas) • 185

Your Planetary Cycles • 190
- Your Sun Cycle
- Your Jupiter Cycle
- Your Saturn Cycle
- Your Cycles of Karma: Rahu and Ketu

Cosmic Cycles for Everyone • 196
- Planetary Practices for the Days of the Week
- Planetary Practices for the Hours of the Day
- Planetary Practices for the Moon Cycle
- Days of the Month: Tithis of the Moon
- New Moon and Full Moon days
- The Moon Nakshatras: The Secrets of Vedic Astrology
- Planetary Practices for the Sun Cycle
- Solstices and Equinoxes
- Eclipses

6 Practicing and Teaching Astrology Yoga • 224

Working with the Planetary Energies • 225

Astrology Yoga and Therapeutics • 226
- Planetary Illnesses and Diseases
- Planetary Unfavorable Expressions
- Planetary Problems with People

Working with the Daily Cycles • 230
- Working with the Moon Cycles
- Other Daily Considerations

Designing Yoga Classes and Practices • 232

Working with the Larger Cycles of Time • 233

The Future of Astrology Yoga • 235

Illustrations and Tables

Illustrations

Sun Salutations • 133
Moon Salutations • 135
Basic Planetary Mudras • 149
Mudra Modes • 151
The Navagraha Mudras • 153
Meditation for the Sun • 163
Meditation for the Moon • 165
Meditation for Mars • 167
Meditation for Mercury • 169
Meditation for Jupiter • 171
Meditation for Venus • 173
Meditation for Saturn • 175
Meditation for Rahu • 177
Meditation for Ketu • 179
Meditation to Correct the Pattern of the Birth Chart • 181

Tables

1-1	Nine Planets (Grahas) Sanskrit Names and Characteristics • 9	
1-2	Twelve Signs (Rashis) and Their Qualities • 29	
1-3	Astrological Signs: Element and Nature • 30	
1-4	Planetary Strengths and Weakness by Astrological Signs • 32	
1-5	Astrological Signs and Their Planetary Rulers • 37	
1-6	Life Goals (Purusharthas) of the Astrological Houses • 42	
2-1	Chakra Locations and Keywords • 56	
2-2	Chakras and Planetary Correspondences • 57	
2-3	Chakras and Sign Correspondences with Ruling Planets • 58	
2-4	Planets and Their Exalted and Debilitated Signs • 59	
2-5	Planets Associated with the Chakras by Exalted Signs • 59	
2-6	Planets Associated with the Chakras by Debilitated Signs • 60	
2-7	Planets to Strengthen to Balance the Chakras • 62	

Tables

3-1	Your Birth Year Group (A to N) • 87	
3-2	Your Birth Month Group (A to N) • 88	
3-3	Birth Day Types and Yoga Practices • 89	
3-4	The 27 Nakshatras: Zodiac Degrees and Sun Nakshatra • 91	
3-5	Signs for Rahu and Ketu Based on Birthdate • 108-111	
3-6	Astrological Profile Worksheet • 122	
4-1	Areas of the Body and Astrological Associations • 127	
4-2	Qualities of the Moon and Sun Postures • 131	
4-3	Categories of the Moon and Sun Postures • 131	
4-4	Attributes of the Moon and Sun Breath • 141	
4-5	Moon and Sun Qualities of the Major Pranayamas • 142	
4-6	Planetary Name Mantras • 155	
4-7	Planetary Bija (Seed) Mantras • 156	
4-8	Planetary Shakti (Power) Mantras • 157	
4-9	Days and Times for Planetary Mantras • 158	
4-10	Mala Gems and Stones With Planetary Mantras • 158	
4-11	Chakra Bij Mantras and Planetary Energies • 161	
4-12	Meditation Planets and Practices for the Rising Sign • 184	
5-1	Length and Sequence of the Planetary Periods (Dasas) • 186	
5-2	Planetary Maturity and Ages • 189	
5-3	Sade Sati Periods for the Natal Moon Sign • 189	
5-4	Planets Associated with the Days of the Week • 197	
5-5	Planets Associated with the Hour of the Day • 204	
5-6	The 30 Tithis of the Moon Cycle • 207	
5-7	Monthly Sun Cycles and Signs of the Zodiac • 219	
5-8	Monthly Sun Cycles and Yoga Practices • 220	
6-1	Weak and Challenged Signs for the Planets • 226	
6-2	Illnesses and Conditions Associated with the Planets • 227	
6-3	Unfavorable Expressions Associated with the Planets • 228	
6-4	Difficult Relationships Associated with the Planets • 229	

Preface

What Is Astrology Yoga?

Yoga and astrology are the oldest knowledge systems developed by the human mind and they show up universally throughout all cultures. Yet it is in the Vedas, or the ancient wisdom of India, that yoga and astrology have enjoyed their most intimate and sophisticated association.

Both were practiced side by side by the ancient seers or rishis of India. To practice yoga without astrology or astrology without yoga was simply incomprehensible to the masters of Vedic thought. To be a great astrologer, one needed to be a good yogi and to progress along the path of yoga, one needed to be an astrologer.

Through astrology we understand the journey of the soul, what karmas it has endured in past lives and which karmas may be encountered in this life. Astrology not only reveals our karmic DNA, it provides the necessary insight to master our destiny and fulfill our greatest potential.

Through yoga we practice the techniques to master the mind, heal the body and live optimally within the cycles of time. Yoga is the technology to manage the change that time brings us and to develop our potentials to meet the challenges an incarnated soul must overcome to reach its ultimate destination of bliss, union and transcendence.

The astrology described in this book may be different than what the Western mind is familiar with. It is more properly called Vedic Astrology, or Jyotish, the Sanskrit term for the science of light. If you are a Western astrologer, or if your knowledge of astrology is limited to knowing what your Sun sign is, this book will give you the foundation to apply Eastern astrology, Vedic astrology, to your practice and teaching of yoga.

The yoga in this book, conversely, is a subset of what the Eastern mind appreciates as yoga. It is more properly called Hatha or Kundalini Yoga, and focuses on the techniques of yoga as commonly practiced in the Western world.

Astrology Yoga brings these two most revered Vedic sciences and teachings together, as they originally complemented each other, to guide us on our spiritual journey through the cosmic cycles of transformation.

How To Use This Book

This book may be enjoyed as an intellectual experience in understanding the connections between astrology and yoga as originally practiced in India, as well as a guide to understanding your astrological makeup as it applies to your practice of yoga.

You will likely need to read the entire book, and then eventually go deeper into understanding your astrological makeup through a personal reading by an astrologer, getting your birth chart done, or researching and reading more about Vedic astrology on your own. Ideally, you will at some point have access to your birth chart to allow you to explore the many possibilities of applying astrology to your yoga practice and teaching.

You can, however, begin to use immediately the many practical suggestions and readily applied information in this book. You do not need to be an astrologer, or indeed, a yoga student or teacher, to gain a deeper understanding of your soul's purpose and journey as you read this book.

There are the six sections in this book:

- The Relationship Between Astrology and Yoga
- Astrology, Yogic Anatomy and Philosophy
- Astrology Yoga Techniques
- Your Astrological Profile
- Your Astrological Life Cycles and Periods
- Practicing and Teaching Astrology Yoga

These sections describe the fundamentals of astrology (planets, signs, houses), yoga philosophy and yogic anatomy (chakras, nadis, gunas, the sutras), the major yoga techniques to balance your planetary energies (asana, mantra, pranayama, meditation and mudra), the different aspects of your personal astrological makeup (sun signs, moon signs, and significant planets), the cycles of time that inform and shape your yoga practice and life journey (daily, weekly, and yearly), and how to create and enjoy more rewarding yoga practices through an appreciation of astrology.

No single book can reveal all the complexities and mysteries of how astrology and yoga work together. After all, these two ancient knowledge systems have been developed, investigated and elaborated by countless masters of both. What this book hopes to accomplish is to give the Western student an appreciation of how astrology and yoga can be used together to accelerate an individual's spiritual journey by applying the fundamental teachings of both.

"A child is born on that day and at that hour when the celestial rays are in mathematical harmony with his individual karma."

Yukteswar Giri
Autobiography of a Yogi

The Relationship Between Yoga and Astrology

"With great respect and love,
the teachings of Yoga instruction are now offered."
Maharisha Patanjali, Yoga Sutras

"I give you the teachings of Astrology which bring good
to those who are peacefully disposed and speak the truth."
Mararisha Parasara, Brihat Parasara Hora Sastra

Our eternal essence is timeless and formless. Yet when we incarnate, we become subject to the laws of time and space, and the soul temporarily forgets its true Self.

Yoga, the original technology of transformation, gives us the means to take care of the bodily form that comes from living in space. Jyotish, the science of astrology from ancient India, instructs us how to navigate the cycles of time we must now understand. Working together, both astrology and yoga allow us to remember our nature and return to our origin.

Our happiness in life, our health, our accomplishments, and our relationships, all depend upon our vitality, our spiritual intent and our karmic actions.

Yoga is the way to insure we remain healthy in body, mind, and spirit so we can successfully travel this path to enlightenment.

Yet without understanding the nature of our innate self and our soul's purpose, the timing and type of our yoga practices may be inappropriate, and the actions we take may be ineffective.

This is the role of Astrology in the practice of Yoga. To understand our basic nature and our life purpose, to realize the gifts and challenges we bring into this journey, and to align ourselves with the cosmic cycles of time to help us move forward.

Yoga and Astrology, as practiced and originated from India, come from the same spiritual source of the Vedic teachings as discovered by the Rishis in their profound meditative and mystical states of super-consciousness.

Both Yoga and Vedic Astrology, or Jyotish, share the same purpose: To enable practitioners to advance in their spiritual evolution and to gain the self-knowledge that leads to liberation.

Whereas Yoga is a technology that relies on personal experience and the employment of techniques, Astrology is a science that relies on observation and interpretation of cosmic laws.

On the spiritual journey, Yoga provides the seeker with the answers to "How" and "What" while Astrology reveals "When" and "Why."

Yoga provides the tools of asana, pranayama, mudra, mantra and meditation and teaches us how to use them. Astrology allows us to understand the karma and the dharma that brought us into this existence and how to interact with our past, present and future.

The great Vedic astrologers, or Jyotishis, used yoga to facilitate the changes in the soul's journey through time and to remedy the challenging cosmic conditions brought about by birth and the natural unfolding of life. Yoga provides the astrologer with the tools to help facilitate the changes brought about by the planetary cycles, as well as techniques to remedy the challenges and to expand the opportunities shown in the birth chart.

The great Yogis used astrology as a method to determine the most effective yoga practices for an individual according to their karmic conditions and how to adapt the practices to the cycles of time. Astrology provides the Yogi with a method to understand and appreciate the unique challenges and opportunities that the cycles of time bring us, as well as providing the yoga practitioner and teacher with a diagnostic tool to determine the most effective practices. More importantly, astrology can reveal the karmic issues to be addressed through the yoga practice.

> "By the practice of all the components of yoga,
> Impurities dwindle away
> And wisdom's radiant light shines forth
> With discriminative knowledge."
>
> Yoga Sutras (II, 28)

Misunderstandings About Astrology

Several misconceptions about astrology are prevalent in the Western world. Many people see astrology as a way to understand and categorize different personality types or to explain someone's psychology or to justify their own actions. Sometimes astrology is seen as fortune telling or a predictive game to tell us when we will get married or become rich. Others reject astrology because it is misinterpreted as a fatalistic approach to life, that the planets are making us do something beyond our will.

In reality, Vedic astrology, or Jyotish, in its original form helps us comprehend our karma and to discover the tendencies of thought and behavior rooted in the subconscious mind that create mental attitudes which prevent us from seeing the truth about ourselves and the world.

Understanding our past conditioning and karmas which keep us locked into repetitive and reactive patterns is the first step to changing our lives and reaching our highest evolution. Rather than being a fatalistic or predictive science, Vedic astrology is a sophisticated tool by which we can understand and master our karmas. There are four types of karma each individual is subject to.

Sanchita Karma

The first is the past collective actions and karmas of the soul that create our destiny or our fate. This karma is called sanchita and it is unchangeable. Sanchita karma is what causes the soul to incarnate into this existence in order to learn the lessons it must understand to become liberated. The sanchita karmas give us our basic nature and temperament, and while we can improve or realize the gifts of this basic nature, it is fixed and what we must work with in this lifetime. This karma can be seen from the birth chart and the soul chooses the time and place to be born in order to have the most appropriate incarnation to work through this karma.

Prarabdha Karma

The second type of karma, like sanchita karma, is also fixed and inescapable. This karma is called prarabdha karma and it is the lessons we are ready to experience and work through in this lifetime. For example, the soul may have a need to experience having children in this lifetime and so this will happen regardless of the present desire a person may have around that issue. Astrology can anticipate the lessons that prarabdha karmas bring us, such as the need to form a particular life relationship or to undergo and overcome illnesses.

Kriyamaya Karma

The third type of karma is created by our current actions in this life and is subject to our freewill. This karma is called kriyamaya karma and it is through understanding our destiny and following our dharma, or life's purpose, that we can successfully interact with this type of karma. Astrology can help us see, for example, that if our path is to be a teacher, then how can we teach and behave in such a manner that we fulfill our life's purpose and move toward liberation. Taking the right action at the right time is one of the main benefits of understanding astrology so that we can execute our kriyamaya karmas to the best of our abilities.

Agama Karma

The fourth type of karma is created by our contemplation of future actions in this life and is also subject to our freewill. This karma is called agama karma and it is most successfully dealt with through meditation and envisioning who we need to become. Astrology allows us to discover our innate gifts and hidden potentials that are part of fulfilling the agama karmas. One can see from the birth chart if a person's destiny, for example, is connected to foreign lands and peoples, or to healing and service. This understanding of the agama karmas can be one of the most powerful uses of astrology as it allows us to understand and then re-create ourselves to realize the fullest potential of this lifetime.

So, far from being fatalistic or predictive, Vedic or Astrology Yoga is revealing and indicative of the karmas we have. The knowledge gained allows us to recognize and understand the karmic patterns that inform our lives, and to work with our gifts to overcome our challenges and express our potentials at the highest level.

And this is where yoga comes in. Once we understand the curriculum for this lifetime that comes from our karmas and which was seeded at the moment and place of our birth, we can direct our awareness and elevate our consciousness through the practice of yoga to fulfill our purpose and achieve liberation from suffering and the illusory cycle of life and death.

Astrology reveals the purpose of this life and yoga gives us the caliber to achieve it.

> "Great is the person who, free from attachment, and with a mind
> Ruling its powers in harmony, works on the path of
> Karma Yoga, the path of consecrated action."
>
> Bhagavad Gita (3,7)

Eastern Astrology Versus Western Astrology

Astrology is the world's oldest science and has appeared in nearly every culture. There are differences in all these systems, yet they all share the common characteristics of using the movement and position of the planets to understand the cosmic cycles that shape our individual and collective lives.

The movements of the Sun and Moon were the most readily observable and significant planets (or more appropriately named, the luminaries) and form the basis of our astrological understanding. In some cultures, like the Babylonians and Greeks, the Sun was considered the prime mover and active force and so Western astrology became a solar-based system with the twelve signs of the zodiac based upon the sun's movements on a yearly basis. In many eastern cultures, such as China and India, the Moon was the primary force in developing astrology and so we have lunar-based systems based upon the movement and phases of the moon on a monthly basis.

While Vedic or Indian or Yoga astrology is based heavily upon the moon cycles and what could be termed the moon signs or star signs (nakshatras), it does borrow from the Western system of the twelve zodiac signs and is better termed a soli-lunar system. Regardless of definition, eastern astrology gives us another powerful set of tools for discovery and understanding with its emphasis on the lunar side of the cosmos.

Perhaps the most obvious difference between Western and Eastern astrology is that people often see their Sun signs change between the two systems. Western Libras become Eastern Virgos, Leos become Cancers, and so forth as many of the planetary positions at the time of birth are adjusted backwards from their Western sign positions by about 23 degrees.

The reason for this difference in sign position is that Eastern Astrology system uses the actual positions of the planets as they currently appear in the zodiac whereas Western Astrology adjusts the planetary positions in order to maintain a consistent correspondence to the procession of the equinoxes. In other words, the Eastern system reflects the true placement of the planets in the zodiac signs. Both systems, however, do give similar characteristics to the signs.

This does not discount the value or authenticity of Western astrology. Both systems are valid in the context of their own paradigms and interpretations. Eastern or Vedic astrology (or Jyotish), however, does reflect yogic philosophy and, in the author's opinion, gives the most accurate results when working with both yoga and astrology together. In this book, the Vedic or Astrology Yoga system is used exclusively and using the Western system will not give the same results.

Another obvious difference between modern Western astrology and ancient Eastern or Vedic astrology is in the planets. Like medieval Western astrology, Vedic astrology only uses the Sun, Moon and the five visible planets – Mercury, Venus, Mars, Jupiter and Saturn. The outer planets, Uranus, Neptune, and Pluto, are not used in the classical system of Vedic astrology.

Vedic astrology, however, does offer two additional "planets" called Rahu and Ketu that are profoundly important in understanding the karmic foundations of our life. Rahu corresponds to the North Node of the moon in Western astrology, whereas Ketu corresponds to the South Node. Both are ecliptic points – that is, points in the zodiac where the solar and lunar eclipses occur in your astrological chart.

For those familiar with Western astrology, the aspects, or relationships, between the planets are also different in Vedic astrology, although the basic natures of the planets remain essentially the same.

Vedic astrology, or Astrology Yoga, is also useful in understanding the different areas of life by using what are called divisional or harmonic charts that are based on the individual birth chart. These charts can allow us to understand the past karma and lives of an individual as well as their future spiritual life, or indeed the next life.

Along with these additional charts, Vedic astrology emphasizes the various planetary periods an individual may be experiencing that will affect all areas of their lives. These particular periods may last from 6 to 20 years and are helpful in understanding the specific changes, challenges and opportunities that come to us on our spiritual and life journey. For example, there is a 7-year period in everyone's life (called the Ketu period or dasa) that often signifies a deep spiritual awakening.

While there are other differences between Western and Eastern astrology, everything in this book is discussed in the context of the practice of yoga. Regardless of your knowledge, or lack thereof, of either of these two systems of astrology, you will gain valuable insights into how you can work with your own astrological energies and cycles of time through the technology of yoga.

The Language of Vedic Astrology

Like yoga, Vedic astrology is a system that requires lifelong study to master. Yet we can understand the basics of astrology by examining its three major components: signs (rashis), planets (grahas), and houses (bhavas).

The astrological signs are the best known. Most people can tell you if they are an "Aries," a "Pisces," or a "Scorpio" or one of the twelve signs by simply knowing the day of the month they were born. In this case, they are using the information of which zodiac sign the sun was positioned in at the time of their birth.

The planets in astrology are less well understood by the average person who may believe that the only important planet is the sun, as in the above example. In reality, there are nine planets in Vedic astrology that make up the language we use to describe a person and their yoga practices.

The houses are the least known but help us understand how the planets and signs affect our individual lives and our specific approaches to spirituality. The term "houses" is used because every planet occupies a certain place in the zodiac, much like we occupy a house. The houses are the twelve areas of life that contain all of the information about our relationships, our career, our family, our spiritual practices, our health, our obstacles and our gifts. Indeed, any question or concern can be understood if we know the nature of the houses.

Think of the planets as actors in your cosmic play. Each planet has a basic function or role to fulfill. The sign it is located in influences how the planet performs. For example, one of the roles of the Sun is to represent the authority figure in your life. If the Sun is located in the sign of Leo, it may perform its authority in a regal or royal manner, like a powerful leader. If the Sun is in Cancer, then it may represent a nurturing authority figure, like a strong mother.

The house it is located in determines where the planet performs in our lives. In our previous example, if the Sun were located in the tenth house, which is associated with career, the Sun would perform its role of authority as a boss.

Each of the nine planets can be in any of the 12 signs as well as in any of the 12 houses, so we start with 1,296 possible combinations in a birth chart. And since there are many, many more mitigating and influencing factors in a birth chart, there are millions of astrological possibilities, which make astrology an incredibly rich and complex science.

But it all begins with the planets, signs and houses, so let's start there.

The Nine Planets (Grahas) of Astrology Yoga

Vedic astrology, or Jyotish, which is the basis for Astrology Yoga, recognizes nine planets or more accurately, the nine grahas. In reality, there are only five actual planets, as defined scientifically, in Vedic astrology: Mercury, Venus, Mars, Jupiter and Saturn. These are the five planets that are visible to the eye.

The outer planets used in Western astrology (Uranus, Neptune and Pluto) are not part of Vedic astrology or Astrology Yoga. The visible planets affect the affairs of the individual soul while the outer planets are considered to be more indicative of cultural or generational change. And since the outer planets are not "visible" to natural human sight, they play no visible role in the individual human's life.

The Sun and Moon are part of the planetary configuration of Vedic astrology, representing the two luminaries, although not technically planets by definition.

The remaining two planets, Rahu and Ketu, have no physical form but exert a powerful influence in the life of every soul. These two planets are points where eclipses occur. In effect, they are actually shadows that obscure the other planets, and are referred to as the Chaya Grahas, or the shadow planets. In Western astrology Rahu and Ketu are associated with the north node and the south node of the moon respectively.

The term graha used for these nine celestial bodies is revealing because the Sanskrit word itself means to "seize, grab, or hold." The nine planets, the nine grahas, basically grab everything. All things in this creation, including human beings, are under the influence of the graha that seizes or holds them in its influence.

For example, a warrior's sword is "grabbed" by Mars as its deserved possession. Venus would grab a flower, the Sun would grab a temple, and the Moon grabs the mother, and so on until everything is ultimately associated with one of these nine grahas or planets. An individual may be under the primary influence of the Sun, or Mars, or any of the planets or grahas, depending upon their birth chart. For example, an individual may be primarily under the influence of Mercury, or is "seized" by Mercury. Such a person would exhibit Mercurial qualities of clever speech, sharp mind, wit, facility for languages and writing, and quick movements.

The nine planets provide a gigantic paradigm to allocate or categorize everything as being under the domain of one of these grahas, and this gives us a powerful language in understanding how astrology works.

To understand Astrology Yoga is to appreciate that everything in the practice of yoga can also be related back to one or more of the planetary energies, and that the planets individually or collectively influence all the specific techniques and styles in yoga.

For example, certain yoga postures are Sun postures (sun salutations), while others are Moon postures (child pose), or Mars postures (warrior pose). Similarly, the nine planets also influence the various pranayama techniques, mudras, mantras and meditations.

The more we understand the basic nature of each of the planets, or grahas, and what they represent and signify in our lives and yoga practices, the more we can consciously align with these energies to transform our consciousness.

The following table illustrates how the different planets possess a wide variety of traits and qualities. There are many more ways to differentiate the nine planets, and this table hints at the myriad ways the planets may be categorized.

Planet	Sanskrit	Sex	Quality	Color	Element	Behaviour
Sun	Surya	M	Sattva	Red, Orange	Fire	Firm
Moon	Chandra	F	Sattva	Opaque White	Water	Changeable
Mars	Mangala	M	Tamas	Bright Red	Fire	Fierce
Mercury	Budha	N	Rajas	Green	Earth	Mixed
Jupiter	Guru	M	Sattva	Yellow	Ether	Benevolent
Venus	Shukra	F	Rajas	Clear White	Water	Easy
Saturn	Shani	N	Tamas	Blue, Black	Air	Harsh
Rahu	Rahu	F	Tamas	Black, Smoky	Air	Ambitious
Ketu	Ketu	N	Tamas	Variegated	Fire	Unusual

Table 1-1: Nine Planets (Grahas): Sanskrit Names and Characteristics

Now let's look at the nine planets in more detail, examining these characteristics and other attributes as they relate to the practice of yoga and the understanding of our lives.

The Sun (Surya): Light of the Soul

While the Sun is known by many names in Sanskrit, it is most commonly called Surya. The Sun represents our health, vitality, ego, self, individuality and soul. It is the king, the father, the authority figure, the government, the boss, and sometimes the teacher.

In the realm of yoga, the Sun is intimately associated with the Soul or Atma. The Atma is the universal soul and so the Sun represents our eternal unchanging nature and the light of our soul (jivatma).

The Sun in yoga also corresponds to the Causal Body (or Karana Sharira). The Causal body is the indestructible nature of the individual that exists beyond the cycles of life and death. It is the inner light of consciousness. In short, the Sun in our birth chart signifies our divinity and our purpose in life (dharma) and as such plays a most important role in shaping our spiritual life.

The yogic quality (guna) of the Sun is purity (sattva). Its Ayurvedic nature (dosha) is pitta (fiery). Among the five levels of existence (koshas) of yoga, the Sun is identified with the realm of bliss and union (anandamaya kosha). The element (bhuta) of the Sun is fire (agni). The type of yoga most identified with the Sun is Raja Yoga.

What the Sun Teaches Us

The Sun helps us learn to relate to power, position and authority in a correct or dharmic manner. Respecting the father, or father figures, and elders, as well as healing the relationship with them is what the Sun wishes to teach.

Ultimately, the Sun is about working out issues with the ego so we can understand who we truly are. The life lesson of the Sun is to create an authentic relationship with the eternal nature of the Soul.

When the Sun Is Weak

When the Sun energy is not fully expressed in your life and your yoga, you lack confidence in your self and often question your choice of yoga practices. Issues of poor self-esteem and self-respect can dominate your actions, creating uncertainty and fear.

Physically, you may experience weak digestion and poor circulation that create low resistance to the cold and damp. You may be easily chilled or come across as lacking personal warmth. A weak Sun can show up in poor eyesight and tendencies to arthritis.

Overall, there can be a lack of vitality and low energy levels that may make it difficult to fully engage in your yoga practice. Another obstacle to your success in yoga from a weak Sun is low motivation and a diminished drive to have a regular practice.

Yoga Practices to Strengthen the Sun

In general, asana practices that warm and activate the body (such as backbends) and the digestive fire (such as twists) strengthen the Sun on the physical level. Meditations that focus on visualizing light inside the body or the image of the sun, as well as meditating both at sunrise and sunset and on Sunday, the day of the sun, strengthen the inner sun.

All forms of Hatha yoga strengthen the Sun, as well as performing austerities, or tapas, to energize the will.

For specific yoga exercises and techniques to strengthen the Sun, and all the other planets, such as asanas, mantras, mudras, and pranayamas, see the chapters on the Planetary Yoga Practices.

The Sun Person

If the Sun is your predominant planet, you are a natural leader and can command the attention of others. There is a strength and nobility in your manner and you are often the center of attention, much like the sun. People are attracted by your natural warmth and ability to bring your light on a situation.

Physically, the heart is strong, the complexion has a glow, and the eyes are bright. The Sun Person may sometimes be balding or alternatively, have a beautiful mane of hair. They tend to be dramatic and have a strong sense of right and wrong. They can be aloof, or people may project upon them a sense of pride or self-superiority. They often have strong opinions and can appear authoritative or even overbearing. Their nature may be somewhat fiery and their most common negative emotion is anger. Yet people also see them as generous, charitable, and dependable.

> "Seeking the Shining Sun, being purified in the highest heavens, the mind is cleared and passionately intoxicated."
>
> Sama Veda

The Moon (Chandra): Light of the Mind

While the Moon is known by several names in Sanskrit, it is most commonly called Chandra. The Moon represents our emotions, personality, happiness, popularity, sociability, inner life and home. It is the mother, the divine goddess, the caregiver and women in general.

In the realm of yoga, the Moon represents the part of the mind known as "manas," or the emotional sensory mind. This aspect of the mind is responsible for our interactions with the external environment and organizes our emotional responses, and so it deeply affects how we experience ourselves in the world.

The Moon in yoga also corresponds to the Subtle Body (or Sukshma Sharira). The subtle body is the vehicle of consciousness in which a person passes from life to life. The chakras, the nadis (energy channels), and the vayus (energies) reside in the subtle body.

The yogic quality (guna) of the Moon is purity (sattva). Its Ayurvedic nature (dosha) is kapha, although its constantly changing nature implies a secondary vata nature. Among the five levels of existence (koshas) of yoga, the Moon is identified with the realm of emotions (manamaya kosha). The element (bhuta) of the Moon is water (jala). The type of yoga most identified with the Moon is Bhakti Yoga.

What the Moon Teaches Us

The Moon helps us learn to control and purify our mind and emotions. The Moon is associated with the mental peace that we can develop through meditation. The Moon, being associated with all things maternal, helps us resolve issues with the birth mother and the universal mother, as well as understanding the relationship of the self with women and children.

Ultimately, the Moon is about uplifting others by learning to channel the emotions through Bhakti yoga and by experiencing the pure love and connection to the Higher Self or Infinite. The life lesson of the Moon is to develop peace, faith, receptivity and surrender to the Divine and turn emotional commotion into spiritual devotion.

> "When the Moon shines, Brahman shines;
> And when the Moon sets, Brahman goes."
>
> Kaushitaki Upanishad 2.11

When the Moon Is Weak

When the Moon energy is not fully expressed in your life and your yoga, you may suffer from emotional instability and weak emotions. There can be feelings of anxiety, a fear of intimacy, or a general lack of friendliness. Often the mind is disturbed or cloudy, and there is accompanying moodiness, depression and negativity. In general, there is an overall feeling of discontent and an inability to be truly happy.

Yoga Practices to Strengthen the Moon

In general, asana postures that cool and calm the body (such as forward bends) strengthen the Moon on the physical level. Meditations that focus on water and those done in the moonlight, particularly the full moon, as well as meditating on Monday, the day of the moon, strengthen the moon.

All forms of Bhakti yoga support the moon, as well as devotional practices and mantras that focus on the feminine energy. Spiritual paths devoted to the Goddess or Divine Mother, and those from the ancient earth traditions, nurture the moon energy.

The Moon Person

If the Moon is your predominant planet, you are a nurturing caretaker and concerned with the welfare of others. Moon people have a natural luminosity about them, but it is softer than the sun, much like the cool reflected light of the moon. People find you sociable, friendly and deeply emotionally.

Physically, there may be a tendency toward a rounded face or body. Moon people have maternal instincts, and think of others as if they were family. They do well interacting with the general public and with women, and can influence the masses. They are sensitive, sentimental, and may be swept away by their feelings. Their moods vacillate daily, or even hour to hour, and they are dominated by the current emotional tone.

Moon people are highly intuitive, sometimes shy, and their true nature is often half-hidden. They may appear calm on the outside, but they can be highly reactive on the inside. They are peaceful, supportive, and comfortable in the role of service. Their idealistic nature often has them working for the good of others.

The Moon person's nature is watery, and their negative emotional response under stress is to become withdrawn and fearful. Yet they can be wonderful diplomats, healers, and administrators. The Moon is most often associated with the mother figure, someone who creates a cozy home or inner emotional environment, and who is the teacher as well as a nurturer.

Mars (Mangala): The Spiritual Warrior

Mars in Sanskrit is known as Mangala, Angaraka or sometimes Bauma. Mars represents logic, vitality, energy, combativeness, courage, strategy, science, and sports. Mars is the brother, the friend, the warrior, the athlete, the enemy and the defender.

In the realm of yoga, Mars represents Virya, or effort, energy, and zeal. Mars gives the yoga practitioner the quality of Abhyasa, the capacity for a constant and regular practice over a long period. In short, Mars gives us the power and strength to both initiate and maintain a daily spiritual practice, our sadhana. Mars is a Kshatriya, a member of the warrior caste, which allows us victory on the battleground of the mind and body.

Mars in yoga also corresponds to the physical body (Sthula Sharira). The physical body is the vehicle used in yoga to achieve spiritual liberation. Mars is the gross expression of the self in the form of muscles, bone and blood.

The yogic quality (guna) of Mars is stability and physicality (tamas). Its Ayurvedic nature (dosha) is pitta (fiery). Among the five levels of existence (koshas) of yoga, Mars is identified with the realm of the gross material plane (annamaya kosha). The element (bhuta) of Mars is fire (agni). The type of yoga most identified with Mars is Hatha Yoga and, secondarily, Kundalini Yoga.

What Mars Teaches Us

Mars helps us to learn to use our physical energy and mental strength in accordance with our spiritual principles. Mars teaches us to develop courage and initiative without a selfish agenda and to use our power appropriately in a just and protective way.

Ultimately, Mars teaches us to relax, calm down, control our anger and achieve a non-violent victory over what oppresses us. Mars can help us destroy negative patterns, conquer our fears and detach from unnecessary possessions.

The main lesson of Mars is to develop a one-pointed mind to stay focused on the purpose of this life and to use our life energy wisely.

> "The person born when Mars is strong is of fiery nature, moving hither and yon, heroic, sharp, fair bodied and opinionated."
>
> Brihat Parashara Hora Shastra

When Mars Is Weak

When the Mars energy is not fully expressed in your life and your yoga, you may suffer from low energy, lack of motivation, and feelings of powerlessness. It will be difficult to start new projects or begin a yoga practice. If you do begin a yoga practice, you may find reasons to abandon it later.

Physically, there could be slow healing, a weakened immune system, impotency, or exhaustion. Psychologically, you may be passive, listless, or easily dominated by others. Fearfulness, timidity, and a lack of self-belief can be attributed to a compromised Mars energy.

Without a strong Mars, progress is challenged in spiritual and yogic undertakings.

Yoga Practices to Strengthen Mars

In general, asana postures that have a martial nature (such as Warrior poses and Archer pose) strengthen Mars on the physical level. Meditations that focus on using the physical body to conquer the mind, such as the holding of a posture for a lengthy time or maintaining a difficult mudra position, can strengthen the inner Mars.

All forms of Hatha yoga and Kundalini yoga strengthen Mars, as well as practices that develop energy and insight. Practicing a kriya, a purifying action or a dynamic yoga practice, strengthens Mars, as does the practice of the shatkarmas, the six cleansing practices of yoga.

The Mars Person

If Mars is your predominant planet, you are confident, aggressive, competitive and bold. You do not shy away from conflicts and debates and will defend those who need it. You enjoy change, action, and having new territories to explore and conquer.

Physically, there may be a tendency toward redness in complexion or hair with angular features. Mars people may have scars from accidents or get injured easily. They usually have good muscle tone but may tend towards infectious diseases.

Mars people are disciplined, although susceptible to impulsive actions, and sometimes a little militaristic in nature. They are logical, scientific, technically oriented and generally good with their hands and working with things. They are very loyal, good at leadership and down to earth.

The Mars person's nature is fiery, like the Sun, but unlike the sun its expression is coarser and pragmatic.

Mercury (Budha): The Scholar

Mercury in Sanskrit is known as Budha or Budh, which means intelligent, clever, and awakened. Mercury represents the intellect, speech, education, business, mathematics, childhood, writing, adaptability, quickness and language. Mercury is the student, the younger sibling, the businessperson, the teacher, the scholar and writer.

In the realm of yoga, Mercury represents the intuitive knowing mind or Buddhi. The aspect of the mind in yoga known as buddhi is the higher faculty of discerning intelligence that allows us to discover the eternal truths and the nature of our existence. It is the area of the mind that is strengthened through meditation. Mercury gives us the mental ability and desire to acquire yogic knowledge.

The yogic quality (guna) of Mercury is activity (rajas), always moving and changing. Its Ayurvedic nature (dosha) is tridosha, meaning that it can assume either a vata, pitta, or kapha nature depending upon circumstances and this further affirms its changeable and versatile nature. Among the five levels of existence (koshas) of yoga, Mercury is identified with the realm of breath (pranamaya kosha). The element (bhuta) of Mercury is earth (prithvi), reflecting its ability to transact commerce and be successful in the material world.

The types of yoga most identified with Mercury is Mantra Yoga and Gyan or Jnana Yoga of knowledge, although Mercury's flexibility and relationship with pranayama also play an important role in the practice of Hatha Yoga.

What Mercury Teaches Us

Mercury helps us learn to control and use our mind and intellect properly. Mercury is associated with applying our intelligence for spiritual and selfless purposes. Mercury, being associated with all things educational, helps us acquire and impart knowledge.

Ultimately, Mercury is about learning discrimination and sublimating the intellect into intuition. The life lesson of Mercury is to use the faculties of the mind in service to the soul.

> "The person born when Mercury is strong is of earthy nature, one who enjoys, firmly happy, strong and patient."
>
> Brihat Parashara Hora Shastra

When Mercury Is Weak

When the Mercury energy is not fully expressed in your life and your yoga, you may experience a lack of self-control or poor self-expression. There is often challenged communication, impaired memory, as well as a vacillating and unfocused mind. It may be hard to stick to one thing (or one yoga practice!) and the tendency is to abandon a task and jump to the next thing of interest. Your challenge will be to focus your mental energy to accomplish your goals.

Yoga Practices to Strengthen Mercury

In general, asana postures that focus on flexibility, agility and movement strengthen Mercury. All mantra practices, and the reading of yogic and sacred texts, improve the condition of Mercury. Consciously regulating the breath through the pranayama practices strengthen the energy of Mercury. Devoting time to spiritual studies and learning sacred languages, such as Sanskrit, and studying philosophy improve Mercury.

Teaching yoga and practicing satsang, truthful spiritual discourse, are excellent ways to make Mercury stronger and more beneficial in your life.

The Mercury Person

If Mercury is your predominant planet, you have a natural tendency to do well with asanas as well as gymnastics and all activities that require flexibility of the body and mind. You impress people with your cleverness of speech and have a witty sense of humor, loving all forms of word play. You can multitask well but may have a hard time holding to a single focus or activity. You would much rather learn the next thing instead of going back over well-covered territory.

Mercury types excel in mental activities and love to live in the realm of ideas and information. They tend to move fast, talk fast, and think fast. They are good writers, teachers, business people, and motivators. They are changeable and dislike repetitive routine. They are inquisitive, analytical and adaptable but may find it hard to hold to any one decision, always willing to change for sake of change.

Jupiter (Guru): The Teacher

Jupiter in Sanskrit is known as Guru or Brihaspati, the lord of prayer and devotion. Jupiter represents wisdom, the righteous laws of the universe, prosperity, wealth, fortune, dharma or life purpose, faith, and all religious and spiritual activity. Jupiter is the advisor, the legal counselor, the teacher, the husband, the minister and priest, the guide and guru, and the minister of state.

In the realm of yoga, Jupiter represents the life's purpose or dharma of the soul. Jupiter reminds us of our highest self and our responsibility to it.

Jupiter gives us joy, enthusiasm, faith, and the ability to hold to our path and develop our higher mind.

The yogic quality (guna) of Jupiter is purity (sattva), reflecting its clarity and righteousness. Its Ayurvedic nature (dosha) is kapha, for its largesse being. Among the five levels of existence (koshas) of yoga, Jupiter is identified with the realm of truth and knowledge (vijnanamaya kosha). The element (bhuta) of Jupiter is ether (akasha), reflecting its expanded, spiritual and ethereal nature.

The type of yoga most identified with Jupiter is Raja Yoga, the royal path of meditation.

What Jupiter Teaches Us

Jupiter helps us to evolve a mature faith, a philosophy and a belief system. Jupiter allows us to understand the true nature of prosperity so that we may be generous, and that there is an abundance of opportunity for us to become self-realized if we aspire and adhere to the highest principles. Jupiter shows us how to respect and support all religious and spiritual values. The teaching of Jupiter is to follow our dharma and to create a proper relationship with our true nature.

Ultimately, Jupiter is about accepting a divine teacher, the guru, and to learn about spiritual knowledge. The life lesson of Jupiter is to live with grace and virtue in accordance with the eternal principle of the cosmic order.

> "The person born when Jupiter is strong is of ethereal nature,
> wise with words and knowledgeable in conduct."
>
> Brihat Parashara Hora Shastra

When Jupiter Is Weak

When the Jupiter energy is not fully expressed in your life and your yoga, you may feel unappreciated, unhappy, and contracted. It may make one a spiritual pretender who does not live what they espouse. Teachers may betray our trust or simply be hard to find. There is a lack of joy, a tendency to be bitter and miserly, and a poverty state of mind. The creative energy is low, children will not bring happiness, and the spouse of a woman may be diminished or unsatisfying. It is difficult to believe, to worship in your own way, and to find your true path in life.

Yoga Practices to Strengthen Jupiter

In general, all meditation practices strengthen Jupiter. The performance of spiritual and religious rituals, the honoring of a teacher, and the creation of altars all improve the state of Jupiter. Practicing the meditative seated asanas, as well as postures such as gurupranam (extended child pose) and yoga mudras that activate the third eye increase our Jupiter energy. Retaining the inhaled breath and expanding the breath capacity contribute to increasing our Jupiter energy.

Teaching yoga and the righteous principles of life, studying the higher teachings, reading spiritual literature and philosophy all bring more Jupiter energy into the life.

The Jupiter Person

If Jupiter is your predominant planet, you are intelligent, philosophical, and religious or spiritual in nature. You possess both spiritual and material wealth and are often the recipient of gifts and good fortune. Finding the correct path in life is of paramount importance to you, and it is difficult, if not impossible, to take actions that are deceptive and unethical. You place a high value on what people think of your reputation and are inclined to be virtuous.

Jupiter types possess a strong faith and belief system that can sometimes lead them into being overly orthodox, opinionated, self-righteous, or even a law unto themselves. There may be an inclination to strictly follow the religious traditions of their culture yet they are also very sincere in their beliefs. They usually enjoy good health and longevity, but can sometimes be misled by their abundance of good fortune that can lead to an overly materialistic life. For the most part, the Jupiter person is optimistic, accomplishes a great deal in both the earthly and spiritual realms, and tries to live happily in all circumstances.

Venus (Shukra): The Divine Lover

Venus in Sanskrit is known as Shukra, which means, "white, bright, clear and pure" and, at the same time, it is also a reference to the body's reproductive fluids. This is a good indication of the deep spirituality and sensuality that is the nature of Venus.

Venus represents love, beauty, art, conveyances, charisma, charm, diplomacy, relationships, marriage, the female reproductive organs, comfort, gems, music, dance, harmony, flowers, ornamentations, and all sensual pleasures. Venus is the spouse of the husband, the divine lover, the partner, the female, and the advising minister.

In the realm of yoga, Venus represents chanting, rituals, kirtan, meditative dance, and the heart-felt devotion to the practice. Venus gives us finesse, elegance, cordiality, refinement and aesthetics.

The yogic quality (guna) of Venus is activity (rajas), reflecting its fascination with the world of the senses. Its Ayurvedic nature (dosha) is kapha, for its sensitivity in relationships. Among the five levels of existence (koshas) of yoga, Venus is identified with the realm of bliss (anandamaya kosha). The element (bhuta) of Venus is water (apas), reflecting its flowing and merging nature.

The types of yoga most identified with Venus are Bhakti Yoga, the yoga of devotion and the heart, and Tantric Yoga, approaching the divine in the form of a beloved.

What Venus Teaches Us

Venus helps us recognize and appreciate all feminine qualities as a manifestation of the divine woman. Venus teaches us to enjoy the pleasure of the senses while realizing they are ultimately the expressions of the divine play of universal love.

Venus is about transforming the need for purely physical love to spiritual love, based upon divine compassion for one's self, one's partner and all of creation. The life lesson of Venus is to enjoy life in a pure way and to recognize the beauty of all creation as an expression of divine grace.

> "The person born when Venus is strong is of watery nature, with affectionate speech and many friends, gentle and learned."
>
> Brihat Parashara Hora Shastra

When Venus Is Weak

When the Venus energy is not fully expressed in your life and your yoga, you may set high standards for happiness and be overly critical of yourself and others. It may be difficult to connect to the other person in a loving and heartfelt way. You may not be able to fully appreciate beauty because of unrealistic standards that keep you unhappy. You may hide your own beauty or reject your femininity. You may also be lacking in taste, grace, and refinement or be unable to enjoy the pleasures of life or the bed. You may have difficulty in creating relationships or you compromise your own needs in a vain effort to please everyone.

Yoga Practices to Strengthen Venus

In general, all devotional practices strengthen Venus, such as chanting from the heart, singing spiritual songs, and creating a relationship with your personal deity. Doing partner asanas and partner meditations increase the Venus energy, as does practicing sacred sex. Flowing, dance-like asana practices increase our Venus energy, as does meditating with malas made of beautiful stones or beads. Wearing refined and tasteful clothes in a yoga practice can strengthen Venus as long as we do not become vain or superficial.

Studying spiritual literature, listening to kirtan, creating mandalas and yantras, and beautifying our yoga space and altar all bring more Venus energy into the life.

The Venus Person

If Venus is your predominant planet, you are charming, persuasive, refined and sensual. You give great importance to aesthetics and are skilled at harmonizing and mediating with people. You have natural attraction and charm, and may possess an alluring sexual energy and beauty. You can become seduced by sensuality and may overspend on beautiful things of high quality. You like the best things in life, and enjoy all the arts and pleasures of the senses.

Venus types have good imaginations and boundless creativity. They are natural diplomats and counselors, giving good advice. In their evolved nature, the Venus person can gain great spiritual knowledge, become excellent astrologers, and be the loving devotee of the divine beloved.

Saturn (Shani): The Yogi

Saturn in Sanskrit is known as Shani which means "the one who moves slowly," a reference to the 29 ½ years it takes Saturn to orbit the sun, the longest of all the visible planets. The slowness of Saturn implies that it is a planet of patience and perseverance and so it signifies these qualities in our lives as well.

Saturn represents the servant, the elderly, the poor, and the renunciate as well as the yogi. From these representations, we also understand that Saturn signifies humility, service, discipline, austerities and a regular spiritual practice (sadhana). Saturn is also associated with limitations, contractions, loss and death, as well as the ability to transcend these qualities through the practice of yoga.

In the realm of yoga, Saturn represents the bandhas (muscular locks), the retention of breath (kumbhaka) and concentration (dharana).

Saturn gives us detachment, commitment and the ability to work on ourselves spiritually. Saturn allows us to develop patience through time and humility through service. It shows us what is ultimately important, liberation (moksha), by removing all the other things in this life that we are attached to.

The yogic quality (guna) of Saturn is stability (tamas), reflecting its heavy and slow moving nature. Its Ayurvedic nature (dosha) is vata, for its cold dryness and acknowledgement that vata increases with aging. Among the five levels of existence (koshas) of yoga, Saturn is identified with the realm of breath (pranamaya kosha) with its focus on breath retention and using the bandhas. The element (bhuta) of Saturn is air (vayu), reflecting the growing insubstantiality of the aged.

The type of yoga most identified with Saturn is Karma Yoga, the yoga of work and selfless service (seva).

What Saturn Teaches Us

Saturn helps us develop responsibility, inner strength and the ability to triumph over the hardships of life. It teaches discipline so we may pursue spiritual practices with an attitude of dutiful service. Saturn allows us to detach from the temporal pleasure of the material world so we may remember the purpose of this earthly life. When we misunderstand this life, Saturn brings us sorrows and limitations so we may redirect ourselves to a higher purpose.

Ultimately, Saturn is about developing an unshakeable inner discipline so that we may become liberated while realizing human love and compassion come from our selfless service.

When Saturn Is Weak

When the Saturn energy is not expressed in your life and your yoga, you may have a lack of commitment and discipline. You may find it difficult to keep a regular yoga practice, or to delay your need for instant gratification to achieve long-lasting rewards. There may be a lack of practicality and practice, with no sustained drive or endurance. You may be arrogant or irresponsible in your actions. Concentration may be difficult and you will be unable to perform the austerities (tapas) of yoga. Obstacles may overwhelm you and you submit to fate rather than realizing your destiny.

Yoga Practices to Strengthen Saturn

All ascetic practices strengthen Saturn, such as restricting diet and speech, performing strong sadhanas (such as holding postures or the breath for an extended period of time), and living simply and humbly. A structured daily yoga and meditation practice keeps Saturn strong. Observing silence, sitting in deep reflection, and making inner and outer pilgrimages all strengthen Saturn energy. Teaching yoga to the poor and elderly is a wonderful Saturn practice as well.

Bringing detachment into our yoga, releasing our expectations, and the willingness to work hard to overcome obstacles makes Saturn strong.

The Saturn Person

If Saturn is your predominant planet, you are serious, hard working, responsible, and can face obstacles and sorrows with strength and determination. There is a sense of maturity, even at a young age, and a desire to achieve and accomplish, particularly in the material world at first and then later in the spiritual realms.

The Saturn person has a good ability to be solitary, which makes them excellent yogis and meditators, but they may have few close friends. There is often emotional repression that facilitates detachment but can bring depression if not engaged in spiritual work. The steadiness of Saturn can sometimes make their lives stagnant and routine and they may remain in unhappy situations too long.

When Saturn people use their better qualities, they become calm, philosophical and meditative and realize the highest state of yoga.

> "The person born when Saturn is strong is of windy nature, difficult to assail and thin bodied."
>
> Brihat Parashara Hora Shastra

Rahu: The Doer and Future Karma

Rahu in Vedic legend is a head without a body, the half of a demon who dared to steal and drink the immortal nectar from the other planetary beings before he was cut in half for his boldness. Rahu thus represents our insatiable ambition, to be better than we are and to become recognized for our actions. Rahu is the ultimate doer, the actor, and the ambitious energy that keeps us hurtling toward an often illusory reward or pinnacle.

In the realm of yoga, Rahu represents the drive and ambition to reach our spiritual goals and achieve liberation through our own actions. Rahu is our present and emerging karma, reminding us to reach the next level and not remain content with our current state of realization. In fact, Rahu is often the source of the divine discontent that causes the soul to constantly incarnate in search of the ultimate accomplishment.

Rahu in the realm of the world represents collective trends, fads, large-scale delusions, epidemics and psychic disturbances. There is often an unusual or futuristic bent to Rahu that gives rise to fascination with the world of fantasy, imagination and illusion as represented by mass media.

The yogic quality (guna) of Rahu is darkness (tamas), reflecting its ability to hide what needs to be discovered. Its Ayurvedic nature (dosha) is vata, for its insubstantiality and illusion. Among the five levels of existence (koshas) of yoga, Rahu is identified with the realm of materialism and physicality (annamaya kosha). The element (bhuta) of Rahu is air (vayu), reflecting its untouchable and fantastic nature.

The type of yoga most identified with Rahu is Bhakti Yoga, the path of devotion to an imagined or real charismatic entity.

What Rahu Teaches Us

Rahu helps us to understand the subconscious and unconscious mind and the hidden aspects of ourselves. It gives us the ability to deeply introspect and self-study and ultimately to detach from the mind's strong desires and fantasies. Rahu can help us overcome our fear and our addictions through our spiritual strength and devotion.

Ultimately, Rahu is about channeling and expressing our personal drives and ambitions toward our highest self and spiritual goals, without becoming obsessive.

> "Gaping mouth, granting wishes,
> sitting on a lion and dark in color is Rahu."
>
> Brihat Parashara Hora Shastra

When Rahu Is Weak

When the Rahu energy is not fully expressed in your life and your yoga, you may feel hypersensitive, moody, anxious, prone to strange fantasies, easily suggestible, and susceptible to addictive or dissipating practices. There can be a strong streak of materialism with such an overriding desire to be successful in the material world that the spiritual needs are ignored. Meditation and discernment may be difficult and you may be more likely to use drugs, alcohol and tobacco. You will tend to live in a world of illusions and fantasy and devote too much time to the world of the Internet, social media, and on-line computer games.

Yoga Practices to Strengthen Rahu

Staying in alignment with an authentic spiritual tradition is the best way to strengthen the energy of Rahu. Constant discipline keeps Rahu in balance. Visiting foreign lands for spiritual purposes is an excellent way to use the energy of Rahu, as is interacting with foreign teachers and philosophies.

Kundalini yoga and systems that work with balancing the energy channels (nadis) ameliorate Rahu, and the practice of alternate nostril breathing is recommended. Bhakti Yoga is a good yoga approach to balance the energy of Rahu, although care must be exercised to not misplace it on a charismatic yet false teacher.

The Rahu Person

If Rahu is your predominant planet, you are mysterious, unknowable and elusive in nature. Rahu people may become therapists, or in need of therapy themselves, and are often connected with the hidden workings of the body, mind and soul. Professions like psychologists, pathologists, and adventurers are Rahu in nature, and often have a connection to unknown lands or foreign concepts. Science fiction writers, computer game developers, movie directors, as well as film actors, are Rahu types.

Rahu people can be unpredictable and elusive. They can be carried away by fantasy and astral forces or be disturbed by mysterious diseases, nervous system disorders, and allergies. They often have unrealistic expectations about life, and other people may in turn place fantastic projections onto them (such as a movie star or internet sensation, the ultimate Rahu type).

Yet the Rahu individual can also be an adventurer, an explorer of unknown lands, and ultimately one who discovers the true meaning of life through their self-absorption.

Ketu: The Renunciate and Past Karma

Ketu in Vedic legend is a body without a head, the other half of Rahu, the demon who dared drink the immortal nectar before he was cut in half. Ketu thus represents detachment from the sensory world, a turning away from the materiality represented by Rahu to an intense longing for spirituality. Ketu is the renunciate, the one who gives up pleasures and possessions and wanders the world to find liberation.

In the realm of yoga, Ketu is our compelling desire to immerse ourselves completely into the search for spiritual realization, forsaking the temptations of the outer world to go inside. Ketu also represents our past karmas, and how we have spent our previous incarnations.

Ketu represents higher knowledge, liberation (moksha), spiritual insight as well as psychic abilities and transformational death. Ketu, of all the planets, represents meditation, the turning inward of the senses.

The yogic quality (guna) of Ketu is darkness (tamas), reflecting its shadowy nature and lack of senses. Its Ayurvedic nature (dosha) is pita, for its ability to sharply discern boundaries and separate from others. Among the five levels of existence (koshas) of yoga, Ketu is identified with the realm of transcendence (anandamaya kosha). The element (bhuta) of Ketu is fire (agni), reflecting its transformational nature.

The type of yoga most identified with Ketu is Gyan Yoga, the path of knowledge to discern the ultimate truths from illusion.

What Ketu Teaches Us

Ketu teaches us to develop concentration, self-inquiry, and meditation. It gives us the ability to see the play of the senses, the maya, and to free ourselves from the illusion that we are simply a body driven by desire. Ketu helps us understand the transitory nature of the material world and the nature of death itself.

Ultimately, Ketu is about renouncing the lower ego and its attachments and clearing the tendencies and impressions from the past (samskaras) so that we may become liberated in this lifetime while still alive (jivamukti).

> "Smoky, two armed with a mace, and riding a vulture,
> Ketu grants blessings."
>
> Brihat Parashara Hora Shastra

When Ketu Is Weak

When the Ketu energy is not fully expressed in your life and your yoga, you may feel disconnected from the realm of spirit. Self-doubt, lack of insight, and the inability to focus the mind on the hidden areas of life may arise. There may be disturbing psychic events, intense visions, possessions or uncontrollable episodes where the past seems to intrude upon the present, producing intense feelings of unfounded guilt. There may be a tendency to live in the past, or feel that past life events are still impinging upon your present life. Uncomfortable isolation, alienation, even imprisonment or confinement can occur when the energy of Ketu is unbalanced or weak.

Yoga Practices to Strengthen Ketu

Spiritualizing your daily life is the best way to strengthen and manage the energy of Ketu. A constant discipline of regular meditation is needed to keep Ketu in balance. Visiting old lands and cultures for spiritual purposes is an excellent way to use the energy of Ketu. The study of ancient spiritual disciplines and the reading of traditional spiritual texts strengthen Ketu.

Kundalini yoga and systems that work with balancing the energy channels (nadis) ameliorate Ketu, and the practice of alternate nostril breathing is recommended. Living in retreats or ashrams, taking yoga vacations in foreign lands, and devoting regular time to beneficial isolation or meditation all beneficially strengthen the energy of Ketu.

The Ketu Person

If Ketu is your predominant planet, you have intense perception and a critical mind, although it may be narrowly focused or highly unusual. Whatever you apply your will to, you can accomplish and often master, particularly if it is somewhat unconventional in nature. There is a strong sense of individualism to the point of eccentricity.

Ketu people can gain the highest spiritual knowledge but, in so doing, may negate everything that others hold dear. They have a developed ability to be alone or live in isolated locales and have low social needs. There is always a distinctly unusual nature to them, as if they were only visiting this world, and are often difficult to understand. Of all the planetary types, Ketu people are the most mysterious and subtle.

The Twelve Signs (Rashis) of Astrology Yoga

While the nine planets, or grahas, are the activating forces in Astrology Yoga, the signs of the zodiac greatly influence their actions. To understand the signs, or rashis, think of the sky as a huge sphere that surrounds our planet. When you look up at the night sky, you see an area that is often described by the grouping of stars or constellation that inhabit that area. In Sanskrit, the grouping is described as a "heap," which is the literal translation of the term "rashi."

This 360-degree circle of sky that surrounds us is divided into 12 sections of 30 degrees each. Each section is denoted as being a sign (rashi) or, more properly, a constellation. As planets move through the sky, as seen from earth, they enter and leave these signs or constellations. On April 18th each year, for example, the sun is in the area of the zodiac we call Aries. The next month, the sun moves into the next sign designated as Taurus, and we say the "sun is in Taurus." Every planet occupies one of the 12 signs and moves through them in successive order over a period of time.

Each sign has specific qualities that affect a planet that occupies that sign. If the planets are the major actors in astrology, the signs affect the way in which the planet acts by imbuing it with its qualities. For example, Mercury in the sign of Aries gives the quickness and initiating energy of Aries to the actions of Mercury, while Mercury in Taurus makes the behavior of Mercury more stable and pragmatic.

The following table shows the twelve signs of the zodiac and the order in which they appear, beginning with the 0 degree of the zodiac, with each sign occupying 30 degrees. Both English and Sanskrit names are given, as well as the keywords that describe the nature of that sign.

While the meanings of the twelve signs of Vedic astrology are essentially the same as the twelve signs in Western astrology, the planets in Vedic astrology may occupy a different sign than Western astrology. This is because Vedic astrology uses a fixed star as the starting point for the zodiac while Western astrologers have tied the starting point to the vernal equinox (usually March 21) which moves forward about one degree every 72 years. Currently there is approximately a 23 degree difference between where the Eastern signs and Western signs begin, so you can convert the Western planetary positions to their Vedic positions by subtracting 23 degrees from their position. This often puts the planets in the sign of a Vedic chart in the previous sign from the Western.

ENGLISH	SANSKRIT	QUALITIES
Aries	Mesha	Energetic, active, impulsive, first, courageous, adventurous
Taurus	Vrishabha	Stable, practical, sensuous, artistic, obstinate, dependable
Gemini	Mithuna	Changeable, intelligent, talkative, studious, business-like, witty
Cancer	Kataka	Nurturing, sensitive, emotional, intuitive, dependent, fluctuating
Leo	Simha	Royal, loyal, generous, arrogant, proud, noble, authoritative
Virgo	Kanya	Critical, precise, organized, pure, shy, self-improving, skilled, serving
Libra	Tula	Balanced, harmonious, diplomatic, fair, indecisive, beautiful
Scorpio	Vrishchika	Intense, powerful, mystical, secretive, forceful, sexual
Sagittarius	Dhanus	Philosophical, ethical, freedom loving, opinionated, ambitious
Capricorn	Makara	Patient, determined, serious, sober, hard-working, persevering
Aquarius	Kumbha	Unconventional, scientific, impersonal, forward thinking, service-oriented
Pisces	Meena	Spiritual, empathetic, psychic, imaginative, impractical, dreamy

Table 1-2: Twelve Signs (Rashis) and Their Qualities

Nature of the Signs

The twelve signs can be further defined as being associated with one of the four elements (Earth, Water, Fire, and Air) as well as one of the three qualities (Fixed, Movable, and Dual). This can help us understand how the planets function when they are in a particular sign, and the following table indicates both the element and the nature of each sign.

SIGN	RASHI	ELEMENT	NATURE
ARIES	Mesha	Fire	Moveable
TAURUS	Vrishabha	Earth	Fixed
GEMINI	Mithuna	Air	Dual
CANCER	Kataka	Water	Moveable
LEO	Simha	Fire	Fixed
VIRGO	Kanya	Earth	Dual
LIBRA	Tula	Air	Moveable
SCORPIO	Vrishchika	Water	Fixed
SAGITTARIUS	Dhanus	Fire	Dual
CAPRICORN	Makara	Earth	Moveable
AQUARIUS	Kumbha	Air	Fixed
PISCES	Meena	Water	Dual

Table 1-3: Astrological Signs: Element and Nature

Earth Signs

Planets in earth signs contribute steadiness, calmness and poise to a yoga practice. Three or more planets in the earth signs (Taurus, Virgo, Capricorn) make it easier to enjoy relaxation as part of your yoga experience. You may tend toward practicality in your approach to yoga, and if your practice produces tangible results, you will stay with it. Be willing to change your yoga routines as you can become fixed in your approach. You will likely enjoy standing and sitting postures, and may be able to hold asanas for a long period of time.

Water Signs

Planets in water signs contribute a flowing and gentle approach to a yoga practice. Three or more planets in the water signs (Cancer, Scorpio, Pisces) make it easy for you to have an open approach to your yoga, content to go with the flow, and to merge with the overall energy of the class. There is an emotional component to your yoga practice, as well as a desire to use yoga to bring harmony and peace to your life. The water signs add a social nature to your yoga practice and you love to take your friends to yoga class.

Fire Signs

Planets in fire signs contribute an active, intense and strong approach to a yoga practice. Three or more planets in the fire signs (Aries, Leo, Sagittarius) give an active and thin body that is energetic and moving. You like challenging yoga practices that build heat and give you a chance for accomplishment. You may enjoy Ashtanga and Vinyasa yoga practices. Like the rest of your life, you bring intensity to your yoga practice that may make you the center of attention.

Air Signs

Planets in air signs contribute an adaptable, flexible and mental approach to a yoga practice. Three or more planets in the air signs (Gemini, Libra, Aquarius) produce a need for change and stimulation in the yoga routines. Meditation may be difficult unless you discover the joys of pranayama and mantra. The practices of Kundalini Yoga appeal to the energy of the air signs.

Fixed Signs

Planets in fixed signs provide the foundation for perfecting the meditative postures. Four or more planets in the fixed signs (Taurus, Leo, Scorpio, Aquarius) can create a steady and long-term yoga practice but you may sometimes find yourself slipping into stagnant routines. Be willing to bring change to your practice.

Movable Signs

Planets in moveable signs contribute to sequencing the movement of asanas and the perfection of vinyasa. Four or more planets in the movable signs (Aries, Cancer, Libra, Capricorn) can give an active practice that enjoys change and innovation but you may need a structure and sustained focus in one area or aspect of yoga to develop mastery.

Dual Signs

Planets in dual signs encourage movement with the breath through the postures, such as Viniyoga and Kundalini Yoga. Four or more planets in the dual signs (Gemini, Virgo, Sagittarius, Pisces) can help you excel at creating a balance between an active asana practice and a seated meditative practice. Both are important for you. Watch for tendencies to vacillate in your routine and second-guess yourself.

Strong Signs and Weak Signs

Knowing the signs that your planets are located in will give you insights into how their energies may be expressed or used. Not only do the planets act differently in the signs, there are signs in which the energy of the planets is more easily expressed (strong) and other signs in which the planetary energy is diminished (weak). For example, the Sun in Leo or Aries is considered to be in a strong sign while the Sun in Libra is often a weaker sign for that planet to be located.

The following table indicates which planets are strong or weak in each of the twelve signs:

	Sign	Strong (exalted/own sign)	Weak (debilitated)
1	Aries	Sun, Mars	Saturn
2	Taurus	Moon, Venus	
3	Gemini	Mercury	
4	Cancer	Moon, Jupiter	Mars
5	Leo	Sun	
6	Virgo	Mercury	Venus
7	Libra	Saturn, Venus	Sun
8	Scorpio	Mars	Moon
9	Sagittarius	Jupiter	
10	Capricorn	Mars, Saturn	Jupiter
11	Aquarius	Saturn	
12	Pisces	Venus, Jupiter	Mercury

Table 1-4: Planetary Strengths and Weakness by Astrological Signs

Aries (Mesha): Initiating Energy and Being

Planets in Aries create a strong desire for self-realization. The sense of self is first strengthened and then transcended as the ego moves from self-centeredness to spiritual awareness. On a more mundane level, Aries energy can sometimes lead one to impulsively and quickly commit to a yoga practice or spiritual path only to leave it later when the newness wears off. The lesson is to couple the strong initiating energy of Aries with a commitment to seeing it through to self-actualization.

Taurus (Vrishabha): Creative Potential and Manifestation

Planets in Taurus provide stability and the capacity to manifest both materially and spiritually. Part of this growth is to learn how to put the material aspects of life into proper perspective with the spiritual journey. Taurus energy must first embrace the world and its sensuality before it can transcend them. With planets in Taurus, one must learn to release attachments and to enjoy the pleasures of the world without becoming ensnared in them.

Gemini (Mithuna): Changing Polarity and Duality

Planets in Gemini allow us to understand the polarity and duality of our ever-changing nature through learning and communication. The mind is first developed through the inquisitive nature and desire to study in a broad-based way. Outward communication eventually evolves into an inner dialogue with self, and the tendency for multiple activities gradually re-focuses into a concentrated effort to understand the underlying unity of all things. In this way, Gemini allows us to use the planetary energies to see beyond our dual nature and to transcend our identification with the changeable nature of the mind.

Cancer (Kataka): Reflective Expansion and Sensitivity

Planets in Cancer give us the ability to develop our intuition and employ our sensitivity to create nurturing external and internal environments that promote the maturation of the soul. The opportunity that Cancer brings us is to understand that our need for security and stability can only be satisfied by finding these qualities within ourselves and not in the outer world. The limiting realm of feelings, reactions, and projections that is the comfortable domain of Cancer quickly expands beyond its narrow scope when we learn to reflect on the eternal nature of the soul that has no boundaries.

Leo (Simha): Radiant Being and Self

Planets in Leo bring warmth, self-confidence, and authority to our yoga practices and teaching. The energy of Leo provides a strong sense of self and self-belief that supports the individual in their spiritual journey, yet the pitfall is that this energy can also be self-aggrandizing and self-centered. There is no ego like the Leo spiritual ego and it can be the cause of their rise or fall. The lesson of Leo is to learn to confront and control the ego so that it becomes the servant and not the master. A realized Leo can be a most charismatic and powerful spiritual teacher if they learn the lesson of humility and service.

Virgo (Kanya): Divine Discontent and Integration

Planets in Virgo give a discerning intelligence and critical mind that can lead to spiritual perfection or material discontent, depending upon where its energies are placed. The organizing and analytical nature of Virgo can be powerful in creating self-improvement practices and pragmatic approaches to living as a spiritual being in the material world. The Virgo spiritual path is often one of service, healing and learning. There is usually a strong intellectual or mental relationship with the higher consciousness that is balanced and integrated by the practice of karma yoga.

Libra (Tula): Harmonious Equilibrium and Balance

Planets in Libra bring a balance to the mind and the practice of yoga and can aid in harmonizing the polarities that exist within all of us. There can be a tendency to over idealize spirituality and this can create an imbalance in the everyday life. The Libra energy can be beneficial in understanding the purpose and nature of forming balanced relationships on our spiritual journey, and the deeper lesson offered by planets in Libra is how to surrender the ego to a divine relationship that transcends the emotional commotion that separates us from our wholeness.

Scorpio (Vrishchika): Mystical Knowledge and Secrets

Planets in Scorpio bring passion and drive for deep inner transformation and the ability to discern the secrets of the universe. Scorpio is considered to be the most mystical sign where the ego can die and the higher self emerge, and so it is a self-destructive energy that must be managed carefully. The Scorpio energy is truly devil or divine, depending upon the consciousness of the individual. This is the sign of the kundalini, the chakras, and the siddhis (yogic powers) that must be encountered respectfully through a continual refinement of the basic power-nature that characterizes this sign.

Sagittarius (Dhanus): Purposeful Living and Knowledge

Planets in Sagittarius bring a strong desire for dharma, philosophy, spirituality, and higher knowledge. There is a seeking for truth and understanding of life's eternal laws, yet there may also be an inclination to moral or spiritual superiority and self-righteous behavior that can be detrimental to their true purpose. Spiritual self-righteousness is the trap of Sagittarius that can be overcome by truly actualizing what they believe rather than demonstrating what they know. The sign of Sagittarius is best expressed when the True Believer evolves into the True Doer (Sat Kartar).

Capricorn (Makara): Material Spiritualism and Structure

Planets in Capricorn allow us to bring our aspirations, both material and spiritual, into a structured and pragmatic realization. The energy here is preserving, ambitious, and hardworking and allows us to accomplish much if we understand the purpose of Capricorn. Spirituality is most often expressed through action, work, and service, and the material plane is where spiritual satisfaction is often found. For realized Capricorns, there is no separation between matter and spirit for they are the bridge builders between these two areas. The true lesson of Capricorn is to release the urgency to achieve and accomplish and thereby realize life's purpose is in the state of being than the act of doing.

Aquarius (Kumbha): Group Consciousness and Service

Planets in Aquarius bring an appreciation for group consciousness, humanitarian efforts and spiritual expression through social reform. The Aquarian energy is one of personal impersonality where community is highly valued yet life is often lived in solitude. Because of the solitary nature of Aquarius, there is the pull toward associating with others who share our spiritual values and a desire to be of service to humankind. The desire for change and the unusual can lead the Aquarian individual to a crisis whereby they must realize that rebellion itself only creates servitude to a different master or belief system. When they surrender their identification with all social, political or spiritual processes, no matter how alternative, then they experience lasting unity with pure consciousness.

Pisces (Meena): Universal Consciousness and Merger

Planets in Pisces provide an empathetic, imaginative and sensitive approach to the life's journey. The Piscean energy is idealized and introspective which can create a religious or spiritual approach to the practice of yoga. Seeing through the illusion, doubt, and personal attachments that this life brings is an important stage for the Piscean seeker. The release of hope and expectations by developing detached self-awareness is the ultimate lesson of the Pisces sign. Rather than seeking higher realms through fantasy and imagination, Pisces individuals can effect a merger with universal consciousness by recognizing and acting upon the possibilities they already have.

The Rising Sign

As the earth revolves, different areas or signs of the zodiac appear to be rising over the eastern horizon. The sign of the zodiac that appears to be rising in the east at the time of your birth is called your "rising sign." The rising sign is the most important sign in your birth chart, even more so than your Sun sign or Moon sign.

So when someone says they have "Gemini rising," it means that the sign of Gemini was on the eastern horizon at the time of their birth. This means that energy of Gemini was prominent at this time and greatly affects the temperament of the individual and how they see the world. Since all twelve signs appear to revolve around the earth over a 24 hour period, a different sign is rising every two hours.

We'll discuss the rising sign more in the next section on the Twelve Houses, or life areas, of Vedic Astrology.

Relationships Between the Signs and the Planets

The most obvious relationship the planets have with the signs is when they occupy them and are affected and influenced by the energy of that sign.

For example, when we say "I'm a Taurus," we mean, "The sun at my birth was in the sign of Taurus." Consequently, the individual exhibits traits associated with Taurus. In this way, the signs affect the planets.

However, you can say that the planets also affect the signs because each sign is also associated with a specific planet. This association of a planet with a sign is called the planetary ruler, or owner, of that sign. In the same way that the planets claim ownership, or dominion, over certain objects or areas, they also claim rulership over the signs. Each sign has a specific planet, or owner, that is said to rule that sign.

Aries, for example, is ruled or owned by Mars. Consequently, the sign of Aries exhibits the Martian properties of impulsivity and combativeness. Any planet in Aries is therefore owned and influenced by Mars.

The following table shows which of the seven visible planets own a particular sign. While Rahu and Ketu are associated with owning signs (and these vary, depending upon the school of Vedic astrology), their rulership is subservient to the primary planet that owns the sign.

SIGN	PLANETARY OWNER or RULER
Aries	Mars
Taurus	Venus
Gemini	Mercury
Cancer	Moon
Leo	Sun
Virgo	Mercury
Libra	Venus
Scorpio	Mars
Sagittarius	Jupiter
Capricorn	Saturn
Aquarius	Saturn
Pisces	Jupiter

Table 1-5: Astrological Signs and Their Planetary Rulers

The Twelve Houses (Bhavas) of Astrology Yoga

As we saw, the twelve signs (rashis) divide the zodiac into twelve sections where the planets in your birth chart are located. Similarly, your birth chart also has twelve houses (bhavas) that divide your life into twelve areas. Each house (bhava) in Vedic astrology is associated with one of the twelve signs, so every area of your life such as health, career, relationships, meditation, family, and so on is linked to a sign and the planets located in that sign.

Each of the twelve houses covers a wide range of areas and people in your life. For example, the fourth house in your birth chart contains information about your mother, your home, your car, your inner emotional life, the abdominal organs, fixed assets, your sense of security, and literally hundreds of other things.

In the practice of yoga, the fourth house may indicate the basic nature of your mind, self-awareness, emotional connectivity to your faith or beliefs, and your capacity to develop inner peace.

The rising sign in your birth chart is associated with the first house. The sign that follows the rising sign in the zodiac is connected to your second house, and so on. For example, if you have Taurus rising in you chart, then your first house will have the qualities of Taurus. The second house would have the qualities of the next sign in the zodiac, which in this example is Gemini.

The planets that occupy the sign associated with a specific house have an impact on the area or affairs of that house. In our example above, if the Moon were located in Gemini then it is also said to be located in the second house (for a Taurus rising) and would bring the energy of a Gemini moon to the area of life indicated by the second house.

One of the areas of life of the second house is speech, so a Gemini moon would tend to bring a talkative and witty nature (Gemini) and a degree of sociability (Moon) to the manner of speaking.

For the purposes of Astrology Yoga, we are only examining the twelve houses as they primarily relate to the practice of yoga, meditation, inner transformation and our spiritual journey.

First House (Thanu Bhava): Incarnated Self

The first house represents the soul in its incarnated state. The sign of the first house indicates your physical body, health, appearance, psychological temperament, and personality, or what astrologers call the rising sign. Any planets located in the sign of the first house affect health, psychology and personality. As a result, the first house reveals both your attitude toward life and your practice of yoga.

To better understand your first house and your yoga practice, you can explore the meaning of your rising sign (the sign of your first house) by looking at the description of the Sun Sign for that sign. In other words, if you are Leo Rising, or have Leo as the sign of your first house, you can read the description for a Leo Sun to begin to investigate the nature of the first house and the type of yoga practice you may be drawn to. Later in this book, you can obtain more information about your rising sign and how it affects your yoga practice.

Second House (Dhana Bhava): Innate Gifts

The second house represents what we are born with, our innate talents, inherited resources, and natural abilities that allow us to embark on a spiritual practice. For example, the second house may give us access to education, family support, or simply natural abilities to learn about ourselves in this life. It also represents what goes in and out of the mouth, our eating and speech habits, which is one of the most powerful ways we create our karmas in this lifetime.

Third House (Sahaja Bhava): Courageous Expression

The third house indicates our courage and bravery in encountering ourselves as spiritual warriors. It is about how we express ourselves as spiritual beings. The third house provides us with the mental stamina to gather information and use the intellect in our yoga practice.

Fourth House (Sukha Bhava): Foundations of Consciousness

The fourth house indicates the basic nature of the mind and the ability to develop self-awareness and the emotional connectivity to faith and beliefs, as well as the capacity to develop inner peace. It gives the security to go beyond our comfort zone as we change and grow. Look to the fourth house for clues to your basic character and life values as well as your potential to experience happiness through spiritual development.

Fifth House (Putra Bhava): Creative Consciousness

The fifth house indicates our creative drive, be it through children, projects, or manifestation of consciousness. This manifestation can occur through the use of mantras, yantras, mystical rituals, affirmations and connection to a personal deity. It may also occur in the form of siddhis, the psychic yogic powers, and an alignment with cosmic forces. Look to the fifth house as well for clues to past life karmic merits (purvapunya) and the gifts we bring into this lifetime. For example, Jupiter, which represents the teacher, located in the fifth house can indicate a beneficial past relationship with a spiritual teacher.

Sixth House (Roga Bhava): Unlimited Spirit

The sixth house indicates what we need to overcome in this lifetime through our self-belief, will, courage and effort. It is what makes us strong and teaches us to use our gifts to overcome our obstacles. It forces us to deal with self-imposed limitations of the physical body and environmental circumstance. It gives the ability to develop critical discernment, a strong sense of service, and practices and habits surrounding health and healing.

Seventh House (Kalatra Bhava): Self and Soul Mate

The seventh house is about the relationship of the self to the other person and what we can learn about our soul's journey as it bonds with another. It is here that self-awareness can become an appreciation of the other person, and where our sense of separateness can dissolve in union with another. In many ways, the seventh house contains the answer to who we are by providing us with both meaningful relationships and a powerful mirror to understand our own projections, self-deceptions, and misimpressions that we form when we are out of harmony with our true self.

Eighth House (Mrityu Bhava): Transformation and Rebirth

The eighth house is the house of yoga, astrology, kundalini, the chakras, and all esoteric spiritual wisdom. If you are reading this book, you obviously have a strong eighth house since this is the area of cosmic transformation, rebirth, and all the mysteries of life. All unconventional paths that lead to realization may be found in the eighth house. The eighth house often brings us significant challenges for it offers the opportunity for both great change and great suffering. There is always the possibility of death with the eighth house but instead of physical death, it can be the transformational dying of the old self and ego into a glorious rebirth.

Ninth House (Dharma Bhava): Truth and Purpose

The ninth house is the house of dharma, our righteous path in life, as well as the teacher. If you are a yoga teacher, or any type of teacher, there is usually a strong connection to the ninth house. This house indicates our beliefs, our philosophy, and our spiritual practices. It shows our ability to work with higher knowledge and wise teachers. A strong ninth house gives us a powerful sense of purpose and destiny. The ninth house also indicates spiritual journeys and foreign knowledge.

Tenth House (Karma Bhava): Self Manifestation

The tenth house is the house of action, particularly in the outer world as in a career or what actions we take that we are remembered for. Recognition, status and success are part of the tenth house and it gives a way to express the purpose of the ninth house. This is why people feel conflicted about their career if it does not align with their life purpose of the ninth house. If we are spiritually aware, it is through the tenth house that we demonstratively reveal our higher inner self in the actions we take in the outer world.

Eleventh House (Labha Bhava): Spiritual Fulfillment

The eleventh house is where we reap the rewards of actions in both the outer and inner world. It is how we are fulfilled and how we gain from our efforts, both materially and spiritually. A strong eleventh house indicates that we can make spiritual gains if we align our actions of the tenth house with the purpose of our ninth house. This house is best expressed when we bring our energies into service to others through our enlightened consciousness.

Twelfth House (Vyaya Bhava): Meditation and Liberation

The twelfth house is the house of solitude and meditation. It is our retreat, our ashram, and our cave of introspection. Planets that occupy or are associated with the twelfth house indicate the types of meditation best suited for us, along with the effects produced by these meditations. This house is called the house of liberation (moksha) for it is the final house and represents the last of the earthly life. It is where the ego can dissolve and merge with universal consciousness.

The Four Goals of Life (Purusharthas)

The twelve houses are characterized according to what Vedic thought calls the Four Goals of Life, or the Purusharthas. Each human existence has four purposes according to the rishis and seers of old: 1) The need to find our path or destiny in this life (Dharma), 2) The need to acquire the necessary resources or abilities to fulfill this destiny and to provide for ourselves (Artha), 3) The need to enjoy the pleasures of this incarnation (Kama), and 4) The need to find enlightenment and liberate ourselves (Moksha).

Each of the twelve houses is associated with one of these four goals as shown in the following table.

LIFE GOAL	HOUSES	MEANING
Dharma	1, 5, 9	Path, Duty, Destiny
Artha	2, 6, 10	Resources, Wealth, Abilities
Kama	3, 7, 11	Desire, Pleasure, Enjoyment
Moksha	4, 8, 12	Liberation, Enlightenment, Union

Table 1-6: Life Goals (Purusharthas) of the Astrological Houses

Where we bring our primary attention in this life is indicated by the distribution of the planets in the houses of our birth chart. If three or more of the nine planets are located in the Dharma Houses (1, 5, 9), there is a strong sense of life purpose of duty and destiny. If three or more planets are located in the Artha Houses (2, 6, 10), there is a focus for obtaining abundance and using our talents to progress. If three or more planets are located in the Kama Houses (3, 7, 11), our life may be spent in the enjoyment of this incarnation and the pleasures of the senses. Finally, if three or more planets are located in the Moksha Houses (4, 8, 12), we are concerned with merging with the greater consciousness.

Another way to understand the purposes of the houses is see the distribution of planets between the first, fourth, seventh and tenth houses (the Kendra Houses) and first, fifth and ninth houses (the Kona Houses). Planets in Kendra houses direct attention toward accomplishments in the material world while planets in Kona houses bring energy to the realm of spirituality and knowledge. More simply, the Kendra houses are conscious behaviors and the Kona houses are unconscious behaviors. It is preferable to have a balance or congruence of planets between these two groups of houses to achieve the maximum results in this life.

Houses of Challenge and Growth

Many books on Vedic astrology, and indeed many astrologers, give intimidating and disconcerting descriptions of the sixth, eighth, and twelfth houses. They are considered malevolent and said to bring bad results to planets located there. Their descriptions as being the houses of illnesses, obstacles, enemies (sixth house), death, endings, secrets (eighth house), and loss, isolation, waste (twelfth house) can be misleading to someone who is on a spiritual path and doing the practices of yoga.

In reality, it is common to see in the charts of spiritual seekers and realized masters a number of planets in these three houses. As you read other books on astrology, it is important to keep this maxim in mind: A spiritual practice (sadhana) changes the way the planets operate in the birth chart. What could be seen as a challenging and difficult birth chart with planets in these three houses can be the roadmap to liberation for one who is willing to do the spiritual work demanded by these houses.

Planets in the sixth house, instead of creating illnesses, can give healing abilities. Instead of creating obstacles, planets in the sixth house help us overcome obstacles. And more important, planets in the sixth house can give a strong capacity for serving others through karma yoga and seva.

Planets in the eighth house, instead of foretelling death and endings, can signify the ability for rebirth and new beginnings, or deep spiritual and therapeutic transformations. Without some energy in the eighth house, either through the planets or planetary associations with the sign of that house, it may be hard to undergo the process of dying of the old self so the new self can emerge.

Planets in the twelfth house, instead of loss and isolation, can also portend a loss of ego and beneficial time spent in solitary meditation. Indeed, planets such as Ketu and Venus when located in the twelfth house are excellent indicators for possible spiritual liberation.

This is one of the distinctions of Astrology Yoga: to see the possibilities and gifts that the planets and birth chart bring to those who are on the spiritual path. When we understand our karmas, our life purpose, and how our challenges exist so we may learn to use our gifts, then we realize the power and potential of astrology to lead the soul to bliss, liberation and reunion with the divine.

Relationships Between the Houses and the Signs

The houses are related to the signs through the rising sign, or the sign that is associated with your first house. The rising sign, or the sign that was ascending on the Eastern horizon at the time of birth, becomes the sign associated with the first house, the house of the body, psychology, personality, and temperament of the individual.

If the area of the zodiac designated as Gemini is rising at the time of birth, then the sign of the first house is Gemini or, as is said, "Gemini Rising." The next sign after Gemini is Cancer, and so Cancer then becomes associated with the next house, the second house. Continuing through the signs and houses, Leo would be the sign of the third house, Virgo the fourth house, until we arrive at the twelfth house that would be associated with the sign of Taurus.

In general, Vedic astrology typically assigns only one sign to a house. In Western astrology (and in a few variations of Vedic astrology), there can be two signs sharing or influencing a single house. For Astrology Yoga, and indeed much of Vedic astrology, the "equal sign, equal house" system is used.

In our above example with Gemini rising and associated with the first house, the eighth house would be Capricorn. In this case, the qualities of Capricorn would influence the eighth house affairs and the planetary ruler of Capricorn, which is Saturn, would also be associated with the eighth house. And so it goes, with all the houses being influenced by the sign associated with it as virtue of the rising sign.

This is the beginning of putting the language of astrology together: planets occupy signs which are in turn associated with houses and which are in turn associated with the planets that rule those signs. Learning to interpret this language is where the complexity of astrology begins and is beyond the scope of this current book.

For now, we will focus on relating the planets, signs, and houses to the practice and technology of yoga.

> "For those who have an intense urge for Spirit and wisdom,
> It sits near them, waiting."
>
> Yoga Sutras (I, 21)

Astrology, Yogic Anatomy, and Philosophy

Many of the philosophical concepts in yoga, including Patanjali's Eight Limbs of yoga as espoused in the Yoga Sutras, as well as all the aspects of yogic anatomy that make up the energetic body, have corresponding associations with Vedic astrology.

Specifically, the shariras (three bodies), the nadis (energy channels), the koshas (sheaths of existence) and the chakras (energy centers) are each linked to one or more of the planets.

By working with the energy of a planet, we can affect its corresponding yogic anatomy component, as well as enhance our understanding of the philosophical concepts and the classical yoga sutras that are also related to the planetary energies.

Here is how the planets relate to the underlying concepts of yoga.

The Three Gunas

According to yoga philosophy, everything in the material world is a mixture of three basic qualities called the gunas. The three gunas are present in varying degrees, and consist of sattva, rajas, and tamas.

In the Bhagavad Gita, they are described like this: "Sattva, Rajas, and Tamas are the three constituent aspects that originate from Prakriti the material plane) and they bind down within the body. Sattva, being pure, luminous, and serene, binds one to happiness and knowledge. Rajas, being impure, creates passions and cravings, and binds one to activity. Tamas, being of the lowest type, causes ignorance, inertia, and bewilderment, and binds one to laziness and illusion."

These qualities are also present in the nine planets, and each planet has a preponderance of one of these gunas, as follows.

The Sun exhibits the quality of sattva because it is luminous and pure. It gives light and its heat purifies. It is steady, bright, and the light of the soul.

The Moon exhibits the quality of sattva because it is luminous and serene. It gives light and its coolness soothes. It is sweet, clear, and the light of the mind.

Mars exhibits the quality of tamas because it is harsh, forceful and self-centered. Its ability to conquer and subjugate darkens its actions.

Mercury exhibits the quality of rajas because it is movable, mutable, and adaptable. It engages in business and commerce based on desire.

Jupiter exhibits the quality of sattva because it is prosperous, benefic, and generous. It follows dharma and seeks the highest knowledge.

Venus exhibits the quality of rajas because it seeks pleasures, enjoyment and creativity. It is susceptible to desire and seeks sensual fulfillment.

Saturn exhibits the quality of tamas because it moves slowly, seeming to stand still, and rules over death and decay.

Rahu exhibits the quality of tamas because it is insatiable and ignorant of the true purpose of life. It also creates illusions with its ability to eclipse.

Ketu exhibits the quality of tamas because it is bewildering, unusual, and causes separation. It also creates darkness with its ability to eclipse.

The Five Bhutas

According to yoga philosophy, everything in the material world contains a mixture of five basic elements that are called the bhutas. The five bhutas are present in varying degrees in all aspects of nature, and consist of earth (prithvi), water (apas), fire (agni), air (vayu) and ether (akash).

Earth has a heavy nature and its qualities are weight and cohesion. It provides support, stability, centeredness and grounding. It is associated with the skin, bones, and blood vessels. Its virtues are forgiveness and patience.

Water has a cool nature and its qualities are fluidity and contraction. It provides contentment, compassion, gentleness and forgiveness. It is associated with all bodily fluids. Its virtues are compassion and fertility.

Fire has a hot nature and its basic qualities are heat and expansion. It provides focus, transformation, understanding and recognition. It is associated with appetite (agni), thirst and sleep. Its virtues are knowledge and leadership.

Air has an erratic nature and its qualities are movement and motion. It provides flexibility, creativity, happiness and clarity. It is associated with muscular expansion and contraction. Its virtues are creativity and love.

Ether has a mixed nature and its qualities are diffusion and space giving. It provides peace, freedom, and expansion of consciousness. Its virtues are bliss and steadfast devotion.

These five elements are present in the nine planets, and each planet has a preponderance of one of these elements, as follows:

The Sun exhibits the element of fire and brings focus and transformation.

The Moon exhibits the element of water and brings gentleness and forgiveness.

Mars exhibits the element of fire and brings recognition and leadership.

Mercury exhibits the element of earth and brings a grounded nature to our speech and interactions.

Jupiter exhibits the element of ether and brings expansion and devotion.

Venus exhibits the element of water and brings fluidity and fertility.

Saturn exhibits the element of air and brings the necessary contraction after movement.

Rahu exhibits the element of air and brings movement and ambition.

Ketu exhibits the element of fire and brings knowledge and understanding.

As we have seen, the twelve signs of the zodiac also bring the bhutas or elements into our lives. There are three fire signs, three water signs, three air signs, and three earth signs, with the fifth element of ether pervading all twelve signs.

The Eight Limbs of Yoga

One of the foundational teachings in yoga philosophy is the concept of the Eight Limbs of Yoga (Ashtanga Yoga) as expounded by the sage Patanjali in the ancient Yoga Sutras.

These eight limbs define the path, or Sadhana Pada, by which yoga is perfected and consist of the following practices:

1. Yamas (Moral Principles for Self-Control)
2. Niyamas (Observances for Personal Development)
3. Asana (Yoga Posture)
4. Pranayama (Regulation of Prana or breath)
5. Pratyahara (Withdrawal of Senses from Their Objects)
6. Dharana (Concentration and Contemplation)
7. Dhyana (Meditation)
8. Samadhi (Merging into Spirit)

Each limb has a planet associated with it. By understanding the nature of the planets, we can appreciate the eight-fold path of yoga.

Although there is no discernable authority on planetary associations with the eight limbs, the following observations are based upon the basic nature and functioning of the planets.

Yamas – The Restrictions of Saturn

The five yamas specified in the yoga sutras can be seen as social ethical guidelines. In other words, the restrictions we place on ourselves to avoid the karmic repercussions of our human interactions. These are the "do nots" of our yogic behavior.

> Do not harm (ahimsa).
> Do not lie (satya).
> Do not steal (asteya).
> Do not disrespect the divine (brahmacharya).
> Do not be greedy (aparigraha).

These guidelines are the controls we use to limit behavior. The planet that is most associated with limitations and restrictions is Saturn. Indeed, one of the deities associated with Saturn is Yama, the god of death that controls our lives by measuring our lifespan like a cord that is then cut.

It is through the discipline and control that Saturn offers us we are able to practice the yamas, the first limb of yoga.

Niyamas – The Dharma of Jupiter

The five niyamas specified in the yoga sutras can be seen as our own personal observances and practices. In other words, how we live our lives to limit the karmic repercussions of our human existence. These are the "dos" of our yogic behavior.

> Do practice purity (saucha).
> Do practice contentment (santosha).
> Do practice spiritual effort (tapas).
> Do practice self-study (svadhyaya).
> Do practice alignment with the divine (ishvarapranidhana).

These practices enhance our behavior and accelerate our spiritual growth. The planet most associated with correct behavior and spirituality is Jupiter. Indeed, the Sanskrit name for Jupiter is Guru, the benefic teacher that immerses in rituals, religious ceremonies, and personal observances.

It is through the spirituality and dharmic behavior that Jupiter exemplifies that we able to perfect the niyamas, the second limb of yoga.

Asana – The Physicality of Mars

The yoga poses, or postures, provide the foundation for the outward practices of yoga. The asanas are the physical manifestation of the progress on the path of yoga. Asana is defined in the yoga sutras as a posture that is stable and steady that can be maintained with comfort and ease. The ultimate purpose of the asana is to furnish a seat for meditation and to prepare the physical body to undertake the rigorous practice of yoga.

Regardless if we see asana as simply a comfortable position for meditation or the means to develop physical health, the focus is on the body as the vehicle for the spiritual journey.

The planet most associated with the physical body is Mars. The necessary will and energy to assume an asana is also the purview of Mars, whether to simply sit for two hours in a meditative pose or perform physical feats of balance and strength necessary for the advanced asanas.

It is through the will of Mars and its realm of physicality that we are able to master asana, the third limb of yoga.

Pranayama – The Movement of Mercury

The breathing exercises of yoga, or pranayama, are said to bring forth a measure of the cosmic vibration that allows us to see the radiant light of the Inner Self. More mundanely, it is the regulation and movement of prana through the breath that furnishes equanimity to the mind and superior health to the body. Ultimately, pranayama is about moving prana, the vital life force of the universe and consciousness.

The great mover among the planets, the planet most associated with movement, is Mercury, the fastest moving of the planets. Mercury controls the movement of prana, the energy that is always in motion, so it is most associated with the practice of pranayama.

It is through the lightness and quickness of Mercury that we are able to master pranayama, the fourth limb of yoga.

Pratyahara – The Negation of Ketu

The fifth limb of yoga, pratyahara or sensory disengagement, takes us into the inner practices of yoga. By removing the attachment of the senses to outward objects, we are able to turn our attention inward and begin the journey to self-realization through concentration, meditation and merger.

When we disconnect from the energy of the senses as they come into contact with objects, we are able to discern the essential nature of pure consciousness. Pratyahara is not the rejection of the sensory nature or denial of material reality. It is the disassociation of the mind from the seduction of sensory impressions that cause separation from our oneness.

The planet associated with disassociation from the senses is the planet Ketu. The ability to renounce the temporal illusion of the senses for the experience of the eternal state of consciousness is one of the facets of Ketu. Liberation through transcendence of material and worldly concerns is what Ketu provides us. The myths of Ketu always describe it as a body without a head. In other words, Ketu represents the senses without the mind.

It is through the negation of the senses that Ketu provides that we are able to master pratyahara, the fifth limb of yoga.

Dharana – The Focus of the Sun

The sixth limb of yoga is dharana or concentration, the first step of mastering the mind by focusing the attention upon an object, or as the sutras describe it, the confining of thought to one point.

Concentration requires steadiness, stability, and an unchanging presence. These are the qualities of the Sun, the ever present shining light that never wavers. It is through this light of the mind, this ray of the sun, that we can focus like a laser beam upon the object. The Sun illuminates the object so the seer can see the seen and hold it in its vision.

It is through the powerful focused energy of the willful Sun that we are able to master dharana, the sixth limb of yoga.

Dhyana – The Reflection of the Moon

The seventh limb of yoga is dhyana or meditation, the penultimate step of mastering the mind by revealing that the subject and object are one and the same, or as the sutras describe it, when a continuous flow of awareness occurs as the thoughts become directed.

Meditation requires the ability to reflect the light of consciousness into the dark areas of the mind, to uncover that which is hidden and to maintain this light regardless of the vacillations and changeability of the mind. The ability to maintain a constant reflected illumination through an ever-changing nature perfectly describes the nature of the Moon. When we discover the constant light that exists beyond the myriad fluctuations of the mind, we have achieved meditation.

It is through the constant reflective energy of the ever-changing Moon that we are able to master dhyana, the seventh limb of yoga.

Samadhi – The Union of Venus

The eighth limb of yoga is Samadhi, or the merger of self into Self, the finite into Infinite, and achieving the union that is yoga. The sutras describe this state as being absorbed into Spirit, where all objects are void of form and only the essence of the object remains.

Samadhi essentially requires that the seer and the seen merge as One and the distinction between Self and Not-Self vanish. Only bliss remains as all sense of separation, alienation, and aloneness disappears in that union with all.

In its lower form, the planet Venus represents relationships on the earthly level and the merger of two lovers in the orgasmic union of bliss. In its most spiritual form, Venus leads us to union with the divine. We no longer seek our Soul Mate but we mate with our soul. The universal love promised by Venus becomes reality when the small sense of self disappears in the embrace of Samadhi.

It is through the ultimate spiritual union promised by Venus that we are able to experience Samadhi, the eighth limb of yoga.

The Three Bodies of Yoga

Yoga philosophy and yogic anatomy has identified three bodies that comprise the human experience. The perfection of yoga requires that we meet the needs of these three bodies, bring them into balance, and use them appropriately to achieve total health and integration.

The three shairas, or bodies, are:

- Physical Body (Sthula Shaira)
- Subtle Body (Sukshma Shaira)
- Causal Body (Karana Shaira)

You can gain insights into the three bodies by understanding the relationship between them and the planets in your birth chart that correspond with these bodies.

Physical Body (Sthula Sharira)

The physical body is the material frame, the tissue, blood, muscles and bones that make up the coarse outer body. It is the body that is subject to the laws of time and space, and its name (sthula) means, "that which decays." The mortal physical body is dependent upon the food we eat, how we use and move the body, and how we protect it from physical disease and illness. It is the essence of physicality.

In Vedic astrology, the planet that is associated with the physical body is Mars. A strong Mars provides the foundation for a robust physical body. Martian yoga practices, such as asanas, strengthen the physical body as well as the bodily cleansing practices (the shatkarmas) that are also ruled by Mars.

For students of astrology, the physical body is also associated with the first house of a birth chart, as well as with the planet that owns or rules the sign of that house (also known as the rising sign).

Subtle Body (Sukshma Sharira)

The subtle body is the psychomental complex that exists independently of and as a supporting structure for the physical body. It is the energetic or the pranic body that cannot be seen by the senses, and it contains the energy centers (chakras) and energy channels (nadis). Through the practice of yoga, we become more aware of the subtle body, the movement of energy through the body, and its relationship to the mind and meditation.

In Vedic astrology, the planet that is most associated with the subtle body is the Moon. A strong Moon provides the foundation for an effective subtle body. Along with the Moon, Mercury (through pranayama) and Venus (through sound) are also associated with the subtle energies.

For students of astrology, the subtle body is also associated with the Moon ascendant (the sign where the Moon is placed) as well as the planet that owns or rules the sign of the Moon in the birth chart.

Causal Body (Karana Sharira)

The causal body is the essence of the soul, our eternal nature beyond time and space. It is the body that "causes" us to incarnate and create a subtle and physical body to experience the earthly realm. Consequently, it is timeless, unchanging, and the seed of our infinite potential.

In Vedic astrology, the planet that is most associated with the causal body is the Sun. A strong Sun provides the foundation for an effective causal body and provides hints about the soul's journey and purpose.

For students of astrology, the causal body is also associated with the Sun ascendant (the sign where the Sun is placed) as well as the planet that rules the sign of the Sun in the birth chart.

The Three Major Nadis: Understanding the Energy Channels

Energy moves through the subtle body through a network of channels called nadis. The nadis carry the energy through the body generated by the pranas and the breath and are similar to, but not identical with, the Chinese meridian model used in acupuncture. Purification of the nadis to increase energy flow through the subtle body is one of the primary purposes of hatha yoga. As the nadis become purified, the subtle body can access this energy to facilitate transformation, healing and enlightenment.

Most yogic texts say there are 72,000 nadis while some indicate 360,000 nadis. There are 14 major energy channels or nadis in the body with origination and termination points at specific vital areas, openings, and organs that are used in the healing practices of ayurveda.

Most yoga practitioners and teachers, however, are primarily concerned with the three major nadis in the body, which are the Pingala, the Ida, and the Sushumna. It is these three nadis that Astrology Yoga discusses in detail.

The Sushumna is the main central nadi that is also associated with the spinal column and the central nervous system of the physical body. It is along the Sushumna that the energy centers, or chakras, are located. It is through the Sushumna that the Kundalini energy moves upward and downward through the chakras.

The Pingala and the Ida are the two major energy channels that run along each side of the spine or Sushumna. The Pingala is associated with the right side, and the sympathetic nervous system, while the Ida is associated with the left side and the parasympathetic nervous system. Both the Pingala and Ida energy channels or nadis originate at the base of the spine and terminate either at the right and left nostrils respectively, according to some yogis, or alternatively at the third eye or sixth chakra.

The Pingala is heating, projective, active, masculine and solar in nature and is associated with the Sun.

The Ida is cooling, receptive, passive, feminine and lunar in nature and is associated with the Moon.

The Sushumna, with its connection to the Kundalini energy, is associated with the planets Rahu and Ketu that are considered to be the head and tail respectively of the Kundalini serpentine energy that curls through the chakras. Ketu embodies the sattvic quality of liberation of the awakened kundalini while Rahu represents the dormant tamasic energy of the sleeping kundalini. Rahu thus represents the base of the spine while Ketu is the top of the spine. Both are associated with the kundalini energy, the astral body, and the Sushumna.

The Ida and Pingala are accessed astrologically by working with Moon and Sun energies respectively, particularly as it relates to the pranayamas performed through the left (Ida) and right (Pingala) nostrils. Alternate nostril breathing, also called Nadi Shodhana or purification of the nadis, is the most common yoga practice used to access the Sun and Moon energies to open the flow through these nadis.

Meditations and yogic exercises that focus on the top of the spine (sixth or seventh chakra) and the base of the spine (first chakra) are used to work with the Rahu and Ketu energies of the Sushumna. One of the old techniques for awakening the Kundalini to enter and move through the Sushumna was to literally beat the buttocks, or base of the spine, on the ground while meditating at the crown chakra.

Understanding the nature of our past karma (Ketu) and present karma (Rahu) are instrumental in the awakening of the Kundalini energy and its entry into the Sushumna.

The Five Sheaths of Existence: Exploring the Koshas

The concept of five sheaths of existence (or koshas) first appears in the Upanishads, some of the earliest yogic texts. The koshas are the layers that hide our true nature and oneness. Yoga is the way to investigate and integrate these layers to realize the essence of our being. Understanding the planets associated with the koshas provides us with another tool to understand these layers of our existence.

The Annamaya kosha is the outermost layer and is the gross physical body. For some, this is where awareness begins and ends. In yoga, we use asanas to break through the illusion that the Annamaya kosha is the only level of existence. Diet, exercise, hydrotherapy, the cleansing practices, and asanas are ways we work with the Annamaya kosha.

In Astrology Yoga, the planets most associated with the Anamya kosha are Mars and the planet associated with the rising sign or the first house in the individual's birth chart.

The Pranamaya kosha is the second layer and is associated with the subtle or energy body. This kosha regulates the vital life force energy as represented by the breath and movement of prana through the energy channels (nadis) and energy centers (chakras). Pranayama, mudras and bandhas are the principal methods to work with the Pranamaya kosha.

In Astrology Yoga, the planets most associated with the Pranamaya kosha are Mercury, which rules the movement of prana and the use of hand mudras, and Mars, which controls the energy of the body. Some scholars posit that Saturn, with its association with breath retention and suspension as well as the bandhas, plays a role in the Pranamaya kosha.

The third layer is the emotional or sensory mind body or the Manamaya kosha. Mana means '"mind" and this kosha is concerned with sensory impressions and emotional feelings. This kosha is where we experience our reactions to the material world. Mantra, music, and affirmations are ways we can work with the Manamaya kosha.

In Astrology Yoga, the planets most associated with the Manamaya kosha are Venus, which rules the feelings associated with sound, music and mantra, and the Moon, which controls the emotional mind and our reaction to sensory impressions. Some scholars also say that Mercury, and its association with mantra and sacred language also plays a role in the Manamaya kosha.

The fourth layer is the wisdom body, or the Vijnanamaya kosha. Vijnana means "knowledge" and this kosha holds the discerning intelligence and intuitive faculty known as "buddhi" in yoga, as well as the wisdom and witness consciousness. This kosha is where we are able to discover the Truth. Meditation is the technique we use to work with the Vijnanamaya kosha.

In Astrology Yoga, the planets most associated with the Vijnanamaya kosha are Mercury, which is closely associated with buddhi mind, and the Sun, which represents the eternal Truth and Light.

The fifth and final kosha is the bliss body, or the Anandamaya kosha. Ananda means bliss, and this kosha contains the true joy, love, peace and ecstasy that is the source of our true self in Oneness. This is the kosha in which we find our union as we merge into universal consciousness and lose our sense of separation from the higher self. Meaningful ritual, in which we connect the finite self with the infinite Self through an action that transcends time and space, is the technique to work with the Anandamaya kosha. An example of this would be the lighting of a candle to connect us to the timeless experience of bringing the One light into our lives.

In Astrology Yoga, the planets most associated with the Anandamaya kosha are Jupiter, which represents the ultimate expansion of the all-inclusive consciousness, and the Moon, which is associated with transcendence beyond the sensory consciousness.

The five koshas are a map to explore all the levels of yoga as we move progressively inward to experience the True Self. Mastering the yogic techniques to work with each of the koshas, as well as coming into proper relationship with the planetary energies of each of the koshas, allow us to achieve an integration and union on all levels of our being.

The Seven Chakras: Planets and the Energy Centers

The chakra system is one of the oldest universal paradigms for working with consciousness. While the chakras appear in some form or the other across many cultures and spiritual traditions, it is in the practices of yoga that they have acquired their most sophisticated and evolved expression.

A chakra is an esoteric psychic center in the subtle anatomy of the body that channels and transforms energy into various expressions and is associated with an organ, a nerve plexus, and endocrine gland in the physical body. Each chakra is also associated with a frequency or color, an element of the material world, a sensory function, a psychological state, and a spiritual function, among many other things.

The chakra system can address all aspects of existence, much like the planetary system, and can be associated with a major function or keyword.

The most common classical representation of the chakras in yoga is the following seven-energy center model that shows their location in the physical body as well as the main keyword that defines the chakra in our human condition.

CHAKRA	AREA OF BODY	KEYWORD
First	Base of spine	Security
Second	Pelvic area	Connection
Third	Navel center	Power
Fourth	Heart center	Compassion
Fifth	Throat	Expression
Sixth	Brow Point	Perception
Seventh	Crown of head	Unity

Table 2-1: Chakra Locations and Keywords

The seven visible planets are associated with the seven major chakras or energy centers. While both Western and Vedic astrologers have different opinions how the planets correlate with the chakras, there is a preferred model among many Vedic astrologers, as shown in the following table.

CHAKRA	NAME	PLANET
First	Muladhara	Saturn
Second	Svadhisthana	Jupiter
Third	Manipura	Mars
Fourth	Anahata	Venus
Fifth	Vishuddha	Mercury
Sixth	Ajna	Sun and Moon
Seventh	Sahasrara	(None)

Table 2-2: Chakras and Planetary Correspondences

Mapping the qualities of the planets to the qualities of the chakras shed light on the relationship between a specific chakra and a specific planet.

For example, the first chakra, or root chakra, at the base of the spine is the foundation for the structure of the chakra system as well as the foundation on which the spine or body rests. Saturn, associated with the first chakra, is considered astrologically to be the planet that provides the structure and foundation in our lives.

The second chakra, positioned in the area of the sexual organs, generates the energy for procreation, for expanding ourselves into the world through reproduction. Jupiter, associated with the second chakra, controls the expansive nature of the universe. Indeed, in Vedic mythology Jupiter was the most prolific of the planets, fathering 17 children through his three wives.

The third chakra, positioned at the navel point or solar plexus, is the seat of our personal power and drive whereby we make the events in life happen. Mars, associated with the third chakra, is the planet of action and energy that moves things forward.

The fourth chakra, or heart chakra, allows us to experience connectivity, love and compassion. Venus, associated with the fourth chakra, is the planet of love, diplomacy, and intimate feelings.

The fifth chakra, located at the throat, is the power of self-expression or speech. Mercury, associated with the fifth chakra, is the planet of communication, speaking, and language.

The sixth chakra, at the third eye point, is the center of higher perception where one can literally see the light, and as such it is appropriate that the two luminaries, the source of light in our lives that allow us to see, the Sun and Moon, are associated with the sixth chakra.

At the sixth chakra, we have two planets relating to that energy center yet no planets are associated with the seventh chakra.

Some Vedic astrologers associate the Moon with the 6th chakra and the Sun with the 7th chakra, perhaps to create a one-to-one planet to chakra mapping.

Along these lines, however, Paramahansa Yogananda, the author of *Autobiography of a Yogi* and student of the great yoga guru and astrologer Swami Yukteswar, indicated that the 6th chakra has both a feminine polarity ruled by the Moon and a masculine polarity ruled by the Sun. In effect, there would be two chakras, one for the Moon (Chandra) and one for the Sun (Surya) but both are situated at the brow point.

The 6th chakra, or third eye, is represented by two-petals or two eyes. The right eye (represented and indicated by the Sun) and the left eye (represented and indicated by the Moon) come together at the third eye to see as One. In this respect, having two planets ruling a chakra where two lights become one seems appropriate.

In addition, some yoga systems consider the seventh chakra to be beyond the realm of human experience and materiality, and in other systems, it is omitted entirely. Consequently, no planet is associated with the seventh chakra.

Several things are noteworthy about this arrangement of planets with the chakras. First, due to their brightness, the Sun and Moon are considered to be the "closest" planets to the self. They are at the top of the chakra system. Then moving outward through the solar system, we have Mercury, Venus, Mars, Jupiter and Saturn in that order, which is the same descending order of the planets through the successive chakras.

The signs of the zodiac, which are ruled by the seven planets, correspond similarly to the chakra system as the following table shows.

CHAKRA	SIGNS	RULING PLANET
First	Capricorn, Aquarius	Saturn
Second	Sagittarius, Pisces	Jupiter
Third	Aries, Scorpio	Mars
Fourth	Taurus, Libra	Venus
Fifth	Virgo, Gemini	Mercury
Sixth	Leo, Cancer	Sun, Moon
Seventh	(None)	(None)

Table 2-3: Chakras and Sign Correspondences with Ruling Planets

In astrology, each planet has a specific sign in which it is strongest, or exalted. When the planet is in its exalted sign, it is able to express its strongest and highest nature. The exalted sign is favorable for the fullest realization of the planet's energy.

Correspondingly, each planet also has a sign in which it is weakened, or debilitated. When the planet is in its debilitated sign, it is unable to express its fullest potential. The following table shows where each planet is exalted or debilitated in a particular sign.

PLANET	EXALTED SIGN	DEBILITATED SIGN
Saturn	Libra	Aries
Jupiter	Cancer	Capricorn
Mars	Capricorn	Cancer
Venus	Pisces	Virgo
Mercury	Virgo	Pisces
Sun	Leo	Libra
Moon	Taurus	Scorpio

Table 2-4: Planets and Their Exalted and Debilitated Signs

Now let's associate the planet to the chakra that contains its exalted sign:

CHAKRA	SIGN	EXALTED PLANET
First	Capricorn	Mars
Second	Pisces	Venus
Third	Aries	Sun
Fourth	Taurus, Libra	Moon, Saturn
Fifth	Virgo	Mercury
Sixth	Cancer	Jupiter

Table 2-5: Planets Associated with the Chakras by Their Exalted Signs

This table reveals a powerful innate relationship of the planets to the chakras if we associate the nature of each planet with the key concepts of the chakra that is connected to the planetary sign of exaltation.

For example, the first chakra is associated with the sign of Capricorn that has Mars as an exalted planet. The first chakra is concerned with security, staying alive, and taking care of the physical body. What better planet to put in charge of defense and physical protection than the warrior planet Mars?

The second chakra is concerned with bonding and connectivity, and Venus, the planet that rules relationships, is exalted in the sign of Pisces associated with the second chakra.

The third chakra is about personal power, manifestation, and vitality or the solar plexus, and so we have the exalted Sun there in the sign of Aries.

The fourth chakra is both about compassion and nurturing, for which we have mother Moon exalted in the sign of Taurus. The fourth chakra is also about selfless service, the higher aspect of an exalted Saturn when it is in the sign of Libra. It is noteworthy that the fourth chakra is the only one with two exalted planets and indicates the primary position the heart chakra has in the human experience.

The fifth chakra is about communication and self-expression. Mercury, which represents intellect, speech and writing does well here in its exalted sign of Virgo.

The sixth chakra is about meditation, perception, and knowledge. It is the place of the inner teacher and is represented by exalted Jupiter, or the Guru, in the sign of Cancer.

In astrology, there is also the sign in which a planet is at its weakest or debilitated, or incapable of full expression. Again, we can learn about the relationships of the planets to the chakras when we associate each planet to its debilitated sign in the various chakras:

CHAKRA	SIGN	DEBILITATED PLANET
First	Capricorn	Jupiter
Second	Pisces	Mercury
Third	Scorpio, Aries	Moon, Saturn
Fourth	Libra	Sun
Fifth	Virgo	Venus
Sixth	Cancer	Mars

Table 2-6: Planets Associated with the Chakras by Their Debilitated Signs

Jupiter, the planet of knowledge and wisdom, is constricted by the demands of the earthly first chakra that emphasizes physicality over spirituality and therefore is debilitated in the corresponding first chakra sign of Capricorn.

Intellectual and analytical Mercury does poorly in the area of feelings and emotions of the second chakra and therefore is debilitated in the corresponding second chakra sign of Pisces.

Saturn, the planet of humility and servility, feels out of place in the assertive third chakra and therefore is debilitated in the corresponding third chakra sign of Aries.

Similarly, the feeling and submissive Moon shies away from the domineering energy of the third chakra and therefore is debilitated in the corresponding third chakra sign of Scorpio.

The Sun, which of all planets is about the strong sense of Self, is uncomfortable in the fourth chakra in which the Self is submerged in deference to the Other, and therefore is debilitated in the corresponding fourth chakra sign of Libra.

Venus, the planet of diplomacy and love, does not enjoy the frankness and bluntness of the fifth chakra and therefore is debilitated in the corresponding fifth chakra sign of Virgo.

And finally Mars, the planet of action, is not well placed in the staid meditative space of the sixth chakra and therefore is debilitated in the corresponding sixth chakra sign of Cancer.

Understanding the Planets and Chakras

A preponderance of planets in one sign, and hence in a chakra, may indicate a need to work with the energy of that chakra, as well as to avoid the tendency to filter life excessively through that energy center.

Exalted planets may make working with the corresponding chakra easier while debilitated planets bring us challenges with that chakra.

Planets associated with one chakra that are located in a sign associated with another chakra will change how that chakra tends to function in our lives. For example, Venus, associated with the fourth chakra and relationships, in the sign of Capricorn, associated with the first chakra and security, may mean that we express our love toward another by providing them with security.

We can also consider the basic energy of each planet located in the sign of a chakra. For example, Saturn indicates contraction or obstruction, so its placement in a sign shows a chakra we may need to expand. located in the sign will make it easier to express that chakra's energies. For example, Jupiter in Leo (the sign associated with the sixth chakra) can provide opportunities for meditation while Saturn in Aries may create blocks in expressing the personal power of the third chakra.

A quick guide to working with the chakras through the planets is simply to balance or strengthen the planet that is exalted (fully expressed) in the sign that is associated with that chakra, as detailed in the table below:

To balance this chakra:	Strengthen this planet:
First	Mars
Second	Venus
Third	Sun
Fourth	Moon and Saturn
Fifth	Mercury
Sixth	Jupiter

Table 2-7: Planets to Strengthen to Balance the Chakras

Your Astrological Profile

The time and place of your birth creates your astrological profile. While there is change and evolution throughout your life, the basic nature and purpose of this lifetime can be understood by examining the birth chart.

The birth chart contains the promises, gifts, challenges, opportunities, karmas and lessons of the soul's journey. It is a karmic DNA map that we can use to navigate this life. Everything that has been or will be is contained in the birth chart, yet all is subject to our free will and awakened consciousness. Without awareness and conscious choices, we become fatalistically ensnared in a sequence of events set into motion by our birth, much like a driver hurtling down a winding road that never sees the road signs or even understands the reason for the trip.

The Birth Chart: Signs, Planets and Houses

The birth chart is a physical representation of where all the planets are positioned at the time and location of your birth. Your birth chart is a unique representation of an event in time and place, the start of your life. At the moment of your birth, the planets and their relationship to each other creates a temporal diagram that is never duplicated again. The birth chart is truly a snapshot of a cosmic clock, consisting of nine planets and twelve signs in an almost endless combination of possibilities.

From the birth chart, we can determine in which sign every planet is located, which area of life, or house, it is affecting, and how the planets themselves are relating to each other and changing each other's energies and manifesting in our life.

The following sections gives an insight into the many dimensions and aspects of your birth chart and how the planets in the various signs and houses affect your life and your yoga practice.

Your Yoga Sun Sign

Most Western people understand their astrological make-up in terms of what sign the Sun was in at the time of their birth. "I'm a Pisces," or "She's a Scorpio," are the common ways to describe a person astrologically.

This system has the advantage of simplicity. Know the day of your birth, and you can read your daily horoscope, analyze your friends' behaviors, or decide if you should ask for that job promotion or simply stay home.

Such an oversimplification of the complexities of an individual's astrological life, however, can be misleading. In Vedic Astrology, your Sun sign is less important than your Moon sign and your rising sign, both of which are more sensitive and precise than the Sun sign. Nevertheless, since the Sun sign is easily obtained by knowing your birth date, it is a convenient place to begin learning about yourself and your yoga practices.

Keep in mind that the sun sign in Vedic Astrology is more about underlying tendencies rather than the outward temperamental characteristics of an individual. In other words, your yoga sun sign gives you information more at the soul level than the psychological level.

For example, your sun sign could be Aries but you may express yourself in your world and interactions as a Virgo (depending if your moon sign, rising sign and other significant astrological considerations had a significant Virgo influence). Yet your soul's journey would be more like the initiating and fiery Aries than the organizing and earthly Virgo.

Another consideration is that the sun signs in Vedic Astrology differ from Western Astrology in that they are based on the actual zodiac positions. As a result, your Eastern or Vedic Sun sign may likely be different from your Western Sun sign. In many cases, your yoga sun sign will be the sign previous to your Western sun sign. Remember this is your soul description and if you open yourself up to having a "new" sun sign, you will see the reflection of your eternal nature in that description.

Finally, the dates given for the Sun sign positions will vary over time, due to the differences between the Western calendar and procession of the equinoxes. The dates in this book are generally good for people born after the mid-twentieth century through the present, but may need to be adjusted by a day forward or backward. If you were born exactly on a day that a sign begins or ends, read the adjacent sign for additional insights.

ARIES Sun (April 14-May 14)

If you were born April 14 to May 14, your birth Sun is in Aries according to Vedic Astrology. This is the most powerful sign for the Sun to be situated. Aries is associated with the planet Mars and is distinguished by its qualities of initiative, independence, ambition, courage, competitiveness, and action. The sign is also characterized by its youthfulness, with all the gifts and challenges that youth brings.

The Aries person wants to be the best in everything and is a natural leader. The have good discretion and a desire to advance quickly both materially and spiritually. They enjoy setting and reaching personal goals and have good tactical intelligence. They may be impatient to get the results of their efforts and can act impulsively.

The Aries Yogi

The Aries Yogi is quick to pick up a yoga practice but may also be quick to drop it as other things compete for attention. They do best with yoga when they set a goal and challenge themselves to accomplish it. They enjoy an athletic approach to yoga that offers physical exercise and the opportunity for accomplishment. The high-energy Aries Yogi can accomplish much if they don't become unyielding or headstrong in their yoga journey. The perceived self-centeredness of the Aries Yogi can lead to heightened self-awareness and a deep quest for spiritual self-realization. Their strong streak of individualism can also evolve into an understanding of the universal self. When they embrace their natural role of the spiritual warrior, they can win on the battleground of the ego.

Because of their independence and self-sufficiency, they can excel in the solitary practice of meditation if they quell their inner restlessness. Their natural element is fire; their key to deep inner transformation, and their innate quality is one of positive action. A strong-will that is applied with focus is the Aries Yogi's greatest strength for the practice of yoga.

TAURUS Sun (May 15-June 14)

If you were born May 15 to June 14, your birth Sun is in Taurus according to Vedic Astrology. Venus is the planet associated with Taurus and brings its sensual nature, love of beautiful things, and appreciation for the arts to this sign. They are earthy and practical people who are at home in the material world and appreciate the play and enjoyment of the senses. They are good at managing their resources and finances and can sometimes become possessive in their things and relationships.

They can be obstinate when pushed, and appreciate a kind and patient approach to life. They work through things carefully and will rarely rush. They have a strong belief in themselves and their abilities. They can be skilled in business and usually marry well. They enjoy food and may have musical talents.

The Taurus Yogi

The Taurus Yogi is practical, stable, resourceful, reliable, patient and will likely enjoy a methodical, pragmatic approach to yoga. They can become fixed in a yoga routine and may not be willing to change their practice. They also have a tendency to choose comfort and sensual pleasures over effort and sacrifice and that can make them avoid doing the work of yoga.

Once they get going with their yoga, however, they will go the distance and stick with a routine. They can bring patience, perseverance and stability to create a lasting practice. It is easier for them to do their yoga in a beautiful and comfortable surrounding, with flowers, incense, and elevating music. Their attachment to materiality does not make for the typical spiritual renunciate. Indeed, a Taurus Yogi sees no conflict in a spiritual path that embraces the pleasures of the material world. In fact, one of the purposes of the incarnation of the Taurus Yogi is to learn to be in the world but not be part of it – to enjoy the play of maya, or illusion of the sensory world, and to see it as such. It is a beautiful sign to first enjoy and then transcend the earthly realm through the sustained practice of yoga.

GEMINI Sun (June 15-July 15)

If you were born June 15 to July 15, your birth Sun is in Gemini according to Vedic Astrology. Mercury is the planet associated with Gemini and brings its quickness and lightness to this sign. They are intelligent with skills and abilities in many different areas and are well educated. They love to read, write, talk and joke. They are good in business and can be skillful with money and are good communicators.

They take a broad-based view of life and prefer to learn a little about a lot of things than a lot about one thing. Because of this wide-ranging interest and constant need for mental stimulation, they tend to do too much at once and can become scattered. They require change and variety in life, and dislike being bored.

The Gemini Yogi

The Gemini Yogi likes variety in the yoga practices and is a fast learner but may try to do too many things at once. Their attention wanders and they like a yoga class with movement as well as music or mantra. They need to learn to be still so they can focus their mind, but even in relaxation their thoughts still race. With sustained practice, yoga can bring the Gemini Yogi the greatest gift needed to fulfill their life, and that gift is focus.

The Gemini Yogi loves partner work and working with the arms in the poses. They can become excellent practitioners of pranayama breath work as well as students of the yogic texts. They love to read about yoga as much as practice it, and they have an affinity for learning and using mantras as well. They can excel at the practice of jnana yoga, the yoga of knowing and knowledge, because they are in love with the intricate nature of the mind. As they use yoga and meditation to master their mind, they gradually detach themselves from its cleverness and discover the power of their intuition to guide them in their spiritual path.

CANCER Sun (July 16-August 16)

If you were born July 16 to August 16, your birth Sun is in Cancer according to Vedic Astrology. The Moon is associated with Cancer and gives its emotional, sensitive and changeable quality to this sign. Cancer people like to live near water, greenery or gardens. They are attached to their home and inner emotional life although they also enjoy traveling. They have excellent intuition and trust their feelings over their thoughts. They have a real need to nurture, teach, and heal and often have connections with children.

The sign of Cancer can make the person mysterious, introspective, changeable, and adaptable. One of their main motivations is to create a sense of lasting security in their homes, their family, and relationships. They are very sensitive as to how physical and emotional environments affect their state of mind.

The Cancer Yogi

The Cancer Yogi is naturally intuitive about their yoga practice. They are ideal candidates for creating a home yoga practice because that's where you will often find them! They are sensitive to their own needs and may gravitate toward emotionally supportive yoga styles and postures. Put them in Child Pose and you will have a happy Cancer Yogi. They enjoy collecting books about yoga and will be fascinated by recipes for yogic meals. They make good yoga friends but can be overly sensitive to any criticisms about their yoga practice.

Yoga can provide the Cancer Yogi with a neutral mind and greater emotional stability, as well as a way to socialize with people of their own interests. They make great children's yoga teachers, as well as prenatal and postnatal yoga teachers. The journey of yoga can provide the Cancer Yogi what they have been seeking all their lives: lasting peace through emotional security. This comes about when they understand true security only comes when they surrender the dependence on outer things to achieve it, be it a home, a job or a relationship, and find the lasting security that comes from true knowledge of the self's infinite nature.

LEO Sun (August 17-September 16)

If you were born August 17 to September 16, your birth Sun is in Leo according to Vedic Astrology. The Sun is associated with Leo and gives a royal, confident and dignified quality to this sign. Leo people are generally strong, attractive, and successful in whatever they set out to do. They can be intense, self-centered, and perceived as being prideful or aloof. They often think they are right, and they usually are, but that may not necessarily endear them to others. They have high goals and ambitions. People are attracted to their natural warmth and generosity.

The sign of Leo is fixed and fiery, like the Sun, and possesses a pure sattvic quality that makes it the ideal placement for a virile, just and independent leader. Leo people enjoy being the center of attention and will happily believe all flattering remarks. They possess both regal and spiritual charisma.

The Leo Yogi

The Leo Yogi likes to do well in yoga class and will be quite willing to demonstrate a posture for their fellow students or talk about their own yoga experiences – or even teach the class themselves! They often become successful yoga teachers because of their natural ability to lead and to perform a role. They are great believers in the yamas and niyamas, the moral precepts of yoga, and like to behave ethically. They do have strong likes and dislikes about their yoga practice, and the different types of yoga, and may need to grow more accepting of all approaches to yoga.

The journey of yoga for the Leo is one in which the ego is directly confronted, tamed, and transcended by the practices of asanas and meditation. When they can accept a teacher, or a higher spiritual authority, the Leo Yogi can escape the entrapment of their own manufactured self-identity and embrace their spiritual ego. For the Leo Yogi, the practices of yoga are not about leaving, negating or dismissing the ego but to use it to become a spiritual light to all those around them.

VIRGO Sun (September 17-October 16)

If you were born September 17 to October 16, your birth Sun is in Virgo according to Vedic Astrology. Mercury is the planet associated with Virgo and gives its intellectual and naturally communicative style to this sign. Virgo people are well educated, enjoy continual learning, and live primarily in the mental realm. They are open, honest and care sincerely for others but can be forceful in their opinions. There is a tendency to criticize that may annoy others but they simply want everyone and everything to be as perfect as this world will allow.

They are well organized and detail-oriented and hate to make mistakes. They are analytical and love to categorize and have an amazing memory for facts and information. They are super-practical and delight in putting the material plane in proper order. They can form strong habits, good and bad, and are happy when they engage in self-improvement practices to enhance their health.

The Virgo Yogi

The Virgo Yogi is a perfect yoga student. They are disciplined, detailed, discerning, and concerned with health. They enjoy a structured and organized yoga practice with attention to specifics, routine, and health-producing benefits. They like to follow instructions and want to get it right. They do need to watch for perfectionist tendencies, getting lost in the details of a posture, and over striving for purity in practice.

The Virgo Yogi needs to harness their critical faculty and avoid being overly critical of their own advancement in yoga. They can accomplish this by engaging in their natural need to be of service to others through karma yoga. The analytical mind needs to be tamed through the regular practice of meditation in which there is a detachment from identification with the thoughts. Intellectualizing needs to be replaced by the experience of the yoga practice, and self-acceptance realized by continual identification with the higher self, through the practice of mantra and the development of the higher discerning intelligence (the buddhi mind) through jnana yoga.

LIBRA Sun (October 17-November 15)

If you were born October 17 to November 15, your birth Sun is in Libra according to Vedic Astrology. Venus, the planet associated with this sign, gives a love of balance, harmony and beauty. Libra people are fair-minded to a fault and may tend to be indecisive as they always consider both sides of any situation. They are relationship oriented, both socially and in their life partnerships. They are straightforward yet diplomatic in their opinions and interactions. They are sensually inclined, like beautiful things, and enjoy social gatherings. Libras will avoid confrontation and arguments and may compromise themselves to the point of resentment to make peace.

For Libras, there can be difficulty in expressing their true sense of self as they are more concerned with the other person than with their own identity and this can lead to low self-confidence and lack of self-belief. They are always seeking to find balance, both in their lives and in the natural harmony of the universe.

The Libra Yogi

The Libra Yogi enjoys a balanced yoga practice that allows for a sense of relationship to other students, teacher and themselves. They are social and may want to go out after class for something to eat or to connect and talk. They may try to be overly pleasing to the teacher and second-guess their own understanding of a posture or practice. They may have a hard time deciding which yoga practice to do, which teacher to study with, and when to practice. They are popular in their circle of yoga friends and benefit from having a yoga friend to practice with.

The beauty of the Libra Yogi is the ability to see all the practices and techniques of yoga as equally valid. They are open to explore all spiritual practices and can advance powerfully through their ability to gain a wide range of yoga experiences if they learn to synthesize. Libra Yogis benefit from the devotional practices of Bhakti yoga and can find that ultimate relationship they seek in the Divine Other.

SCORPIO Sun (November 16-December 15)

If you were born November 16 to December 15, your birth Sun is in Scorpio according to Vedic Astrology. Mars, the planet associated with Scorpio, brings its qualities of intensity, passion, and inner strength to this sign. Scorpio people are attractive with lives full of drama and excitement. They tend to be private, almost to the point of deeply secretive, and hide their thoughts and may take actions without considering the implications.

Scorpios have a strong interest in solving mysteries and exploring the hidden side of life. They have a deep perception and strong will to achieve transformation on a deep level, whether through mystical practices, sexuality, or mind-altering substances. They are charismatic and deeply influence people on mental, physical and emotional levels. The shadow side of Scorpio is its self-destructive nature that reflects their fascination with the eternal transformational process of death and sudden endings.

The Scorpio Yogi

The Scorpio Yogi is energetic, persevering, intense, and passionate about their yoga practice. They enjoy an athletic yoga practice that allows for movement, self-discovery, and intensity and may experiment with Ashtanga and Vinyasa yoga. They are drawn to the transformational practices of tantra and the hidden side of yoga. They have a special affinity for working with the chakra system and may be attracted to the practice of Kundalini Yoga.

Scorpio Yogis need to watch for their hidden agendas being brought into a yoga practice, as well as tempering their emotional intensity. They may find themselves drawn into yoga romances and flirtations as they work to find a balance in their relationships. When they beneficially harness the deeply transformational energies of this sign, Scorpios discover the real power they have always been seeking; the power to shed their old skin and their old way of life and be reborn like the phoenix from the ashes.

SAGITTARIUS Sun (December 16-January 13)

If you were born December 16 to January 13, your birth Sun is in Sagittarius according to Vedic Astrology. Jupiter, the planet associated with Sagittarius, gives this sign its qualities of morality, expansiveness, adventure, and freedom. Sagittarius people are generous, optimistic, philosophical, and like to lead ethical lives. They have a strong sense of faith and, consequently, people have faith in them. They have sound judgment and a strong desire to know and speak the Truth.

They set high goals and are capable of achieving success. They are natural advisors and counselors, and sometimes become teachers, lawyers, or credentialed professionals. They are respected for their wisdom over time and viewed as knowledgeable and wise. They enjoy traveling, the outdoors, and living a carefree existence.

The Sagittarius Yogi

The Sagittarius Yogi is expansive and enthusiastic about their yoga practice. They enjoy an active yoga practice that allows for achievement that is based on spiritual principles. They may grow restless in the confines of a yoga classroom and would actually prefer to be practicing in nature or visiting spiritual sites. They have luck in finding good yoga teachers and may become a yoga teacher themselves. They love to explore the philosophical aspects of yoga, often reading the Yoga Sutras or delving into the other sacred texts.

An important aspect of a yoga practice for the Sagittarius Yogi is that of ritual, altars, and religious trappings. They love to exhibit the outward expressions of the inner practices, and they will often have an altar in their home with a picture of their spiritual teacher. They do need to be cautious about holding tightly to the certainty of their beliefs or descending into religious dogma or self-aggrandizing their own spiritual ego. Their relentless quest for higher knowledge finds its ultimate expression in the personal experience of yoga when they realize they already possess the highest truth and authentic knowledge they have been seeking externally.

CAPRICORN Sun (January 14-February 12)

If you were born January 14 to February 12, your birth Sun is in Capricorn according to Vedic Astrology. Saturn, the planet associated with Capricorn, gives this sign its qualities of responsibility, patience, and perseverance. Capricorns take it slow and sure, one step at a time, as they climb their personal mountain to reach their goal. They are achievement oriented, career conscious, and hard working. They tend to be sober, sometimes somber, and often serious. They are concerned about providing their families with security and may appear externally dispassionate that masks their need for emotional affection.

They are interested in philosophical concepts along with their materialistic predisposition. They may hold a position of status and are reserved in their emotional expression. They tend to shine later in life after methodically progressing on their own merits.

The Capricorn Yogi

The Capricorn Yogi is practical, responsible, patient, and hardworking about their yoga practice. They may be overly cautious or rigid about their relationship to yoga. They need to watch for an inability to change a yoga routine or try something differently; otherwise their yoga practices can become static and routine. They need to schedule spontaneity into their daily practice. They do enjoy a disciplined yoga practice that allows for steady achievement through hard work. With their work ethic, they make excellent karma yogis, finding their spirituality in service and accomplishments that benefit others.

They tend to channel their spiritual impulses into the material world, and want to see the practical results of their spiritual journey. Capricorn Yogis want their yoga practice to have a lasting impact on the outer world. Their breakthrough in spiritual realization occurs when they realize they cannot do anything to become enlightened, and that it is the surrender to their own inner stillness that brings them to the truth.

AQUARIUS Sun (February 13-March 13)

If you were born February 13 to March 13, your birth Sun is in Aquarius according to Vedic Astrology. Saturn, the planet associated with Aquarius, gives this sign its qualities of service, idealism, and humanitarianism. Aquarius people are good communicators and writers. They learn quickly and finish their jobs properly. They have an active mental nature and think about befitting others while also initiating social reforms. They are unconventional, and bring a unique philosophical attitude to the challenges they meet in life.

They may lead a life of service or teaching and often have eccentricities and an appreciation for the unusual or futuristic. They may scatter their energy with all of their inventive ideas and exhibit a strong progressive nature that considers the welfare of others.

The Aquarius Yogi

The Aquarius Yogi is idealistic, friendly, humble, and inventive. More than likely, they were doing yoga before any other people in their social group as they like to take the lead in adopting new technologies and knowledge systems. They enjoy an unusual approach to yoga practice that allows for self-discovery, sharing, and group relationships. You may find an Aquarius yogi in a yoga teacher-training program where they enjoy the community of the training as much as the yoga. Sometimes they exhibit eccentric behavior and their free spirit in their yoga practice. Yoga is never weird enough for them!

The Aquarian Yogi often progresses spiritually through cultivating group consciousness. While they have an aptitude for solitude that is beneficial for meditation, they also have a need for a collective spiritual practice that reaches out to all humanity. Because of their naturally impersonal yet friendly style, they make excellent yoga teachers. The spiritual breakthrough for the Aquarius Yogi occurs when they realize that their constant need to expand the consciousness of all those around them is simply an outer projection of their deep need to experience the pure consciousness of their own being.

PISCES Sun (March 14-April 13)

If you were born March 14 to April 13, your birth Sun is in Pisces according to Vedic Astrology. Jupiter, the planet associated with Pisces, gives this sign its qualities of spirituality, compassion, empathy, and imagination. Pisces people are kind, helpful, and well liked. They are intelligent and have gentle personalities that may cause them to be taken advantage of. They are respectful of others and sometimes lack confidence in themselves. There is a strong emotional and intuitive nature that if unbridled causes a tendency towards escapism.

They can be creative and mystical and express these qualities artistically. Because of their desire for other states of consciousness, they may develop addictive personalities and substance abuse problems. They are tolerant, compassionate and adaptable to all people and situations and can be natural healers and possess psychic abilities.

The Pisces Yogi

The Pisces Yogi enjoys doing yoga with friends and is attracted to the otherworldly experiences that yoga can provide. They sometimes need direction in their yoga and may find themselves vacillating in their practice. They are easily influenced by others and may do yoga because people they like are doing it or they recommend it to them.

They enjoy a flowing yoga practice that allows for creativity with mystical underpinnings, rituals, and inspirational insights. They love to do yoga near water, and enjoy the emotional connection that yoga provides.

The challenge and opportunity for the Pisces Yogi is to use yoga to pierce the strong wall of illusion they create for themselves. By cultivating detached awareness through meditation, and not overly identifying with their emotional states, they can get in touch with that eternal self that lurks beneath their own murky waters. Yoga can help them realize that the world of fantasy they live in is only a substitute for the limitless world they discover when they transcend their moods, fears, and illusions.

Your Yoga Moon Sign

In Vedic astrology the moon represents the mind and the emotions whereas the sun represents the soul. The position of the Moon in the birth chart indicates the way the person thinks and feels, the important areas in their life, and their mundane relationship with the external world. In the world of everyday life, the Moon sign is considered to be more important than the Sun sign in understanding your nature.

Being born during the waxing Moon usually gives a more extroverted mind and personality, while the waning Moon leads to a more introverted mind. The full moon is considered to be favorable and rich in its action in a birth chart while the new moon is hampered in its full expression.

Afflictions and challenges to the moon at the time of birth are generally experienced more strongly than with the other planets for the condition of the moon often indicates the condition of our happiness. The planet that owns or rules the sign that the moon is located in at the time of birth also plays an important role in the person's life and yoga practice.

The following is a summary of the influence of the Moon in each of the twelve signs for a birth chart. Keep in mind that these summaries are by nature superficial and are always modified by other aspects of the birth chart.

Because the Moon moves through a different sign every 2 ½ days, you need to know your birth time to discover your moon sign as it may often be in two different signs on the same day. If you know your Western moon sign and degree, you can subtract 23 degrees from that to find your Vedic moon sign.

Once you know your moon sign, the following descriptions help you understand another part of your astrological make-up and how it relates to the practice of yoga, particularly in the realm of emotions and everyday affairs.

Moon in Aries

The moon in Aries is ruled by Mars. This gives an energetic and lively personality that can make independent decisions. Strong in ambition, firm in belief, and hurried by nature, there may be a lack of patience and an uncompromising attitude. Physically strong, enthusiastic and self-centered, this individual can advance far in yoga if they can focus their mind, hold to one course of action, and be willing to learn from their teachers. Aries love to be the first in everything, including their own practice of yoga and can be inspiring to their friends.

Moon in Taurus

The moon in Taurus is ruled by Venus. This is an auspicious sign for the moon that allows for a full expression of emotions and an appreciation of the senses, art, and nature. Patient, practical, and tolerant, there can also be an obstinate nature that holds to a fixed thought or position. Physically and mentally forbearing, this individual can create a long lasting yoga practice that is steady and rewarding if they can overcome a tendency toward indulgence and laziness.

Moon in Gemini

The moon in Gemini is ruled by Mercury. This is a highly mental sign with a broad interest in many things and a love of learning, reading and writing. Flexible, adaptable and usually blessed with a youthful body, this is a good sign for asana and pranayama practices. Yet it is concentration and meditation that the individual must work on to focus the mind and develop the patience that a lifelong yoga practice requires.

Moon in Cancer

The moon in its own sign of Cancer gives an intuitive and imaginative nature. This is an emotional and sensitive sign that runs on feelings and possesses deep nurturing energy. The hypersensitivity toward criticism and a tendency toward indulgences, particularly food and drink, can make the practice of yoga difficult for this individual yet it will be ultimately rewarding as it is the best way to manage the fluctuating moods of the Cancer native.

Moon in Leo

The moon in Leo is ruled by the Sun and this brings a sense of purpose and determination to achieve goals. There is an independence and benign self-centeredness that can make it challenging to follow the directions and dictates of others, so it will be important to practice humility and a willingness to listen to the teacher. The practice of yoga can help to marginalize egoistic and prideful tendencies, and the individual has a wonderful capacity to be a charismatic yoga teacher.

Moon in Virgo

The moon in Virgo is ruled by Mercury and this indicates a brilliant and analytical mind that is discerning and critical. There is an interest in education, self-improvement, attention to details, communication, health and service, all of which can make for an excellent yoga student and teacher. The practice of yoga, and the resulting lessening of egoistic judgment, can do much to soften the self-critical nature and relieve the self-doubt and nervousness that is common with the moon in this sign.

Moon in Libra

The moon in Libra is ruled by Venus and this indicates a love of beauty, harmony, and peace. There is a strong interest in finding the balanced way in life and in reconciling the material needs with the spiritual needs. While there is a definite tendency toward indulging the senses, this is also a mental orientation to life, often living in the realm of ideas. Libras do best with a yoga practice that follows an established routine or tradition with a good balance of asanas, pranayama and meditation. They can use yoga to find the true sense of self that is independent of a relationship.

Moon in Scorpio

The moon in Scorpio is ruled by Mars and is challenged by this sign as it can create a restless or overly emotional mind. They bring their intensity to the yoga practice and that can drive them to accomplishment. Because of their private or even secretive nature, they can go deeply into the mysterious realms of the spirit if they channel their sexuality into transformational practices. Scorpios need the practice of yoga to positively harness their need for a deep union that transcends simple physical passion.

Moon in Sagittarius

The moon in Sagittarius is ruled by Jupiter and indicates a positive, righteous, and expansive way of dealing with others. One of the most philosophical signs, Sagittarius produces great teachers and counselors, as well as large spiritual egos. There is an attraction to rituals, ceremonies, and orthodoxies and yoga practices can help integrate the fascination for new thoughts with these old traditions. They must watch that their love for high thinking, philosophical discourses, and rarified idealism does not take them away from applying the practical techniques of yoga.

Moon in Capricorn

The moon in Capricorn is ruled by Saturn and brings ambition, devotion, and hard work to the yoga practice. They tend to be systematic in their approach to yoga, and take each step after deep thought. They will rarely rush into yoga but once they commit, they make good progress through their own efforts. They can be overly serious or even pessimistic about their lives and their yoga, and that can be balanced by studying the lives of saints and yogis who overcame their hardships. Their natural introversion and impersonality can actually help in the practice of yoga.

Moon in Aquarius

The moon in Aquarius is ruled by Saturn and gives a strong interest in philosophy, psychic perceptions, meditation and yoga. Their love of the untraditional and nonconventional make them natural seekers, and their need for solitude can accelerate their spiritual progress. They have an impersonal style that can make them good teachers, yet it is difficult to know or appreciate what is going on in their minds. Yoga can help them change the world by first changing themselves.

Moon in Pisces

The moon in Pisces is ruled by Jupiter and gives strong principles and morals like Sagittarius but also an element of vacillation, indecision and susceptibility to being easily influenced by others. They have a respectful relationship with teachers and deep spiritual interests, yet their tendency to fantasy, escapism, and gullibility can lead them away from their path. Pisces benefit from good friends, and especially good friends who do yoga and who help them make good decisions. Yoga can be a way to realize their powerful dreams.

> "By the practice of meditation on the Moon,
> Knowledge of the organization of the stars is given."
>
> Yoga Sutras (III, 28)

Your Rising Sign

At the time of your birth, there is a zodiac sign that is "rising" over the eastern horizon, much like the sunrise. This rising sign imbues the incarnated soul with its energies and shapes the basic temperament of an individual for life. The rising sign is also called the ascending sign, or the ascendant, and in Vedic astrology, it is known as the rashi lagna.

Your rising sign at birth is a powerful indication of your health, personality, physical body, and fundamental psychology. It creates a framework in which the entire life is played out, and is instrumental in understanding our relationships, career, and spiritual journey.

The rising sun changes every two hours and is very sensitive to the birth time. An incorrect birth time of only a few minutes can mean that the rising sign will not be the true one. Astrologers can use methods to rectify an uncertain birth time in order to calculate the rising sign.

For an advanced understanding of your astrological makeup and its effects on your yoga practice, discovering the rising sign is an important step to take. For this reason, it is recommended you find out your birth time as exactly as possible. Hospital documents are usually more helpful than family memories in fixing the time of birth.

If you do not have a birth chart or know your rising sign, you can sometimes approximate your rising sign in this way: Take your birth time and then for every two hours after sunrise, add a sign to your Sun sign. For example, if you were born May 18 at 12:30 pm and sunrise was 6:30 am that day, then the sun sign of Taurus was rising at 6:30 am and six hours later, the rising sign would be Leo, or three signs after Taurus (remembering that the rising sign advances every two hours). This method will at least get you within one sign of your rising sign.

Even if you do not know your exact birth time, you may be able to figure out your rising sign by reading the descriptions of the 12 signs to see which one most closely describes you.

Aries Rising

If your rising sign is Aries, your yoga practice will need a strong degree of physicality and challenge to keep you interested. However, you need to also back off on your aggressive approach in your personal practice and not push your body too hard. You may need to intentionally slow your practice down, and watch carefully that you do not create yoga injuries through competing with yourself. Remember that yoga is about enjoying the journey and not racing to an imagined destination.

Aries Rising Yoga Personality: Swami Muktananda

Taurus Rising

If your rising sign is Taurus, your yoga practice will prosper when you make it a daily affair because you have a tendency to be fixed in your habits as well as your movements. You will, however, have to find a way to motivate yourself to actually get moving and get started. Once you have the habit, however, you may tend to become routine in your practice so avoid stagnation by switching out your practices. It is important that you have a beautiful location for your practice with art, flowers, and attractive yoga props to connect to your love of the senses.

Taurus Rising Yoga Personality: Sri Krishna

Gemini Rising

If your rising sign is Gemini, your yoga practice will never be boring because you love to change your routines and always try something new. Reading about yoga is almost as good as practicing yoga – but not quite! Avoid the tendency to over analyze or intellectualize about yoga and remember it's primarily an experiential and personal journey. Yoga is very important for those with Gemini rising because it is easy for them to get out of the physical body and live in the mental realm. Pranayama, as well as other practices that soothe and strengthen the nerves, is important for Geminis. They do make good teachers and speakers, and have a deep desire for a spiritual mate.

Gemini Rising Yoga Personality: Dalai Lama

Cancer Rising

If your rising sign is Cancer, you will likely have a wonderful home practice where you will feel secure and nurtured. Retreating into their shells and enjoying the seclusion of familiar surroundings can be excellent qualities of Cancer rising to develop the meditative mind. You have the capacity to be your own teacher because there is powerful intuition associated with Cancer rising. One challenge for Cancer rising is to make time for themselves and their yoga practice. They are very concerned about their families and friends and are often caregivers and nurturers. Yoga can give them the opportunity to nurture themselves and to better manage their changeable nature and fluctuating emotions.

Cancer Rising Yoga Personality: Sri Aurobindo

Leo Rising

If your rising sign is Leo, your yoga practice will have an element of performance, even if only you are the audience. There is a fondness for dance, music and drama, as well as sports and games. You may set high standards for yourself and your yoga practice, and there is a strong sense of sincerity and involvement, as well as independence in your spiritual path. They usually excel in the physical practices of hatha yoga, but they must watch their fiery nature for signs of impatience or even anger. While they usually become accomplished yogis, they must realize that yoga is not about what we accomplish but what we help others to accomplish.

Leo Rising Yoga Personality: Paramahansa Yogananda

Virgo Rising

If your rising sign is Virgo, your yoga practice will succeed as soon as you make it a habit. There is a love of self-improvement health routines, and Virgos are attracted to yoga for the physical benefits it provides. There is a fascination with diet and hygiene, and Virgos must watch the tendency to become judgmental with themselves and others about strictly following all the yogic percepts. They want to get their yoga "right," and they may ask many questions and get lost in the details of a practice. Like Gemini rising, they need variety and change in their yoga routines, and like Cancer rising, they can create a spiritual home that caters to their shy and reclusive nature. Learning to relax is an important yoga lesson for their excessive mental and nervous energy that can sometimes dissipate them.

Virgo Rising Yoga Personality: Sri Ramana Maharshi

Libra Rising

If your rising sign is Libra, your yoga practice will be centered on friends and social groups. There is an enjoyment of travel, and yoga can be a great reason to go places and have adventures. They make excellent yoga teachers because they are well liked and understand their students' needs. If they teach yoga, however, they need to be aware of their strong opinions, and not become overzealous in their own yoga practice. They do love peace and harmony, however, and will rarely argue their beliefs. There is a strong sensual nature to Libras that can lead to yoga affairs and becoming distracted by the pleasures of the senses. As is the case with Libras, making decisions is one of their big challenges, so sometimes it is better to simply have a fixed daily yoga routine rather than decide what to do every day.

Libra Rising Yoga Personality: Mahatma Gandhi

Scorpio Rising

If your rising sign is Scorpio, you are strongly attracted to yoga, astrology, and all the transformational and secretive practices associated with the mysteries of life. There is a deeply mystical side to you that can either be devil or divine. They are often forceful, intense and competitive people so they must carefully monitor these tendencies in their yoga practice. They are excellent one-on-one yoga teachers but must learn to control their need to exert power over others. There is usually a fascination with the chakras and Kundalini yoga as well as the development of the siddhis, or yogic powers, which can derail their spiritual progress. As they learn to use yoga to control their instincts and desires, they gain the ability to truly solve the greatest mystery of life – themselves.

Scorpio Rising Yoga Personality: Sathya Sai Baba

Sagittarius Rising

If your rising sign is Sagittarius, your yoga practice tends to be active, enthusiastic and spiritual. There is a strong concern about following the correct path and yoga practice, and there is an underlying philosophical fascination with all higher knowledge. It is very likely that spiritual journeys, pilgrimages, and quest for self occur throughout life. They love outdoors and traveling but do require a quiet spiritual home base. They would do well to follow a yogic diet as their health can suffer from indulgences. There is an optimistic, cheerful and physical engagement with life and their yoga practices give them a strong sense of ethics and dharma that is also so important to them.

Sagittarius Rising Yoga Personality: Mother Teresa

Capricorn Rising

If your rising sign is Capricorn, you tackle your yoga practice with determination, seriousness and perseverance. There is a natural fascination for older cultures and ways of thinking that attracts them to yoga if they are able to overcome their fundamentally conservative nature. With a tendency toward teeth and bone problems, Capricorns do well with a vegetarian or yogic diet that can prevent calcium loss. Sometimes they enter yoga later in life but they can actually look younger as they get older. They are often successful in the business world, and are great examples of how to bring a healthy dose of materialism to spirituality in a way that benefits many.

Capricorn Rising Yoga Personality: Yogi Bhajan

Aquarius Rising

If your rising sign is Aquarius, your yoga practice will be free-spirited and group oriented. You will have a natural gift for teaching yoga and are an avid learner all your life. They usually work hard behind the scenes, preferring to help the welfare of others rather than making a name for themselves. They are humble, eccentric, humanitarian, and often prefer isolation even though they are attracted to group consciousness and service to others. They are highly philosophical, and find yoga, as well as all on-the-edge technologies, to be fascinating. Yoga can provide them with the tools to overcome their melancholy tendencies as well as an avenue for their need to go where no others have gone before.

Aquarius Rising Yoga Personality: Sri Ramakrishna

Pisces Rising

If your rising sign is Pisces, your yoga practice is another way for you to dream, imagine and reach far away places in your mind. Your challenge will be to bring a dose of practicality to your psychic sensibilities to actually do a yoga practice. Overcoming vacillation and indecision by fully committing to a regular yoga practice, or yoga teacher-training program, can be the best thing for your spiritual growth. There is a strong sense of empathy and spirituality, yet if it cannot be properly channeled through yoga or some other discipline, there will be an urge for escapism through fantasy, drugs, food or alcohol. Yet the Pisces individual has the powerful potential to truly merge into the universal consciousness and achieve liberation in this lifetime.

Pisces Rising Yoga Personality: Baba Sitaram

> "There is a Light that shines beyond all things on earth,
> Beyond us all, beyond the stars, beyond the planets,
> Beyond the very highest heavens.
> This is the Light that shines in our heart."
>
> Chandogya Upanishad 3.13.17

Your Birth Day Planet

The planet associated with your day of birth gives insight into your basic nature and temperament. The Sun is associated with Sunday, Moon with Monday, Mars with Tuesday, Mercury with Wednesday, Jupiter with Thursday, Venus with Friday, and Saturn with Saturday. If you were born on Tuesday, for example, Mars will be a significant planet for you.

In Western culture, one of the best-known associations of the days of the week with personality types and an individual's destiny was a children's rhyme known as Monday's Child that helped children learn the seven days of the week. Although there were several versions, the following became the most popular rendition and was formalized in the 19th century:

> Monday's child is fair of face.
> Tuesday's child is full of grace.
> Wednesday's child is full of woe.
> Thursday's child has far to go.
> Friday's child is loving and giving.
> Saturday's child works hard for a living,
> But the child who is born on the Sabbath Day
> Is bonny and blithe and good and gay.

While the content was stretched to make a rhyme, there are several striking similarities with the astrological natures of the seven planets that ruled the respective days (as well as two completely wrong attributions).

For Monday's child, people who are heavily influenced by the Moon often do indeed have a "fair" or pleasantly rounded face.

Tuesday's child, however, ruled by the energetic and combative Mars might be hard-pressed to exhibit "grace."

Wednesday's child similarly is misattributed the quality of "woe" since its ruling planet Mercury is more likely to bring intelligence and learning.

Thursday's child as "having far to go" can be related to Jupiter who rules Thursday as is associated with long-distance travels, particularly pilgrimages.

Friday's child, ruled by Venus, the sensual planet of love and earthly pleasures, is certainly tagged correctly as "loving and giving."

Saturday's child, ruled by the disciplined, patient and preserving Saturn, is also well described as "working hard for a living."

Sunday's child would also likely exhibit the qualities of "bonny" good health as well as the shining "gay" optimism of the Sun.

For a quick look at your astrological profile, discover the day of the week you were born and the planet that rules that day. Then read about that planet in the section, The Nine Planets of Astrology Yoga.

Important: The day in Vedic tradition begins at sunrise, not midnight, and lasts until sunrise the following day. For example, if you were born at 2:00 am Tuesday, Vedic astrology considers you to be born on Monday since Tuesday begins at sunrise, not after midnight.

With that in mind, you can find the day of week you were born by using the following two tables to discover your "birth day."

Discovering the Day You Were Born: Your Birth Year Group

Using this table, find the year you were born and then get the corresponding group letter next to that year. For example, if you were born in 1966, your group letter is "F".

Year	Group	Year	Group	Year	Group	Year	Group	Year	Group
1920	K	1940	H	1960	L	1980	I	2000	M
1921	F	1941	C	1961	G	1981	D	2001	A
1922	G	1942	D	1962	A	1982	E	2002	B
1923	A	1943	E	1963	B	1983	F	2003	C
1924	I	1944	M	1964	J	1984	N	2004	K
1925	D	1945	A	1965	E	1985	B	2005	F
1926	E	1946	B	1966	F	1986	C	2006	G
1927	F	1947	C	1967	G	1987	D	2007	A
1928	N	1948	K	1968	H	1988	L	2008	I
1929	B	1949	F	1969	C	1989	G	2009	D
1930	C	1950	G	1970	D	1990	A	2010	E
1931	D	1951	A	1971	E	1991	B	2011	F
1932	L	1952	I	1972	M	1992	J	2012	N
1933	G	1953	D	1973	A	1993	E	2013	B
1934	A	1954	E	1974	B	1994	F	2014	C
1935	B	1955	F	1975	C	1995	G	2015	D
1936	J	1956	N	1976	K	1996	H	2016	L
1937	E	1957	B	1977	F	1997	C	2017	G
1938	F	1958	C	1978	G	1998	D	2018	A
1939	G	1959	D	1979	A	1999	E	2019	B

Table 3-1: Your Birth Year Group (A to N)

Discovering the Day You Were Born: Your Birth Month Group

The next table helps you determine what day of the week occurred on the first day of the month in which you were born. Using the group letter from the previous table, move across the row until you get to the column with the month of your birth. That will be the **first day of that month** in the year you were born.

Now count from that first day of the month to the actual day you were born. That will give you the day of the week on which you were born.

For example, suppose you were born March 10, 1966. Using the previous table, you find that for 1966, your birth year group letter is "F." Now look in the table below until you find the row that begins with "F." Look across the "F" row until you get to the column for March ("Mar") and you will see that that day is listed Tuesday ("Tu").

This means that March 1, 1966 was a Tuesday. Now count the days from Tuesday, March 1, until you reach your birthday on March 10. You will find that March 10, 1966 is on a Thursday. **Remember:** If you were born before sunrise Thursday, then your day of birth would be Wednesday.

Here's another example. A person was born August 6, 1976. From our previous table, the year group for 1976 is "K". For the "K" group, August 1 was Sunday. Counting 6 days from Sunday to August 6, we see that the day for August 6, 1976 is Friday.

	Jan	Feb	Mar	Apr	May	Jun	Jul	Aug	Sep	Oct	Nov	Dec
A	Mo	Th	Th	Su	Tu	Fr	Su	We	Sa	Mo	Th	Sa
B	Tu	Fr	Fr	Mo	We	Sa	Mo	Th	Su	Tu	Fr	Su
C	We	Sa	Sa	Tu	Th	Su	Tu	Fr	Mo	We	Sa	Mo
D	Th	Su	Su	We	Fr	Mo	We	Sa	Tu	Th	Su	Tu
E	Fr	Mo	Mo	Th	Sa	Tu	Th	Su	We	Fr	Mo	We
F	Sa	Tu	Tu	Fr	Su	We	Fr	Mo	Th	Sa	Tu	Th
G	Su	We	Fr	Sa	Mo	Th	Sa	Tu	Fr	Su	We	Fr
H	Mo	Th	Fr	Mo	We	Sa	Mo	Th	Su	Tu	Fr	Su
I	Tu	Fr	Sa	Tu	Th	Su	Tu	Fr	Mo	We	Sa	Mo
J	We	Sa	Su	We	Fr	Mo	We	Sa	Tu	Th	Su	Tu
K	Th	Su	Mo	Th	Sa	Tu	Th	Su	We	Fr	Mo	We
L	Fr	Mo	Tu	Fr	Su	We	Fr	Mo	Th	Sa	Tu	Th
M	Sa	Tu	We	Sa	Mo	Th	Sa	Tu	Fr	Su	We	Fr
N	Su	We	Th	Su	Tu	Fr	Su	We	Sa	Mo	Th	Sa

Table 3-2: Your Birth Month Group (A to N)

Your Birth Day Description

Now that you know the day of the week you were born, you know which planet has a major influence in your life. This planet indicates general qualities you may possess and yoga practices that may be appropriate.

Remember you will likely have other prominent planets that modify the effects of your birthday planet. The planet that is associated with the day of the week on which you were born, however, often does show how we act in this life, how our soul encounters this incarnation, and the nature of the planetary energy that we run on throughout each day.

DAY	PLANET	DESCRIPTION	YOGA
Sunday	Sun	Strong, generous, stable, loyal, energetic, popular, visionary	Hatha, Mantra
Monday	Moon	Nurturing, peaceful, calm, flexible, passionate, idealistic	Meditation, Restorative
Tuesday	Mars	Confident, competitive, athletic, combative, tactical, impetuous	Hatha, Asanas
Wednesday	Mercury	Well-spoken, wealthy, charming, witty, intellectual, adaptable	Gyan, Pranayama, Mudras, Mantra
Thursday	Jupiter	Virtuous, spiritual, ethical, pure, prosperous, powerful, instructive	Meditation, Teaching
Friday	Venus	Beautiful, sensuous, artistic, refined, diplomatic, creative	Tantric, Kirtan,
Saturday	Saturn	Responsible, hard-working, stoic, mature, humble, materialistic	Karma, Bandhas, Pranayama

Table 3-3: Birth Day Types and Yoga Practices

Read the description of the planet associated with your birthday. The weekday you were born is your lucky day because others are more in alignment with your native energies on that day.

While your birthday planet colors your life, influences from other planets modify this. For example, a person born Wednesday has Mercury energy and you would expect them to be talkative and playful. However, if there is a strong Saturn influence in their birth chart, they may be more restrained and measured while still exhibiting the mental alacrity of Mercury.

Your Yoga Star Sign

Before the twelve zodiac signs, ancient Indian astronomers divided the cosmos into 27 divisions based upon the fixed stars called nakshatras, which means "that which does not decay and is eternally fixed." Each nakshatra is distinguished by the major star located in its division of the sky, and is in effect a "star sign."

While the 12 zodiac signs are based on the movement of the Sun during the year (one sign per month), the 27 nakshatras, or star signs, are divided based on the movement of the Moon during the month (approximately one nakshatra per day).

Since the moon travels approximately 13 degrees and 20 minutes each daily period, the nakshatras are the same length. When you divide this number into the 360 degrees of the zodiac, you get 27, or the number of nakshatras or "star signs." Within this 13-degree and 20 minute range of the zodiac, there are various stars associated with that nakshatras (just like a constellation is associated with a sun sign). Like the 12 zodiac signs, the 27 nakshatras also have their own names, symbols, and meanings.

All the planets occupy one of the 27 nakshatras, and are affected by the energy of that nakshatra. The most important planet affected by a nakshatra is the Moon since the nakshatras are where the moon travels each day. The nakshatra of your Moon can be used like the Sun sign or Moon sign to understand your temperament, gifts and challenges.

You can find out the nakshatras occupied by the planets in the birth chart by having your Vedic birth chart done by an astrologer. Alternatively, if you know the sign and degree your planets occupy in Western astrology, you can subtract approximately 23 degrees from that position and get the location of your planets in Vedic astrology and hence determine its nakshatra by using the table in this chapter.

Once you know the nakshatra where your moon, sun, or any other planet is located at birth, you can read the descriptions of that nakshatra, or star sign, that the planet occupies to understand yourself and your yoga practices.

You can, however, easily determine the nakshatra where your sun is located at birth by finding your birth date in the following table. Reading the description for the nakshatra associated with your sun can give you more insights about your astrological self. As you locate the nakshatras for your other planets, see if an overall pattern emerges as you read the descriptions for all of them as well.

	Nakshatra	Zodiac Degree Range	Birth Date Range for the Sun Nakshatra
1	Ashwini	0 - 13 Aries	Apr 14 – Apr 27
2	Bharani	13 - 27 Aries	Apr 27 – May 11
3	Krittika	27 Aries - 10 Taurus	May 11 – May 24
4	Rohini	10 - 23 Taurus	May 24 – Jun 8
5	Mrigashirsha	23 Taurus - 7 Gemini	Jun 8 – Jun 21
6	Ardra	7 - 20 Gemini	Jun 21 – Jul 5
7	Punarvasu	20 Gemini - 3 Cancer	Jul 5 – Jul 19
8	Pushya	3 - 17 Cancer	Jul 19 – Aug 3
9	Ashlesha	17 - 30 Cancer	Aug 3 – Aug 16
10	Magha	0 - 13 Leo	Aug 16 – Aug 30
11	Purva Phalguni	13 - 27 Leo	Aug 30 – Sep 14
12	Uttara Phalguni	27 Leo - 10 Virgo	Sep 14 – Sep 27
13	Hasta	10 - 23 Virgo	Sep 27 – Oct 10
14	Chitra	23 Virgo - 7 Libra	Oct 10 – Oct 24
15	Swati	7 - 20 Libra	Oct 24 – Nov 6
16	Vishakha	20 Libra - 3 Scorpio	Nov 6 – Nov 19
17	Anuradha	3 - 17 Scorpio	Nov 19 – Dec 2
18	Jyeshtha	17 - 30 Scorpio	Dec 2 – Dec 15
19	Mula	0 - 13 Sagittarius	Dec 15 – Dec 28
20	Purva Ashadha	13 - 27 Sagittarius	Dec 28 – Jan 10
21	Uttara Ashadha	27 Sag - 10 Capricorn	Jan 10 – Jan 23
22	Shravana	10 - 23 Capricorn	Jan 23 – Feb 5
23	Dhanishtha	23 Cap - 7 Aquarius	Feb 5 – Feb 19
24	Shatabhisha	7 - 20 Aquarius	Feb 19 – Mar 4
25	Purva Bhadrapada	20 Aquarius - 3 Pisces	Mar 4 – Mar 17
26	Uttara Bhadrapada	3 - 17 Pisces	Mar 17 – March 31
27	Revati	17 - 30 Pisces	Mar 31 – Apr 14

Table 3-4: The 27 Nakshatras: Zodiac Degrees and Dates for Sun Nakshatra

For example, if you were born on November 23rd, then your sun would be in the nakshatra of Anuradha (in the sign of Scorpio). For a September 28th birthday, the sun nakshatra is Hasta (in the sign of Virgo).

Understanding the Nakshatras

All nine planets in Vedic Astrology are placed in one of the 27 nakshatras at the time of your birth, in the same way they appear in one of the 12 signs of the zodiac. As with the signs, the nakshatras modify the effects of the planets.

In addition, your ascendant, or exact degree of your rising sign, also is located within a nakshatra. The ascendant, the sun, and the moon typically express the nakshatras most strongly in our lives and yoga, but all the planets in your birth chart activate the energy of the nakshatra they occupy. If planets are close together in your birth chart, then they may also occupy the same nakshatra, making that energy more potent in your life.

The nakshatras are said to be older in origin that the signs of the zodiac and are unique to Vedic astrology. As we'll see later, the nakshatras not only reveal different aspects of your self and soul's journey, they may also be used to select the best times for yoga practices and indeed all activities.

The following description of the 27 nakshatras may also be helpful in understanding your career choice or dharma in the world. The characteristics of each nakshatra can support and enhance our worldly, as well as our spiritual, activities, and the descriptions of suggested careers have been modified from the ancient texts for modern occupations.

The nakshatras have also been used by teachers to discern the spiritual name of the individual, and is still used in India to determine the most favorable sound for a newborn's name.

Later in life, marital and sexual compatibility are also determined by examining the nakshatras that the moon is in for each spouse.

Finally, where the moon is located at birth in a nakshatra sets into motion the major planetary periods of our lives, starting a sequence of events that show up all through our lives and making it possible to discern the likely times for major life events to occur.

The following 27 nakshatras are presented in the order they occur in the zodiac, along with the exact degrees of the zodiac sign they occupy, and the name or description that has been attributed to the major star in that area.

For now, you can read the nakshatra for your sun (obtained from the previous table), and then return for more information as you discover the nakshatras for your other planets as well as your ascendant.

The quotations at the end of each nakshatra are from the ancient text Hora Ratnam and provide a traditional flavour to the more modernized descriptions.

1. ASHWINI
The Star of Adventure (Aries 00 00' to 13 20')

Planets in this nakshatra indicate natural healing abilities. The healing is transformational and revitalizing and has a therapeutic or mystical nature. You may be impulsive, adventure seeking, and self-initiating. You may also have a low tolerance for boredom and possess a free spirited nature that can lead to quickness and rash behavior.

You will need to stick with a yoga practice in a responsible way which may be difficult, but ultimately rewarding. Be willing to listen to your teachers and put yourself under their discipline. Holding postures for extended periods of time will help balance you. You will be able to use your yoga for healing work, as a therapist or counselor, and will enjoy the opportunity to travel and share your spiritual journey. You may have a natural gift for using herbs. Acupuncturists often have a planet in this nakshatra.

> "Those born with the Moon in Ashwini are charming, fortunate, skillful, intelligent, fond of ornaments and valorous."

2. BHARANI
The Star of Creativity (Aries 13 20' to 26 40')

Planets in this nakshatra give a passionate and artistic temperament coupled with potent creative energy that may be sexual in nature. There will be an ability to be focused and goal-oriented that can allow you to master your sometimes turbulent nature. Personal transformation occurs when you exert self-control and willpower to overcome obstacles.

You will need to practice Brahmacharya, the yogic yama of divine conduct, as well as exercise responsibility in your intimate relationships. There can be benefits from periods of celibacy, yet you can also progress through the sexual tantric practices of yoga if there is maturity of the soul. Your mind can be easily focused through meditation, and you will enjoy postures and other yogic practices that require an application of your will. This is a good position for planets if you are interested in astrology, yoga and shamanism.

> "Those born with the Moon in Bharani are skillful in sexual acts, truthful, resolute in undertakings, bereft of sickness, fortunate and eat limited food."

3. KRITTIKA
The Star of Fire (Aries 26 40' to Taurus 10 00')

Planets in this nakshatra make you forthright in your truthfulness and honesty yet also gives a sharp side to your nature that can be cutting or critical. One of the powers of this nakshatra is the ability to burn away negativity to get to the truth and to cut through illusions that we surround ourselves with. There is ambition and intensity present, along with sharp wit and high imagination.

You will benefit from developing a connection between your throat chakra and your heart chakra so that the sometimes blunt words of truth can be filtered through compassion. Understand that the true meaning of Satya is not simply truthfulness but bringing your word and thought into conformity with your present situation. Fire worship and pujas come easily to you. Finally, this is an excellent position for a spiritual teacher who can confront the student about what needs to be accomplished.

"Those born with the Moon in Krittika are splendorous, intelligent, liberal, avid eaters, fond of opposite sex, sagacious, skillful and honorable."

4. ROHINI
The Star of Sensuality (Taurus 10 00' to 23 20')

Planets in this nakshatra give you an appreciation of the material world and all its elements as experienced through the senses. There is a love of beauty, art and culture and the fine things in life. You have a philosophical side to your practical earthiness and the ability to speak well about your firm views. The yoga practice of pratyahara, the disengagement of the senses from the outer world to awaken the inner senses, will be a powerful practice for you, as well as following a mono-diet (eating only a single food) for short periods of times.

You will benefit from developing your ability to nurture growth and creativity and to avoid the temptation of overindulgence in comfort and luxury. This is an excellent position for those who work with herbs and food for healing, a well as writers, artists, actors and designers. Consultants and people in positions of authority benefit from planets placed in this nakshatra. Yoga teachers with this placement tend to be charming and artistic in their teaching.

"Those born with the Moon in Rohini are charming in appearance, firm in disposition, honorable, enjoy pleasures, affable in speech and brilliant."

5. MRIGASHIRSHA
The Star of Searching (Taurus 23 20' to Gemini 06 40')

Planets in this nakshatra give the ability to explore deep spiritual truths. There is a passion to investigate, to seek, even to chase after the illusory nature of matter or the ultimate truth of reality. There is a quickness and lightness associated with this placement, much like a deer, which is the symbol for this nakshatra. Sometimes this quickness and searching creates a restless nature that is always on a quest. It may give a changeable nature that can lead to having few firm views. There is a desire to move, travel, and avoid confrontation.

You need to develop your focus through concentration and meditation. While you may prefer a moving yoga practice, you should perfect the seated asanas for stability. You can be an excellent student of yoga, and your communication skills can lead you to become an effective teacher or proponent of yoga. This is an excellent position for teachers of all types, as well as writers, researches, mystics, psychics and astrologers.

> "Those born with the Moon in Mrigashirsha are enthusiastic, timid, peace-lovers, seek purity, unstable, and learned in secret lore."

6. ARDRA
The Star of Clarity (Gemini 06 40' to 20 00')

Planets in this nakshatra indicate a capacity to comprehend the workings of the universe and the nature of one's mind. Yet there can be a pull between using the mind to find material fulfillment and to gain spiritual knowledge. The practice of the yoga of discernment, Gyan Yoga, comes easily to people with planets in this nakshatra. While there can be great material and spiritual rewards, these only come through focused and persistent effort and by learning to deal with your emotional nature.

You will benefit by developing patience, perseverance, and pertinacity. Your thirst for knowledge can make you an excellent writer or speaker, but you must restrain your impulsive nature. Resist the temptation to jump from yoga style to yoga style. A daily pranayama practice will bring peace and effectiveness. This is an excellent position for those who work in healing, particularly in pain management, hospitals and hospice work. Teachers, social workers, and people involved in humanitarian projects also benefit with planets placed in this nakshatra.

> "Those born with the Moon in Ardra are deft in magic rituals, adventurous, skillful in trading, fierce and sometimes ungrateful."

7. PUNARVASU
The Star of Renewal (Gemini 20 00' to Cancer 03 20')

Planets in this nakshatra give a philosophical and spiritual outlook. There is a friendly and flexible attitude toward life that comes out in the yoga practices. You will likely enjoy mystical poetry and have artistic tendencies. There is a sensitivity and appreciation for the material world but you can be content with very little materially. You often have the resources you need and feel that you are abundantly blessed.

In your meditation, release your anxiety over small things your concern for making everyone happy. Realize you have the ability to bring spiritual light into darkness, and you are a natural counselor. You may travel much in your life, but you also have a strong attachment to home, family and friends. This is an excellent position for spiritual teachers, psychologists, philosophers and mystics. Those who work in technical fields, as well as social workers, entertainers, writers and publishers, benefit from planets placed in this nakshatra.

> "Those born with the Moon in Punarvasu are handsome, patient, happy, contented and walk fast."

8. PUSHYA
The Star of Nourishment (Cancer 03 20' to 16 40')

All planets in this nakshatra become nurturing and supportive. You are excellent at encouraging and helping others to grow, and respected in your family and liked by your friends. It is said that the ability of this nakshatra is to create spiritual energy. There is a mature and ethical predisposition that pulls you toward humanitarian goals. Karma Yoga can be an excellent path for you as you do best in selfless service that brings peace of mind. Because you control your emotions and have good speaking abilities, you are an excellent teacher with a caring yet impersonal style.

Planets in this nakshatra bring wisdom and generosity, as well as a capacity for creativity, especially when helping others. This is an excellent position for spiritual teachers, religious leaders and the clergy, as well as those who deal with spiritual and earthly laws. Business leaders, politicians, defenders of public welfare., and those in the creative and art fields benefit from planets placed in this nakshatra.

> "Those born with the Moon in Pushya are fortunate, famous, adventurous, kind, charitable, wealthy, and have artistic tastes."

9. ASHLESHA
The Star of the Serpent (Cancer 16 40' to 30 00')

Planets in Ashlesha create a philosophical and penetrating intellect that explores the hidden areas of the soul. The symbol for this nakshatra is the coiled serpent at the base of the spine or the kundalini energy. Hence yoga practices involving the chakras and working with kundalini energy are favored. The Buddha had his ascendant in this nakshatra, and there is desire for mystical exploration and seeking enlightenment. This can be a difficult energy for many unless they are meditators and yogis because it gives a reclusive and independent nature that makes normal socializing challenging. There is strong intuition when planets occupy this nakshatra, and working with the sixth chakra comes easy.

This is an excellent position for yoga teachers (especially Kundalini). Planets in this nakshatra are beneficial for astrologers, mystics, and psychics and those interested in the occult. Therapists and counselors in the areas of addiction and sexuality do well with planets here.

> "Those born with the Moon in Ashlesha are mischievous, lascivious, crafty, mystical and seeking self-restraint."

10. MAGHA
The Star of Power (Leo 00 00' to 13 20')

Planets in Magha indicate strength and spiritual leadership and often bring success to the house, or area of life, that this nakshatra occupies. The great Indian saint, Paramahansa Yogananda had his Moon and rising sign in this powerful nakshatra. There is a desire to follow the path of your ancestors or to adhere to a spiritual lineage of established tradition. Power, wealth, and resources come to this placement and it may distract you from your yoga path. There can be greatness but also restlessness and passion that must be acknowledged and understood. You will need to channel your ambition and accomplishments to serve others and to grow your spirituality. Karma yoga, the yoga of selfless service, can balance the tendency toward real or perceived spiritual egoism by bringing humility and kindness to your manner.

This is an excellent position for the dramatic arts, and supports those in the public eye, such as teachers and yoga instructors. Planets in Magha benefit self-employed people, as well as those in research and history.

> "Those born with the Moon in Magha are radiant, honorable, with irascible temper, respectful to the gods and possessing oratorical abilities."

11. PURVA PHALGUNI
The Star of Pleasure (Leo 13 20' to 26 40')

Planets in this nakshatra bring creative energy and a love of pleasure. Often there is skill in the fine arts, as well as an importance placed on erotic love and partnerships of all kinds. It has been described as an excellent placement for a "love goddess" and so we find that the singer Madonna has both her Ascendant and Moon in this nakshatra.

Besides simple passion, this nakshatra also brings affection and a love of life and sensual pleasures in general. This sociable and diplomatic nakshatra brings good fortune and fulfillment, and the challenge is to not overindulge in all the pleasures it brings you.

Because this nakshatra brings luck, you can develop a tendency to not put forth your own efforts. To balance this, you can develop the "tapas" or yoga austerities in your practice. This could mean holding postures for longer period of times, working with longer breath retention, or even taking cold morning showers before your yoga practice. Fasting one day a month or dressing simply can balance the inclination to self-sabotage through over indulgence.

This is an excellent position for those who perform, such as actors, singers, dancers, models, artists and musicians, and those in the media, such as radio, film and photography. Planets in this nakshatra are common for teachers and professors, as well as therapists who specialize in relationships.

> "Those born with the Moon in Purva Phalguni are brilliant, wanderers, charitable, adept at art and dance, discerning and skillful."

12. UTTARA PHALGUNI
The Star of Service (Leo 26 40' to Virgo 10 00')

Planets in this nakshatra give a compassionate nature and desire to help others. There is a kindness and generosity that brings friends and you enjoy relieving the suffering of others.

The other focus of this nakshatra is on the joy that love, marriage and relationships can bring. In fact, you may have such a strong desire to never be alone that you may stay in relationships that no longer serve you, particularly if you are a rescuer. Your strong interest in the spiritual life, however, can balance your tendency to lose yourself in another person.

Learning to be beneficially alone, such as in a yoga practice or during meditation, brings peace of mind to your relationships and your service-oriented life. Devoting the fuits of your labor to the highest good, as in the practice of karma yoga, is a good way to use this energy. With care, you can practice tantra and sexual mysticism as part of your spiritual path.

This nakshatra is excellent for social workers and those who do charitable work. Healing of all types, including relationship counseling, as well as public health is favored. Writers, astrologers, media personalities, public relations and sales people benefit by planets in this nakshatra.

> "Those born with the Moon in Uttara Phalguni are victorious, happy, enjoy pleasures, passionate, poetic and arty, truthful and scholarly."

13. HASTA
The Star of Skills (Virgo 10 00' to 23 20')

Planets in this nakshatra bring physical and mental skills, as well as support a strong spiritual nature. The symbol for this nakshatra is the palm of the hand, reflecting its ability to manifest what one seeks and place it in their hands. You are industrious, capable of hard work, and can grasp many things with your mind – and your hands! You will be good in crafts, have a degree of dexterity, and a desire to create through the hands, be it writing, art or music. Issues of control, indecisiveness, and holding on to things can create problems with planets in this nakshatra.

Yoga practices that follow a routine and do not require decisions will be helpful for you. You will enjoy all the postures that use the hands prominently, and you will also benefit from exploring the practice of hasta mudras, or the hand positions in yoga.

This nakshatra is excellent for crafts people, artists and writers. Teachers, students, advisors, counselors, psychotherapists, astrologers, healers and palm readers all benefit from planets in this nakshatra. Sales people, communication professionals, events planners, and those in the travel industry are influenced by this nakshatra.

> "Those born with the Moon in Hasta are learned, enthusiastic, servile, travellers living abroad, valorous and highly sexed."

14. CHITRA
The Star of Opportunity (Virgo 23 20' to Libra 06 40')

Planets in this nakshatra give a sense of design and proportion, allowing for artistic expression, originality, and personal flair. The symbol for Chitra is a brilliant gem that allows you to shine, either in your ideas, elegance, or personal charisma. There is a balanced mind with an analytical slant that makes you an excellent student. You can bring artistic organization to the material world in a beautiful and pragmatic way.

The desire for originality may make it difficult for you to follow a yoga routine or your teacher's suggestions. You may bring your own slant to your practice and teaching that can lead to an egotistical relationship with your yoga. For this reason, you should follow and teach from an authentic yoga tradition.

This nakshatra is excellent for architects, interior designers, jewelers, and fashion designers, as well as creative business people and artists. People who desire a deeper knowledge of the scriptures, as well as writers, publishers, and those in the media, benefit from planets in this nakshatra.

> "Those born with the Moon in Chitra are splendorous, wealthy, enjoy pleasures of the bed, scholarly in outlook yet glamorous and bejeweled."

15. SWATI
The Star of Learning (Libra 06 40' to 20 00')

Planets in this nakshatra bring a love of learning and beauty. There is a connection with artistic activities and business skills. Your greatest joy is to travel for educational purposes and that meets your need for positive change. You possess excellent communication skills, but there is a restless aspect that can scatter your energies and make it hard to stay on track.

Meditation and commitment to a regular yoga routine is a must to harness your powerful intellect. You have a need for periods of solitude and meditation in order to keep your sensitive constitution healthy.

This nakshatra is excellent for people who like to work independently on their own and assume positions of leadership. Yoga and meditation teachers, as well as spiritual guides, benefit greatly from planets in this nakshatra. Serious students and people who follow ascetic practices are aided by planets located in Swati.

> "Those born with the Moon in Swati are righteous, eloquent, expert traders, lustful, highly celebrated or learned, self-restrained and educated."

16. VISHAKHA
The Star of Purpose (Libra 20 00' to Scorpio 03 20')

Planets in this nakshatra create ambition and determination to accomplish one's goals. There is an ability to gain knowledge and to acquire a deep understanding of life. Sometimes the sense of purpose associated with this nakshatra can make you unaware of others or unable to balance your activity. Success and power are alluring, and you can become fanatical in beliefs and methods, although there is an ability to achieve much.

Yoga is essential for your health as it will create a way to relax and rebalance your life. Practicing restorative yoga, relaxation techniques, and pranayama can keep you from burning yourself out. Meditation helps you connect you to the higher purpose behind your strivings.

Teachers, writers of literature, researchers, scientists, politicians, and lawyers are helped by this nakshatra. Those who have strong ideas or ideologies, such as those who believe strongly in humanitarian causes, will benefit from planets in Vishakha.

"Those born with the Moon in Vishakha are masters of many languages, ferocious to enemies, spiritually inclined, controller of senses."

17. ANURADHA
The Star of Success (Scorpio 03 20' to 16 40')

Planets in this nakshatra give a talent for dealing with people and forming friendships that lead to success. You have good organizational skills, an affinity for numbers, and an ability to recognize opportunities. You often bring people together for business, social or spiritual purposes. Your sensitivity and low tolerance for frustration can create emotional upset.

Pranayama practices, such as alternate nostril breathing, and other emotional balancing breathing techniques are excellent for those with planets in this nakshatra. Meditation can bring needed emotional control to your life and keep your strong appetite in check.

This nakshatra is excellent for business management, event planners, and all professions that require organizational skills. Politicians, lawyers, pubic speakers and those in the travel and import business benefit from this nakshatra. Actors, musicians, dentists, surgeons and medical technicians are also aided by planets in Anuradha.

"Those born with the Moon in Anuradha are heroic, in the royal service, travel and live abroad, loved by all, charming, secretive and tawny."

18. JYESHTHA
The Star of Wisdom (Scorpio 16 40' to 30 00')

Planets in this nakshatra bring understanding to the hidden areas of life. People with the energy of Jysehta may be mystical, subtle and skillful and seek knowledge from deep and dark places. The personality is strong, and can range from arrogance and overbearing to reclusiveness and timidity. There may be issues of jealously or betrayal, yet those with planets in Jyeshta are powerful protectors and receive protection. When wisdom is gained, it comes from real life experiences.

Kundalini yoga and all practices that work with the chakras are recommended. Karma yoga, particularly when helping the powerless, is a superb way to manage this energy. To avoid being swept away by their own searching, strong spiritual teachers are essential.

This nakshatra is excellent for creative and eccentric individuals and those self-employed. Intellectuals, philosophers, researchers, dancers, musicians, and models often have planets in Jyeshta. On the other side, the protector element of this nakshatra favors military leaders, detectives, and police. This nakshatra benefits shamans and tantric masters.

> "Those born with the Moon in Jyeshtha are wealthy, strong in temperament, libidinous, revengeful, protective and knowledgeable."

19. MULA
The Star of Foundation (Sagittarius 00 00' to 13 20')

Planets in this nakshatra bring a deeply inquisitive nature to the person who always wants to get to the root of all things. Indeed, its name "mula" translates as "root." There is often a scientific or philosophical nature that facilitates deep research and analysis. There can be a powerful and passionate nature that may be expressed through oratory or writing, such as with Martin Luther King who had his career planet located here.

Meditation is essential to bring emotional balance and peace to the mind, as is developing a spiritual or philosophical approach to life. A daily yoga practice helps you through the highs and lows you may experience.

This nakshatra is excellent for doctors and healers (especially herbalists and pharmacists), as well as philosophers, spiritual teachers, lawyers, public speakers, and writers (especially those who write speeches).

> "Those born with the Moon in Mula are honorable, capable, crisis managers, lustful, slim, wealthy and can cause difficulties."

20. PURVA ASHADHA
The Star of Invincibility (Sagittarius 13 30' to 26 40')

Planets in this nakshatra bring patience, spirituality and power over others. There is a strong desire to improve one's circumstances or to self-improve. In either case, there is a sense of invincibility that often makes for success. Victory may sometimes occur through aggression, but fortunately there is also an empathetic and intuitive nature that modifies the power exerted over others. There is a watery side to this nakshatra that gives an emotional depth and softness as well.

The success and power of this nakshatra to bring material success can sidetrack you from your spiritual journey. To counter this tendency, living a simple life and practicing the yoga restraint (yama) of non-possessiveness (aparigraha) will bring great benefits.

This nakshatra is excellent for teachers, writers, and lawyers. Because of its connection to the element of water, all professions connected with water, such as boating, shipping industry, the navy, marine matters, and even water utility workers may have planets in Purva Ashadha.

> "Those born with the Moon in Purva Ashadha are monogamous, firm in friendship, heroic, grieving and honorable."

21. UTTARA ASHADHA
The Star of Victory (Sagittarius 26 40' to Capricorn 10 00')

Planets in this nakshatra bring ambitions and principles connected to social goals and humanitarian causes. There is an idealism and restlessness that creates the archetypical reformer. A common quality is a streak of independence and a sense of loneliness, as exhibited by Abraham Lincoln who had his moon in this nakshatra. Generally there is psychological insight that allows them to be good communicators, along with an ability to organize and take on responsibility in a mature and thoughtful way.

Because this nakshatra creates difficulty in completing plans, committing to a daily yoga practice is an excellent way to balance the intensity and diametrical apathy that occurs with this nakshatra.

This nakshatra is excellent for government jobs, social workers, doctors and scientists. All people who fight for a cause, be it a social reformer, a military person, benefit from planets in Uttara Ashadha.

> "Those born with the Moon in Uttara Ashadha are grateful, upright, modest, can charm anyone, and blessed with excellent spouse."

22. SHRAVANA
The Star of Learning (Capricorn 10 00' to 23 20')

Planets in this nakshatra bring a desire for knowledge and arriving at the truth. It is the sign of the student, and its name translates as "the hearing," an indication of this deep desire to learn, often from oral traditions. There is a brilliance to the mind that understands different cultures and spiritual traditions that enables them to connect to others through speaking or writing.

While people with planets in Shravana may be drawn toward Gyan or Jnana, the yoga of discernment and knowledge, they benefit from a more experiential approach to yoga that is more doing than studying. They make excellent yoga teachers and students for their ability to work in the oral tradition and enjoy participating in satsang, or spiritual discussions.

Teachers, speech therapists, and linguists all benefit from planets in Shravana, as do astrologers, religious scholars, priests, and old-time politicians. People in the recording and media industry, particularly working with sound or broadcasting, often have planets in this nakshatra.

> "Those born with the Moon in Shravana are illustrious with a competent spouse, learned in scriptures, orator, poetical and great givers."

23. DHANISHTHA
The Star of Symphony (Capricorn 23 20' to Aquarius 06 40')

Planets in this nakshatra bring a love for music and rhythm and its symbol is the cosmic drum. This is an optimistic and liberal nakshatra with ambition and motivation. Planets here enhance prosperity and recognition. There may be a need to control and exert power that can create impatience and self-absorption. It is important to keep the bigger picture in mind and work with others to accomplish the good you desire.

Yoga practices that incorporate music and rhythm are successful, such as chants and incantations, drumming and particularly playing the gong, the instrument of the Yogi. Practices that require extended periods of stillness, such as meditation, or holding the breath and postures to develop patience, all benefit the person with planets in Dhanishtha.

Musicians, drummers, poets, healers, and those who deal in real estate, benefit from planets in this nakshatra. People who engage in charitable projects and humanitarian work often have planets in Dhanishta.

> "Those born with the Moon in Dhanishtha are philanthropic, great speakers, enjoy music and dance, insist on peaceful methods at work."

24. SHATABHISHA
The Hundred Stars (Aquarius 06 40' to 20 00')

Planets in this nakshatra create an independent, mystical and reclusive nature with a tendency to self-isolate. Science, metaphysics, psychology, therapy and unconventional healing hold a special attraction. The power of this nakshatra is the ability to heal, and those with planets here undergo a healing transformation in their own lives. There is an intellectual slant to this nakshatra that may remove you from the outside world. You may experience some extremes in life that lead to a deep self-realization.

Understanding the yogic healing science of Ayurveda can benefit those with planets in Shatabhisha. Meditation practices can remove them from the world, so this must be balanced with karma yoga and service to others.

Astrologers, astronomers, physicians, nurses, healers, pathologists, writers, researchers, nuclear scientists and electricians benefit from planets in Shatabhisha which can also give organizational and business skills.

> "Those born with the Moon in Shatabhisha are heroic,
> have fluctuating fortunes, great fortifications, and enjoy vices."

25. PURVA BHADRAPADA
The Star of Truth (Aquarius 20 00' to Pisces 03 20')

Planets in this nakshatra emphasize purification and transformation. There is an element of fire that creates change, much like the phoenix rising from the ashes. Planets here give good speaking abilities and an opinionated nature. There is interest in the unusual, the mystical, and the eccentric. Because of the strong personal and social vision this nakshatra creates, there can be a tendency toward a critical nature toward those who are unable to see life's injustices. Moderating your impetuousness and suspicion help you realize your search for lasting truth.

It is important for those with planets in this nakshatra to cultivate diplomacy and to speak tactfully and subtly.

Planets in this nakshatra bring benefit to those in the business world, such as administrative planners, statisticians, and managers. Healers involved in geriatrics, hospice work and nursing often have planets in Purva Bhadrapada, as do ascetics, visionaries, astrologers, occultists, tantrics, and the black arts magicians.

> "Those born with the Moon in Purva Bhadrapada are crafty,
> defeated by women, impatient, heroic, and indulge in sorrows."

26. UTTARA BHADRAPADA
The Warrior Star (Pisces 03 20' to 16 40')

Planets in this nakshatra bring writing and speaking skills that can be passionate and influential. There is insight into the hidden areas of life that creates a mystical nature. There is a need to be alone to develop your wisdom and intuition. You are generally protected in the financial areas of life, having what you need and able to obtain resources for others.

This nakshatra represents where the Kundalini energy can be awakened so yoga practices that work with the chakras and nadis, including all types of Kundalini Yoga, are beneficial.

Those who do charitable work, as well as those in non-profit organizations, benefit from planets in this nakshatra. Religious workers, saints, astrologers, mystics, writers, philosophers, teachers, and researchers often have planets in Uttara Bhadrapada, as do those who deal with death and transformation or the practices of tantric yoga.

> "Those born with the Moon in Uttara Bhadrapada are great speakers, vanquish their foes, always satisfied, clear goals and blessed with progeny."

27. REVATI
The Prosperous Star (Pisces 16 40' to 30 00')

Planets in this nakshatra create a nurturing and helpful personality. There is an artistic and creative nature that may take you away from materialistic goals, preferring to provide help and healing. This nakshatra is about marking time, particularly the end of time, and is associated with the end of all things, as is fitting for the last nakshatra. The symbols for Revati are a cosmic fish and a drum. The fish is a symbol of spirituality and the drum is a marker of time. This is a protective and hospitable nakshatra concerned with offering sustenance to both worldly and spiritual travelers.

This nakshatra supports the quest for spiritual liberation, and planets here bring benefit from meditating on the endings of all things. Revati also supports using the gong in yoga meditation and relaxation.

Those who work with time, from clock makers to historians, as well as those who provide help for travelers, benefit from planets in this nakshatra. Mystics, musicians, empathetic healers, and all those who take care of others often have planets in Revati.

> "Those born with the Moon in Revati are very desirable, rich, enjoy pleasures, scholarly, proud, travel and live abroad or in isolation."

Your Karmic Planets: Rahu and Ketu

Rahu and Ketu are called the shadow planets (Chaya Grahas) because they represent the ecliptic points in your birth chart where the moon and sun are put into shadow or eclipsed. Like shadows, these two planets conceal more than they reveal and indicate the part of the self that is not easily known, such as the past and future karmas.

At the time of your birth, Rahu and Ketu signify the major karmic issues of your life and the areas in which they will manifest. Rahu and Ketu are always located in opposite signs of the zodiac from each other, forming an axis between our present and past karmas.

Rahu is the karma of this present life, where we spend our energies, fulfill our ambitions, and express our obsessions. Ketu represents the past life work, what we have accomplished, where we have been, and what we already have known and experienced.

Typically we bounce back and forth between the extremes of the two opposite signs these planets occupy, seeking to balance our karmas by swinging in one direction, often too far, and then ricocheting back in the other direction, trying to find a balance in the middle.

The primary work in this life is to find a way to reconcile the seemingly opposite nature of these two planets into a consistent expression of our true nature. For example, Ketu in Libra (the sign of relationships) and Rahu in Aries (the opposite sign of self) may indicate a life in which it is important to find the balance between the tendency to submerge one's needs in deference to a relationship and the opposite intense search for self-identity that excludes a relationship. The balance would be to find one's sense of self within a relationship, thus satisfying the needs of both signs these planets occupy.

To find out where Rahu and Ketu are in your birth chart, use the following table and locate the year you were born and find the birth date and the corresponding signs they occupied. You can then read what this placement tells you about your major karmic issues.

For example, if you were born April 15, 1975, then the following table shows that at the time of your birth Rahu is in the sign of Scorpio and Ketu is in the sign of Taurus.

Year	Date Range	Rahu / Ketu Signs
1925	Jan 1 – Dec 31	Cancer / Capricorn
1926	Jan 1 – Mar 25	Cancer / Capricorn
	Mar 26 – Dec 31	Gemini / Sagittarius
1927	Jan 1 – Sep 22	Gemini / Sagittarius
	Sep 23 – Dec 31	Taurus / Scorpio
1928	Jan 1 – Dec 31	Taurus / Scorpio
1929	Jan 1 – Mar 14	Taurus / Scorpio
	Mar 15 – Dec 31	Aries / Libra
1930	Jan 1 – Nov 24	Aries / Libra
	Nov 25 – Dec 31	Pisces / Virgo
1931	Jan 1 – Dec 31	Pisces / Virgo
1932	Jan 1 – Jun 1	Pisces / Virgo
	Jun 2 – Dec 31	Aquarius / Leo
1933	Jan 1 – Nov 27	Aquarius / Leo
	Nov 28 – Dec 31	Capricorn / Cancer
1934	Jan 1 – Dec 31	Capricorn / Cancer
1935	Jan 1 – May 28	Capricorn / Cancer
	May 29 – Dec 31	Sagittarius / Gemini
1936	Jan 1 – Dec 31	Sagittarius / Gemini
1937	Jan 1 – Jan 31	Sagittarius / Gemini
	Feb 1 – Dec 31	Scorpio / Taurus
1938	Jan 1 – Aug 9	Scorpio / Taurus
	Aug 10 – Dec 31	Libra / Aries
1939	Jan 1 – Dec 31	Libra / Aries
1940	Jan 1 – Feb 1	Libra / Aries
	Feb 2 – Dec 31	Virgo / Pisces
1941	Jan 1 – Aug 17	Virgo / Pisces
	Aug 18 – Dec 31	Leo / Aquarius
1942	Jan 1 – Dec 31	Leo / Aquarius
1943	Jan 1 – Apr 16	Leo / Aquarius
	Apr 17 – Dec 31	Cancer / Capricorn
1944	Jan 1 – Oct 15	Cancer / Capricorn
	Oct 16 – Dec 31	Gemini / Sagittarius
1945	Jan 1 – Dec 31	Gemini / Sagittarius
1946	Jan 1 – Apr 9	Gemini / Sagittarius
	Apr 10 – Dec 31	Taurus / Scorpio

Table 3-5: Signs for Rahu and Ketu Based on Birthdate

Table 3-5 (Continued): Signs for Rahu and Ketu Based on Birthdate

Year	Dates	Signs
1947	Jan 1 – Dec 14	Taurus / Scorpio
	Dec 15 – Dec 31	Aries / Libra
1948	Jan 1 – Dec 31	Aries / Libra
1949	Jan 1 – Jun 24	Aries / Libra
	Jun 25 – Dec 31	Pisces / Virgo
1950	Jan 1 – Dec 21	Pisces / Virgo
	Dec 22 – Dec 31	Aquarius / Leo
1951	Jan 1 – Dec 31	Aquarius / Leo
1952	Jan 1 – Jun 17	Aquarius / Leo
	Jun 18 – Dec 31	Capricorn / Cancer
1953	Jan 1 – Dec 31	Capricorn / Cancer
1954	Jan 1 – Feb 20	Capricorn / Cancer
	Feb 21 – Dec 31	Sagittarius / Gemini
1955	Jan 1 – Sep 1	Sagittarius / Gemini
	Sep 2 – Dec 31	Scorpio / Taurus
1956	Jan 1 – Dec 31	Scorpio / Taurus
1957	Jan 1 – Feb 24	Scorpio / Taurus
	Feb 25 – Dec 31	Libra / Aries
1958	Jan 1 – Aug 27	Libra / Aries
	Aug 28 – Dec 31	Virgo / Pisces
1959	Jan 1 – Dec 31	Virgo / Pisces
1960	Jan 1 – May 7	Virgo / Pisces
	May 8 – Dec 31	Leo / Aquarius
1961	Jan 1 – Nov 7	Leo / Aquarius
	Nov 8 – Dec 31	Cancer / Capricorn
1962	Jan 1 – Dec 31	Cancer / Capricorn
1963	Jan 1 – May 3	Cancer / Capricorn
	May 4 – Dec 31	Gemini / Sagittarius
1964	Jan 1 – Nov 14	Gemini / Sagittarius
	Nov 15 – Dec 31	Taurus / Scorpio
1965	Jan 1 – Dec 31	Taurus / Scorpio
1966	Jan 1 – Jul 17	Taurus / Scorpio
	Jul 18 – Dec 31	Aries / Libra
1967	Jan 1 – Dec 31	Aries / Libra
1968	Jan 1 – Jan 13	Aries / Libra
	Jan 14 – Dec 31	Pisces / Virgo
1969	Jan 1 – Jul 10	Pisces / Virgo
	Jul 11 – Dec 31	Aquarius / Leo
1970	Jan 1 – Dec 31	Aquarius / Leo

Year	Dates	Signs
1971	Jan 1 – Mar 12	Aquarius / Leo
	Mar 13 – Dec 31	Capricorn / Cancer
1972	Jan 1 – Sep 23	Capricorn / Cancer
	Sep 24 – Dec 31	Sagittarius / Gemini
1973	Jan 1 – Dec 31	Sagittarius / Gemini
1974	Jan 1 – Mar 20	Sagittarius / Gemini
	Mar 21 – Dec 31	Scorpio / Taurus
1975	Jan 1 – Sep 17	Scorpio / Taurus
	Sep 18 – Dec 31	Libra / Aries
1976	Jan 1 – Dec 31	Libra / Aries
1977	Jan 1 – May 22	Libra / Aries
	May 23 – Dec 31	Virgo / Pisces
1978	Jan 1 – Nov 30	Virgo / Pisces
	Dec 1 – Dec 31	Leo / Aquarius
1979	Jan 1 – Dec 31	Leo / Aquarius
1980	Jan 1 – May 26	Leo / Aquarius
	May 27 – Dec 31	Cancer / Capricorn
1981	Jan 1 – Nov 24	Cancer / Capricorn
	Nov 25 – Dec 31	Gemini / Sagittarius
1982	Jan 1 – Dec 31	Gemini / Sagittarius
1983	Jan 1 – Aug 9	Gemini / Sagittarius
	Aug 10 – Dec 31	Taurus / Scorpio
1984	Jan 1 – Dec 31	Taurus / Scorpio
1985	Jan 1 – Feb 3	Taurus / Scorpio
	Feb 4 – Dec 31	Aries / Libra
1986	Jan 1 – Aug 3	Aries / Libra
	Aug 4 – Dec 31	Pisces / Virgo
1987	Jan 1 – Dec 31	Pisces / Virgo
1988	Jan 1 – Jan 31	Pisces / Virgo
	Feb 1 – Dec 31	Aquarius / Leo
1989	Jan 1 – Oct 17	Aquarius / Leo
	Oct 18 – Dec 31	Capricorn / Cancer
1990	Jan 1 – Dec 31	Capricorn / Cancer
1991	Jan 1 – April 11	Capricorn / Cancer
	April 12 – Dec 31	Sagittarius / Gemini
1992	Jan 1 – Oct 9	Sagittarius / Gemini
	Oct 10 – Dec 31	Scorpio / Taurus
1993	Jan 1 – Dec 31	Scorpio / Taurus

Year	Dates	Signs
1994	Jan 1 – Jun 4	Scorpio / Taurus
	Jun 5 – Dec 31	Libra / Aries
1995	Jan 1 – Dec 23	Libra / Aries
	Dec 24 – Dec 31	Virgo / Pisces
1996	Jan 1 – Dec 31	Virgo / Pisces
1997	Jan 1 – Jun 18	Virgo / Pisces
	Jun 19 – Dec 31	Leo / Aquarius
1998	Jan 1 – Dec 16	Leo / Aquarius
	Dec 17 – Dec 31	Cancer / Capricorn
1999	Jan 1 – Dec 31	Cancer / Capricorn
2000	Jan 1 – Aug 29	Cancer / Capricorn
	Aug 30 – Dec 31	Gemini / Sagittarius
2001	Jan 1 – Dec 31	Gemini / Sagittarius
2002	Jan 1 – Feb 27	Gemini / Sagittarius
	Feb 28 – Dec 31	Taurus / Scorpio
2003	Jan 1 – Aug 26	Taurus / Scorpio
	Aug 27 – Dec 31	Aries / Libra
2004	Jan 1 – Dec 31	Aries / Libra
2005	Jan 1 – Feb 21	Aries / Libra
	Feb 22 – Dec 31	Pisces / Virgo
2006	Jan 1 – Nov 7	Pisces / Virgo
	Nov 8 – Dec 31	Aquarius / Leo
2007	Jan 1 – Dec 31	Aquarius / Leo
2008	Jan 1 – May 4	Aquarius / Leo
	May 5 – Dec 31	Capricorn / Cancer
2009	Jan 1 – Nov 1	Capricorn / Cancer
	Nov 2 – Dec 31	Sagittarius / Gemini
2010	Jan 1 – Dec 31	Sagittarius / Gemini
2011	Jan 1 – May 1	Sagittarius / Gemini
	May 2 – Dec 31	Scorpio / Taurus
2012	Jan 1 – Dec 31	Scorpio / Taurus
2013	Jan 1 – Jan 13	Scorpio / Taurus
	Jan 14 – Dec 31	Libra / Aries
2014	Jan 1 – Jul 13	Libra / Aries
	Jul 14 – Dec 31	Virgo / Pisces
2015	Jan 1 – Dec 31	Virgo / Pisces
2016	Jan 1 – Jan 9	Virgo / Pisces
	Jan 10 – Dec 31	Leo / Aquarius

Rahu in Aries / Ketu in Libra

This karmic axis in the birth chart brings the focus of the present life on the self and indicates past karmas incurred through relationships.

There is a need to balance self and other, particularly in areas of service and life partner relationships. There is an intense need for self-discovery and an accompanying self-absorption that can lead to experiences of deep meditation and accomplishment of significant inner work, provided that one does not become lost in spiritual ego.

You must find a way to harness your competitive and adventurous nature through a responsible and committed yoga practice. Physical activity is highlighted in your yoga, as is the need to listen to your higher self and rely on your own judgment when it comes to how you practice. Be careful that you do not try to please everybody, including your teacher, when you engage in the practice of yoga. There needs to be a balance between your personal agendas in your yoga practice and your tendency to look toward others for your sense of spiritual fulfillment.

One way to deal with the challenges of this karmic placement is to lose your natural self-centeredness in healthy spiritual relationships. Karma Yoga, the yoga of service, is an excellent path for this karmic axis.

Since Mars rules Aries, the sign occupied by Rahu, and Venus rules Libra, the sign occupied by Ketu, working with these two planetary energies can help in resolving karmic issues.

Paramahansa Yogananda, the author of *Autobiography of a Yogi*, has this sign placement of Rahu and Ketu which manifested in his life as a famous yogi with a strong sense of identity (Rahu in Aries) who created strong connections to others (Ketu in Libra) in his spiritual mission.

Rahu in Taurus / Ketu in Scorpio

This karmic axis in one's birth chart brings the focus of the present life between exploring a purely materialistic path and a deeply spiritual one. One of the main concerns in this life is create physical, mental and spiritual stability.

There is a need to balance the practical with the search for the mystical. Often there are extremes present here in that a person may become a devout materialist, refusing to engage spirituality, or an extreme spiritualist, ignoring material concerns.

It is possible to become an enlightened materialist with this placement, finding the spiritual in doing the practical work. It is also possible to bring an element of pragmatism, or realism, to spiritual pursuits where the spiritual journey brings material rewards.

There is often a strong interest in the mystical or transformational realms that needs a practical reason to indulge. When that reason is found, then transformation can occur on a deep level and the mysteries of life are discovered.

The past life (Ketu) may have been spent searching for mystical and yogic powers, and it is likely that there was an exploration of the kundalini energies (Scorpio). Now the present life (Rahu) may be concerned with finding a way to put those past life experiences to practical purposes (Taurus).

Ultimately, there must be a recognition that the search for material satisfaction is not in conflict with the spiritual yearnings of the soul.

Since Venus rules Taurus, the sign occupied by Rahu, and Mars rules Scorpio, the sign occupied by Ketu, working with these two planetary energies can help in resolving karmic issues.

Ramakrishna Paramahamsa, the famous mystic of 19th century India, has this sign placement of Rahu and Ketu which provided him with a materially secure life (Taurus in Rahu) simply because he had so few material needs in comparison to his all-consuming mystical journey (Ketu in Scorpio). It is interesting that he did suffer from throat cancer that can be an unfortunate result of Rahu being in Taurus (the sign of the neck and throat) and was a way in which he paid off the karma of his incarnation.

Rahu in Gemini / Ketu in Sagittarius

This karmic axis in one's birth chart brings the focus of the present life on spiritual experiences (Ketu in Sagittarius) and the ability to communicate them effectively (Rahu in Gemini). One of the main concerns in this life is to develop the ability to express through speaking, writing and communication. There will also be a focus on developing companionship, intellectual ability, and even improving flexibility (Gemini). When this occurs, usually later in life, there will be an outpouring of innate wisdom and knowledge that the soul has gathered over the past lives.

The past life revolved around higher learning, spiritual teachers, and dharma. The person may have been a great teacher in his or her own right. Possibly, however, there was an overindulgence in the realm of pure philosophy or spiritual learning that was not fully shared with others.

In the present life, you likely have a reservoir of passive knowledge from a previous life but you need to find a way to activate it and bring it into the world. You have the need to find a teacher to guide you to use this knowledge, yet you have problems staying with a teacher. You may also find yourself continually embracing and then rejecting various spiritual paths and philosophies.

There may be a tendency to over-intellectualize your spirituality or spend time reading about rather than following your spiritual path. The attention on your spiritual journey may waver as you vacillate between multiple possibilities.

The lesson of this placement is to find a way to express your knowledge in a meaningful way and to work on developing your power to communicate your spiritual insights. Spiritual journaling will be an excellent practice, as well as engaging in a structured way to develop your ability to deliver your innate vast knowledge, such as perhaps taking a yoga teacher training course.

Lord Krishna, according to the Vedic texts, has this sign placement of Rahu and Ketu, which manifested in his clever use of language and charming ways (Rahu in Gemini) to lead people into the realization of the divine law (Ketu in Sagittarius).

Since Mercury rules Gemini, the sign occupied by Rahu, and Jupiter rules Sagittarius, the sign occupied by Ketu, working with these two planetary energies can help in resolving karmic issues.

Rahu in Cancer / Ketu in Capricorn

This karmic axis in the birth chart brings the focus of the present life on learning to live in both the material and emotional realm while moving toward a spiritual path. One of the main concerns in this life revolves around the need to accept responsibility while recognizing the inclination to reject discipline. In early years, there may be confusion as to the purpose of this life as the pull toward the inner realms seems in conflict with the need to create material stability.

The past life (Ketu in Capricorn) was centered on pursuing worldly goals and ambitions where career, pragmatism, practical realization, and achieving recognition were paramount. A focus was on paying karmic debts, shouldering responsibility, and denying the emotional realm.

In the present life (Rahu in Cancer), success with this placement comes when duties are discharged without attaching to the fruits of the effort, or in practicing service and karma yoga, particularly in the areas of healing, nurturing, home and family life, and maternal issues.

There may be a tendency to intellectualize your emotions and to ignore karmic responsibilities by disconnecting from the world. The task is to respect your emotions and develop the softer side of your nature.

The lesson of this placement is to learn to accept emotional happiness without fear of consequences and to balance the tendency toward self-denial with self-trust. The challenge will be to bring a humanitarian perspective into work in the outer world and so be recognized for the caring nature rather than their worldly achievements.

Mahatma Gandhi has this sign placement of Rahu and Ketu, which allowed him to use his soft and nurturing nature (Rahu in Cancer) to create a peaceful revolution that had far-reaching practical results (Ketu in Capricorn).

Since the Moon rules Cancer, the sign occupied by Rahu, and Saturn rules Capricorn, the sign occupied by Ketu, working with these two planetary energies can help in resolving karmic issues.

Rahu in Leo / Ketu in Aquarius

This karmic axis in one's birth chart brings the focus of the present life on developing a strong sense of self while being in service to others. Leo is the sign that has the strongest sense of the individual self and individual consciousness while Aquarius is the sign of the universal self and group consciousness. One of the main concerns in this life is to find the sense of self and identity while living in a state of group consciousness.

The past life may have been spent in service to others and submerging the individual needs to the needs of the group. There was little concern for personal accomplishments or even establishing a distinctive identity or presence of ego. Helping others brought the greatest sense of personal satisfaction. Sharing in friendship and seeking knowledge through idealism and philosophy was the purpose of the incarnation.

The lesson of this placement is to learn to serve through leadership. Like the benign monarch who has the best interests of her subjects at heart, the individual with Rahu in Leo and Ketu in Aquarius must realize that there is a powerful place in time and space where the needs of the individual and the group are in alignment and by serving one, the other is also served.

Madam Helena Blavatsky, the founder of the Theosophical Society and a leading proponent of bringing Eastern thought to the Western world, has this sign placement of Rahu and Ketu. She was able to create a larger than life presence and identity for herself (Rahu in Leo) that was instrumental in spreading new age and esoteric wisdom (Ketu in Aquarius) to the masses.

Since the Sun rules Leo, the sign occupied by Rahu, and Saturn rules Aquarius, the sign occupied by Ketu, working with these two planetary energies can help in resolving karmic issues.

Rahu in Virgo / Ketu in Pisces

This karmic axis in one's birth chart brings the focus of the present life on organizing the material realm so that the search for enlightenment can be realized. One of the main concerns is to find the proper balance between the material side of life (Virgo) and the spiritual side (Pisces). There can be a struggle between being overly mental and overly emotional, between earthly duties and spiritual aspirations, between looking at the little details while not forgetting the big picture. There will also be a focus on developing material success while engaging in personal growth. When this ability is developed, there will be an effortless movement between this world and the next, achieving success in both realms.

The past life was consumed by a search for enlightenment, so much so the details and responsibilities of everyday life were forgotten. The fantasy of liberation erased the practicality of earthly living, and this could have created some suffering in your life and in the lives of those around you.

In the present life, you have a need to serve humanity and fulfill the karmic obligations of a human birth, with all of its material needs. Paying attention to the physical body is essential; yet resist the temptation to see that everything is simply flesh.

There may be a tendency to strive for material success yet unless this success finds a way to benefit others, it will only bring emptiness.

The lesson of this placement is to realize that spirit is carried in matter, and that every small action in the earthly realm, no matter how insignificant, is ultimately an expression of the divine. There is a need for karma yoga, as Rahu in Virgo requires that service be done, and Ketu in Pisces can see this as a path to merging with the unknown.

John Lennon, English musician and songwriter, has this sign placement of Rahu and Ketu that allowed him to bring his critically discerning and creative mind (Rahu in Virgo) to create a unique musical expression of high imagination (Ketu in Pisces). His song "Imagine" is a perfect expression of these two energies, bringing the vision of a dreamer into a practical earthly utopia.

Since Mercury rules Virgo, the sign occupied by Rahu, and Jupiter rules Pisces, the sign occupied by Ketu, working with these two planetary energies can help in resolving karmic issues.

Rahu in Libra / Ketu in Aries

This karmic axis in one's birth chart brings the focus of the present life on relationships and individuality. One of the main concerns is to balance independence and self-expression with the needs and the consideration of others. There will be a focus on developing a balance between self-sufficiency and dependence. When this ability is developed, you can form healthy and spiritually satisfying relationships without neglecting your own needs.

The past life was a continual fight for the fullest sense of self-expression and where the needs of others were subordinated to your quest for spiritual freedom.

In the present life, you may swing in the other direction and become the ultimate people-pleaser, reluctant to state your needs and eager to keep everyone happy. There may also be a tendency to sublimate the self and shy away from the past life role of a spiritual warrior who took no prisoners.

The lesson of this placement is not to live for others, or even live for yourself, but to live spiritually through ethical deeds and thoughts where others are taken into consideration yet not at the expense of your spiritual journey.

Guru Maharaj Ji, the meditation teacher and founder of the Divine Light Mission in the 1970s, has this sign placement of Rahu and Ketu which manifested in his ability to create a strong spiritual persona that became the centerpiece of his teachings (Ketu in Aries) and allowed him to create an expansive world-wide relationship (Rahu in Libra) with millions of disciples.

Since Venus rules Libra, the sign occupied by Rahu, and Mars rules Aries, the sign occupied by Ketu, working with these two planetary energies can help in resolving karmic issues.

Rahu in Scorpio / Ketu in Taurus

This karmic axis in one's birth chart brings the focus of the present life on idealistic love versus passionate sexuality, comfortable stability versus intense change, and readily apparent beauty versus secretive dark mysteries. One of the main concerns in this life is to understand the deepest inner workings of the psyche and soul and to search wholeheartedly for spiritual liberation through transformational practices. There will be a focus on developing exciting new experiences that give a taste of the Scorpionic realm of regeneration, renewal, and profundity.

The past life was focused on sensual pleasures and comforts, where satisfying the material and earthly needs was of paramount importance, perhaps to the neglect of exploring the realms of hidden knowledge and transformation. There may have been guilt from overindulgence that is now replaced by an urgency to rush headlong down any avenue that offers an experience beyond the ordinary realms of pleasure and consciousness.

The lesson of this placement is to learn your spiritual lessons through worldly experiences, balancing the urgency for transformation with a more placid and calm approach that allows you to feel comfortable in this material world while realizing this will not detour you from your mission to experience and unravel the deepest mysteries of this life.

Swami Vivekananda, an Indian Hindu monk who played a major role in bringing yoga to the West in the late 19th century, has this sign placement of Rahu and Ketu. His success with mystical practices in foreign lands (Rahu in Scorpio) allowed him to build the Vedanta societies in England and the America (Ketu in Taurus).

Since Mars rules Scorpio, the sign occupied by Rahu, and Venus rules Taurus, the sign occupied by Ketu, working with these two planetary energies can help in resolving karmic issues.

Rahu in Sagittarius / Ketu in Gemini

This karmic axis in one's birth chart brings the focus of the present life on spirituality, ethics, dharma, teachers and higher knowledge. One of the main concerns in this life is to gather information and explore new ideas. There will also be a focus on developing one's own unique philosophy that may embrace foreign or non-traditional views. When this ability is realized, the person may either become a great intellectual who communicates a new way of thinking, or an iconoclastic individual who has little respect for the ideas of others.

The past life was spent deep in the realm of the mind, trying to bring order to the inner life through analysis and logic and perhaps not altogether succeeding.

In the present life, you feel that spirituality will come through good actions and correct knowledge. There may be a tendency to reject advice and to come up with your own solutions to your spiritual dilemma, yet you need to acknowledge that a spiritual teacher is essential to untangle you from the webs your mind incessantly weaves.

The lesson of this placement is to develop a philosophical attitude and to allow your intuition to guide you.

Sri Ramana Maharshi, an Indian spiritual master who taught during the first half of the 20th century, has this sign placement of Rahu and Ketu. He advocated the practice of self-inquiry and Jnana Yoga (Rahu in Sagittarius) while preferring to teach through silence (Ketu in Gemini).

Since Jupiter rules Sagittarius, the sign occupied by Rahu, and Mercury rules Gemini, the sign occupied by Ketu, working with these two planetary energies can help in resolving karmic issues.

Rahu in Capricorn / Ketu in Cancer

This karmic axis in one's birth chart brings the focus of the present life on ambition, accomplishment and career. One of the main concerns in this life is to achieve success, however the individual may define it. There is an inner fear of failure that keeps pushing you to achieve your goals, and while you may be outwardly successful, you remain inwardly reclusive, and withdrawn from the world.

The past life is very present in the this life, with a strong connection to emotions, maternal issues and the home. There is a natural ability and need to nurture and to help others, and this often translates into being successful so you can satisfy the material needs of others if not necessarily their emotional ones.

In the present life, you work very hard and need to find a balance through fun and relaxation. There is also a need to come to an understanding of your emotional nature and not let your emotions gain the upper hand over your life.

There may be a tendency to never feel content or happy with whatever success you achieve because as soon as you crest your mountain, you are looking at the next mountain to climb.

The lesson of this placement is to learn to fulfill your emotional and spiritual needs in the outer world, by seeing no difference between material accomplishments and spiritual satisfaction. Develop the yogic niyama of santosha, or contentment, and you will find your balance in life.

Albert Einstein has this sign placement of Rahu and Ketu that allowed him to discover the mysteries of the material universe (Rahu in Capricorn) through his developed intuitive powers (Ketu in Cancer).

Since Saturn rules Capricorn, the sign occupied by Rahu, and the Moon rules Cancer, the sign occupied by Ketu, working with these two planetary energies can help in resolving karmic issues.

Rahu in Aquarius / Ketu in Leo

This karmic axis in one's birth chart brings the focus of the present life on group activity, revolutionary ideas, life philosophy, and creativity, generally of the unusual kind. One of the main concerns in this life is to reconcile the drive to change the outer world with the need to explore the inner world. There will be a need to create a sense of identity through a humanitarian or group consciousness endeavor. There is both a desire to save the world and to save one's self.

The past life was spent as a powerful personality who may have dominated others, or subordinated the needs of the group to their own agenda. In the present life, you need to take care that you do not mistrust or ignore your personal power as you move in the other direction. Realize that you may have to satisfy a material ambition before you can aspire toward your spiritual goals. There is some confusion between idealism and outward change that must be reconciled to avoid inner conflict. You can change the world by first changing yourself.

The lesson of this placement is to embrace your personal power and then use it to make this world a better place for everyone.

J. Krishnamurti, the prolific spiritual author, had this placement of Rahu and Ketu which allowed him to spread the new age and esoteric teachings (Rahu in Aquarius) through a powerful presence that was remarkably devoid of personal ego (Ketu in Leo).

Since Saturn rules Aquarius, the sign occupied by Rahu, and the Sun rules Leo, the sign occupied by Ketu, working with these two planetary energies can help in resolving karmic issues.

Rahu in Pisces / Ketu in Virgo

This karmic axis in one's birth chart brings the focus of the present life on the mystical, the intuitive, and the worlds of both imagination and higher consciousness. There is an inner conflict here as the most materialistic planet, Rahu, is in the most mystical sign of Pisces, and similarly spiritual Ketu is in earthly Virgo. At first the individual may seek spiritualism through accomplishments in the outer world, or become frustrated as the practicalities of this world derail their spiritual longings.

The past life was spent lost in the realm of everyday life and details to the exclusion of spiritual pursuits, and now there is a resulting rejection and a reversal that can also be equally limiting if you do not let go of your preconceived ideas of how spirituality should be.

In the present life, you may at first attempt to find your answers through ambition, success, and indulging in intoxicants that can lead to an addictive personality.

The lesson of this placement is to release your expectations of how enlightenment is to be achieved, or even the idea that it is somehow achievable. Be open to what life is revealing to you, and realize that all is coming if you only do the practice. Enlightenment will not be grasped, bought or found. It will only come when you can see that there is truly no conflict between your material concerns and your spiritual journey. All is one.

Ram Das (Richard Alpert), the American spiritual teacher who began his journey into expanded consciousness with Timothy Leary and LSD, had this placement of Rahu and Ketu. The use of hallucinogenics (Rahu in Pisces) was the beginning of his transformation from Richard Alpert into Ram Das yet it was through his writings and ultimately his service through the Seva Foundation, an international health organization (Ketu in Virgo), that he achieved his standing as a spiritual leader.

Since Jupiter rules Pisces, the sign occupied by Rahu, and Mercury rules Virgo, the sign occupied by Ketu, working with these two planetary energies can help in resolving karmic issues.

"There are three ways to conduct your destiny: Through the law of karma, action and reaction. Or you can tune into the magnetic field of the earth and just float with it – a freeloader. Or your life can be run by that magnetically attracting, very positive, creative, meditative, neutral mind. That way you can do very well."

Yogi Bhajan
7/23/87

Your Astrological Profile Worksheet

Use this table to begin filling out your astrological profile. While some information requires a birth chart based on your birth time and location, you can get significant information based only on your birth date.

Notice that your planetary type can be determined by you after reading their descriptions in the section of the Planets of Vedic Astrology. Your current age will be useful as you look at the section on the planetary cycles later in the book.

ASTROLOGICAL PROFILE	DATA NEEDED	YOUR INFORMATION
SUN SIGN	Birth Date	
MOON SIGN	Birth Date & Time	
RISING SIGN	Birth Date & Time	
RISING SIGN PLANET	Birth Date & Time	
BIRTH DAY PLANET	Birth Date	
RAHU/KETU SIGNS	Birth Date	
SUN STAR SIGN	Birth Date	
MOON STAR SIGN	Birth Date & Time	
PLANETARY PERIOD	Birth Date & Time	
PLANETARY TYPE	Your Opinion	
YOUR AGE	Birth Date	

Table 3-6: Astrological Profile Worksheet

Astrology Yoga Techniques

The yoga techniques described in this section are taken from the Hatha and Kundalini yoga practices that originated from the tantric traditions that emphasized the physical body as the vehicle for enlightenment.

There are five major techniques common to these yoga practices: **asanas**, or the physical postures, **pranayama**, or what is often called breath control, **mudras**, or the hand and body locks (including the bandhas), **mantra**, or the use of sacred sound, and **meditation**.

These techniques are often practiced together, and the first four techniques are instrumental in producing the fifth technique of meditation. These techniques are discussed separately in the following section for the sake of categorizing and explaining. The results of using them are more profound, however, when they are practiced as a system together or through a process sometimes referred to as **kriya**.

The planetary associations with the yoga techniques are not derived from one authoritative source, but from the teachings of astrologers and yogis through time. By nature, some of these associations are intuitive or discerned by the practitioner and are not arbitrary or dogmatic.

The descriptions are far from exhaustive because of the richness and complexity of both astrology and yoga, and you are encouraged to use your own understanding of both sciences to go deeper into this area.

Ultimately, you will have to judge by the results of your practice, which is true for all yoga and astrology, if these techniques are effective for the planets you wish to work with.

As with all yoga practices, the intention behind the practice is as important as the practice itself. In fact, it is likely that any yoga practice, done in the proper consciousness with focused intention, can balance and strengthen any of the planets.

These categorized techniques, however, are as good a place as any to begin your familiarity with the practices of Astrology Yoga.

Planetary Postures: Asanas of Astrology Yoga

Most yoga practices in the Western world are based on the postures, or asanas, of Hatha Yoga and are a good introduction to understanding how yoga techniques are related to Vedic astrology concepts.

The origins of the classical asanas in Hatha Yoga are shrouded in mystery and myth, going back to the god Shiva who is said to initially have taught 8,400,000 postures representing the 8,400,000 life forms the soul travels through to achieve enlightenment (depending upon interpretations, this number has also been represented as 840,000 and 84,000). Of these, 84 asanas were said to be distilled by Shiva to cover all aspects of the human existence.

Unfortunately, there is no authoritative listing of these 84 asanas. Various ancient texts describe a number of postures in detail: Hatha Yoga Pradipika (14 postures), Yoga Pradipa (21), Gheranda Samhita (32), Vishva Kosha (32), and Anubhava Prakasha (50). Various traditions have come up with their own list of 84 postures, including the lineage of Bishnu Ghosh that contains the 26 postures used in the Bikram yoga practice, and an early Western listing of the 84 postures compiled by Alain Danielou in 1949 (*Yoga: The Method of Reintegration*).

The Evolution of Asanas and How the Planets Affect Them

Classical yoga was one of the major schools of ancient knowledge and philosophy in India known as the Vedas. The other schools focused on logical thinking, rational skills, cosmic principles, metaphysics, and sacred actions. Along with the Vedic schools were six limbs of the Vedas known as the Vedangas that were the main tools used to interpret this sacred knowledge. The Vedangas included mantras, rituals, and Jyotisha, or what we now call Vedic astrology.

The Vedas also evolved into specific teachings known as the four Upavedas that consisted of the arts (Gandharaveda), architecture (Vastu), healing arts (Ayurveda), and the martial arts (Dharnuveda).

The practice of asanas in Yoga was influenced by the martial art practices of Dharnuveda as well as the meditative postures described in the early yogic texts. Indeed, many asanas commonly practiced today in the West are derived from gymnastic postures or wrestling practices.

The practice of martial arts comes under the province of Mars, as do all physical and athletic practices for improving the body. For the most part, Mars is the principle planet of the cultural or physical asanas, while Saturn with its patience and discipline rules the meditative asanas.

Mercury, which rules agility and flexibility, also works with Mars on the physical postures, particularly those requiring gymnastic skills. Jupiter, the planet of wisdom and cosmic expansion, similarly pairs with Saturn to insure success in the meditation postures.

The physical postures need the vitality of the Sun to succeed and the meditative postures depend upon the Sun for its steadiness. The Moon brings the needed ease and resilience to the physical asanas while offering peace of mind for holding the meditative asanas. Venus brings grace and art to the physical movements and gives the qualities of devotion and compassion to the meditative postures.

Rahu provides the drive and ambition to achieve the full promise of asanas while Ketu reminds us that we are ultimately doing them to become liberated and not merely to achieve.

Categorizing Asanas Astrologically

There are many approaches to categorizing asanas. The two broadest categories are the Cultural Postures (as in active physical culture that works on improving the body's health) and the Meditative Postures (stationary sitting). Mars, Mercury, Sun, and Rahu are associated with the cultural asanas while Saturn, Jupiter, Moon, Ketu and Venus are associated with the meditative asanas.

Broad-based body movements, such as Standing, Sitting, Supine, Forward Bend, Back Bend, Twist, and Inversions, may also group postures. In a general way, we can associate the static sitting and standing postures with the two largest and slowest moving planets, Saturn and Jupiter. The twists are associated with the Sun (solar plexus) and Mars (agni or digestive fire). Supine and relaxation postures, as well as forward bends, tend to be associated with the calm and receptive Moon. The energizing backbends are associated with the Sun (vitality) and Venus (heart chakra). The handstands and arm balances are associated with Mercury while inversions have a connection to both the solar and lunar areas of the head (Sun and Moon).

We can also categorize asanas according to the planets and astrological signs by following these guidelines:

- Associations of the planets, signs and houses with the different areas of the body to the postures that affect those areas.

- Significations of a planet and its energetic effect that associated it to a posture with a similar energetic effect.

- Significations of an astrological sign that associate it with a posture.

- Name of an asana or its energetic effect that associate it with a planet or sign.

While no ancient texts explicitly address the astrological and asana correspondence, we can use these guidelines to understand how the different yoga postures interact with the planets and signs.

Vedic Astrology and Areas of the Body

As the asana system is orientated around the physical body, insights into how various yoga postures connect astrologically can be discovered by noting the planets, signs, and astrological houses that are associated with, or signify, different areas of the body.

The table on the next page is derived from several texts on Vedic astrology and relates the three major astrological factors of planets, signs and houses to general areas of the body.

One of the ancient branches of Vedic astrology called Angvidya focused on the study of the physical body in relation to the planets. It is from this knowledge system, we can hypothesize the relationships of the planets to the body and the asana practices.

These astrological associations with the body form the basis of medical astrology and are used diagnostically in the practice of Ayurveda. By understanding how the asanas affect major body areas, we can associate the postures with their astrological components.

For example, asanas that work on the neck and shoulders, such as Gomukhasana, have a relationship with the sign Gemini, the planet Mercury, and the third house of the birth chart. Hip opening postures, such as Malasana, come under the sign of Sagittarius as well as the planet Mercury.

Given these astrological associations and an understanding of a yoga practitioner's birth chart, asanas may be employed therapeutically if an inherent weakness is observed in the chart.

For example, if Capricorn, the natural sign of the knees, or Saturn the planet associated with knees, is unfavorable in the birth chart of an individual, then difficulties with the knees could be anticipated and caution observed in attempting advanced seated postures such as Lotus Pose. This would be even more significant if the tenth house (knees) was also involved.

AREA OF THE BODY	SIGNS	HOUSES	PLANETS
Head, top and back	Aries	First	Sun, Mars (head)
Face, Throat, Right eye, Teeth	Taurus	Second	Moon (face) Venus (face) Mercury (throat)
Shoulders, Neck, Arms, Hands, Cervical spine	Gemini	Third	Mercury (neck) Rahu (hands)
Upper chest, Thoracic spine, Heart, Lungs, Diaphragm, Breasts	Cancer	Fourth Fifth (also heart)	Mars (chest) Sun (heart, back) Moon (breasts) Mercury (lungs)
Stomach, Heart	Leo	Fifth (Fourth)	Moon
Small intestine	Virgo	Sixth	Mercury
Large intestine, Lumbar spine	Libra	Seventh	Jupiter (abdomen)
Sexual organs, Rectum, Sacrum	Scorpio	Eighth	Venus (sexual organs, pelvis)
Thighs, Hips	Sagittarius	Ninth	Saturn (thighs) Mercury (hips)
Knees (spine in general)	Capricorn	Tenth	Saturn
Legs	Aquarius	Eleventh	Saturn (calves) Ketu (legs)
Feet, Left eye	Pisces	Twelfth	Jupiter

Table 4-1: Areas of the Body and Astrological Associations

How Postures Are Associated with the Planets

We can associate postures with the planets by understanding the basic nature and significations of each planet. An obvious example is Warrior Pose (Virabhadrasana) that is associated with Mars, the planet that rules battles and warfare. Dancer Pose (Natarajasana) is associated with Venus, the planet of the arts and dance. Perhaps more subtle is the association of Child Pose with the Moon which represents the mother and nurturing.

Some poses like the Half-Moon posture (Ardhachandrasana) and Sun Salutations (Suryanamaskar) contain the Sanskrit name of the planet within the asana name.

Another approach is to consider the energetic effects of an asana and how it may be related to a planet. For example, Mercury, associated with speech, has a relationship to any asana that works with the throat. Jupiter with its association with the second chakra has a relationship with any asana that works on opening the pelvic area.

Take the major characteristic of any planet and see which asana it may indicate. For example, Mercury is quickness, and a signification of Mercury is the arms. Therefore, the quick flowing vinyasa "jump through" transition in the Ashtanga series that uses the arms is a Mercury asana.

In this way, every asana can be tied to one or more of the nine planets in Vedic astrology and their practice can aid in strengthening and balancing our planetary energies.

How Postures Are Associated with the Signs

Similarly, yoga postures can be associated with the 12 signs of the zodiac through name, meaning, symbol, or body area association.

For example, Lion pose (Simhasana) shares the name of Leo while Scorpion pose (Vrschikasana) shares the name of Scorpio. Fish pose (Matsyasana) comes from the symbol for Pisces while Bow pose (Dhanurasana) shares the symbol and name (Dhanus) for Sagittarius.

Perhaps less obvious is the association of Eagle pose (Garudasana) with the sign of Scorpio which is represented by the eagle or phoenix, the mythical bird of transformation. Similarly, Corpse pose (Savasana) is also associated with the sign of Scorpio with its theme of transformation through death.

Using the names and symbols of the signs, we can relate Tolasana (Scales Pose) to the sign Libra, the sign of the scale of balances. Similarly, Makarasana (Crocodile Pose) refers to the sign of Capricorn that is symbolized by an animal with the upper body of a deer and the lower body of a crocodile. Vrishasana (Bull Pose) refers to Taurus, symbolized by the bull.

Learning to See Postures Astrologically

There are many ways we can learn to discern how a yoga posture may be associated with an astrological element such as a planet or sign. The more we know about the significations of the planets and signs, the better we can understand how the postures work. To help you think astrologically in terms of the asanas, let's look at some advanced examples.

Two of the more popular asanas in Western yoga classes are Downward-Facing Dog (Adho Mukha Svanasana) and Upward-Facing Dog (Urdhva Mukha Svanasana). These two postures are often done together in Hatha yoga classes and form a large part of the Ashtanga Yoga and Vinyasa Yoga sequences.

The dog is often associated with the shadow planet Ketu. In Vedic astrology, there are also two Moon signs (Nakshatras) that are associated with the dog as well: Mula (located in the sign of Sagittarius) and Ardra (located in Gemini). Mula is said to be a "downward nakshatra" (or a downward moving sign) and is also associated with Ketu. On the other hand, Ardra is an "upward nakshatra" (an upward moving sign) and associated with the other shadow planet called Rahu. In addition, Rahu is associated with a downward glance while Ketu signifies an upward glance.

Both Downward-Facing Dog (Adho Mukha Svanasana) and Upward-Facing Dog (Urdhva Mukha Svanasana) can be associated with the planets Rahu and Ketu. Just as these two planets always move together in tandem, so do the two "dog" postures with their upward and downward movement and glances that bring a complementary effect to their practice.

Here's how other asanas can be related to the planets and the signs:

Trikonasana (Triangle Pose) can be associated with Mercury because Mercury rules, or is associated with, the shape of a triangle and the use of the arms is prominent.

Gomukhasana (Cow Face Pose) can be associated with the Moon because the Moon is associated with the face and the milk cow. Since the posture also uses the arms and shoulders extensively, it too can be related to Mercury.

Paschimottanasana (Seated Forward Bend) literally means the "western facing" asana, as the yogis were stretching the west side of the body as they bent away from the sun. Saturn is associated with the western direction and hence this asana can be referred back to that planet.

Purvottanasana (Upward Plank Pose) literally means the "eastern side" and the yogis were stretching the east side of the body as they stretched toward the sun. The Sun is associated with the eastern direction and hence this asana can be referred back to that planet.

Bhujangasana (Cobra Pose) can be seen as a reference to the serpentine energy of Kundalini that is associated with the two shadow planets, Rahu and Ketu.

Notice that more than one planet or sign may be associated with a posture. A posture may work on a chakra ruled by a planet, a body area within a specific sign, or be associated with a symbol of another sign or a secondary planetary energy.

Finally, the most important tool in discerning how these asanas work astrologically is the intuition of the yoga teacher and astrologer, as well as the experience of the practitioner. This chapter is a starting point for exploration and not a dogmatic dictum.

Sun and Moon Asanas

The Sun and Moon play a central role in all astrology systems as well as in the Hatha Yoga practice (the word Hatha, or Ha-Tha, literally means Sun and Moon). Because of their major influence in astrology and yoga, the sun and moon can be associated with every asana by understanding the primary effect that each posture produces.

In the practice of Hatha Yoga, the fundamental principles of Brimhana, Langhana, and Samana can be applied to the practices of asana and pranayama. Brimhana is expanding, projective, and heating. Langhana is lightening, calming and cooling. Samana is a balance between these two. This concept is important in the therapeutic application of asana as an Ayurvedic tool.

So a "Brimhana" posture would be heating and projective (masculine) and a "langhana" posture would be cooling and receptive (feminine). Brimhana is a quality of the Sun while Langhana is associated with the Moon.

All the asanas may be classified as being primarily Brimhana or Laghana (Sun or Moon) and hence each asana is fundamentally a Sun posture or a Moon posture.

MOON POSTURES	SUN POSTURES
Cool	Warm
Relax	Activate
Release energy	Build energy
Promote elimination	Promote strengthening
Affect parasympathetic nervous system	Affect sympathetic nervous system
Increase sensory activity	Increase motor activity
Aid in treatment of tension, insomnia, constipation, headaches, chronic pain, irritability, arthritis, stroke, allergies, inflammation, herpes, stress	Aid in treatment of fatigue, lethargy, diarrhea, depression, asthma, chronic fatigue, apathy, poor circulation, low vitality, weakness

Table 4-2: Qualities of the Moon and Sun Postures

If we use the traditional categorization of asanas according to body position or movement, we can associate groups of asanas with how they work more or less with the Sun and Moon energy.

The following table shows the relative expression of the Moon and Sun energy with the strongest energy producing postures for each planet at the top of the table and the least at the bottom.

The supine postures have the most moon energy while handstands and arm balances have the most sun energy. The inversions have an equal balance of sun and moon energy, and headstand (sirsasana) is often cited as the classical posture (samana) for balancing Sun and Moon energies.

MOON POSTURES	SUN POSTURES
Supine (most)	Handstands, Arm Balances (most)
Sitting	Back Bend
Twisting	Abdominal
Forward Bend	Standing
Inversions (least)	Inversions (least)

Table 4-3: Categories of the Moon and Sun Postures, Most to Least

Surya Namaskara (Salutation to the Sun)

The most obvious asana-oriented Sun practice is the classical Sun Salutation. The origins of this practice in which a sequence of postures are done to welcome the energy of the Sun at sunrise has been traced back at least 2500 years when it was done as a form of worship or prostrations. Even so, this was not considered part of the original set of Hatha asanas and was incorporated only later as a dynamic yoga practice.

There are many versions of the Sun Salutation practice, modified by teachers over the last 100 years to suit their particular practice or lineage, but the classical version consists of 12 postures or positions:

1. Pranamasana (Prayer pose)
2. Hasta Utthanasana (Raised arm pose)
3. Padahastasana (Hand to foot pose)
4. Ashwa Sanchalanasana (Equestrian pose)
5. Parvatasana (Mountain pose; also Downward Dog)
6. Ashtanga Namaskara (Eight Point Bowing)
7. Bhujangasana (Cobra pose)
8. Parvatasana (Mountain pose; also Downward Dog)
9. Ashwa Sanchalanasana (Equestrian pose)
10. Padahastasana (Hand to foot pose)
11. Hasta Utthanasana (Raised arm pose)
12. Pranamasana (Prayer pose)

These 12 positions are practiced twice to complete one round, changing sides (right leg, left leg) during Ashwa Sanchalanasana.

While there are variations on these 12 poses (such as Upward Dog instead of Cobra, or Plank Pose instead of Eight Point Bowing), there are always 12 positions performed.

The 12 positions relate to the twelve zodiac or solar phases of the year (the "sun signs"). The sequence may be done facing the direction of the sun and is often repeated for 12 rounds for the twelve directions of the compass and the twelve signs of the zodiac. An advanced practice is to repeat the sequence for 108 rounds, 12 times for each of the nine planetsß.

Surya Namaskara

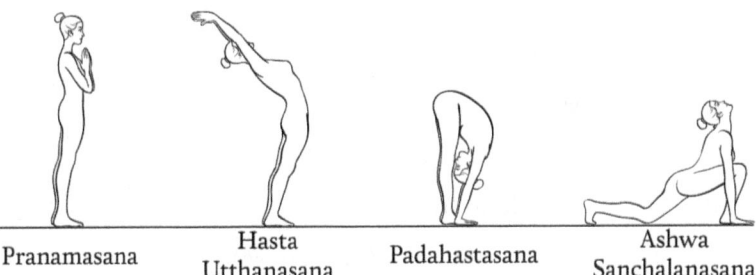

Pranamasana — Hasta Utthanasana — Padahastasana — Ashwa Sanchalanasana

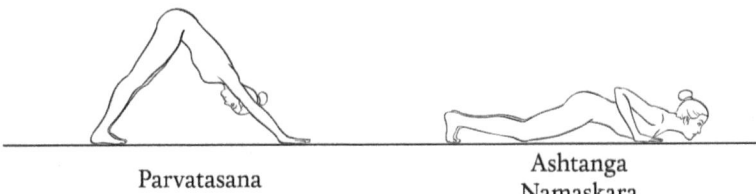

Parvatasana — Ashtanga Namaskara

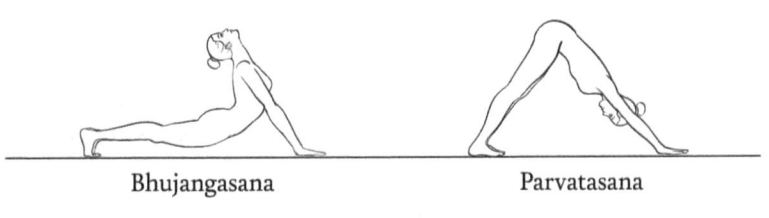

Bhujangasana — Parvatasana

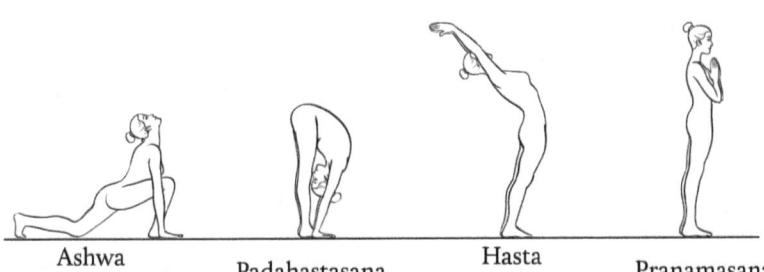

Ashwa Sanchalanasana — Padahastasana — Hasta Utthanasana — Pranamasana

Chandra Namaskara (Salutations to the Moon)

The sequence of Moon Salutations known as Chandra Namaskara is similar to the traditional Sun Salutation series but with an additional posture Ardha Chandrasana (Half Moon Pose) after Ashwa Sanchalanasana, as follows:

1. Pranamasana (Prayer pose)
2. Hasta Utthanasana (Raised arm pose)
3. Padahastasana (Hand to foot pose)
4. Ashwa Sanchalanasana (Equestrian pose)
5. Ardha Chandrasana (Half Moon pose)
6. Parvatasana (Mountain pose; also Downward Dog)
7. Ashtanga Namaskara (Eight Point Bowing)
8. Bhujangasana (Cobra pose)
9. Parvatasana (Mountain pose; also Downward Dog)
10. Ashwa Sanchalanasana (Equestrian pose)
11. Ardha Chandrasana (Half Moon pose)
12. Padahastasana (Hand to foot pose)
13. Hasta Utthanasana (Raised arm pose)
14. Pranamasana (Prayer pose)

These 14 positions are practiced twice to complete one round, changing sides (right leg, left leg) during both Ardha Chandrasana and Ashwa Sanchalanasana, for a total of 28 postures in one round.

Whereas the twelve positions of Surya Namaskara relate to the 12 zodiac signs, the fourteen positions of Chandra Namaskara relate to the 14 lunar phases. In the lunar calendar, there are 14 days before the Full Moon and 14 days after and before the New Moon. These days are called tithis and play an important role in the astrological calendar of India.

The first sequence of 14 postures done on one side represent the increasing light on the 14 tithis from New to Full Moon and the second sequence done on the other side represent the decreasing light on the 14 tithis from Full to New Moon.

Chandra Namaskara is often done at night when the moon is visible or at the time of the full moon at dawn.

Chandra Namaskara

ASTROLOGY YOGA: COSMIC CYCLES OF TRANSFORMATION

Additional Planetary Postures

The following asanas can be used to work with other planetary energies.

Mars Asanas

Asanas that focus on the navel point and promote courage and focus activate and balance the energy of Mars. A few examples include:
- Virabhadrasana I, II, III (Warrior Pose)
- Akarna Dhanurasana (Archer Pose)
- Paripurna Navasana (Boat Pose or Cantilever Pose)

Mercury Asanas

Asanas that focus on the shoulders, arms and neck, and promote flexibility activate and balance the energy of Mercury. A few examples include:
- Pincha Mayurasana (Forearm Balance)
- Kantasanchalana (Neck rolls, head turns)
- Vinyasa Jump-Throughs (Flowing sequences)

Jupiter Asanas

Asanas that focus on preparing the body for meditation activate and balance the energy of Jupiter. A few examples include:
- Guru Pranam (Extended Child Pose)
- Yoga Mudra (Seal of Yoga)
- Padmasana (Lotus Pose)

Venus Asanas

Asanas that focus on the heart center and balance the emotions activate the energy of Venus. A few examples include:
- Ustrasana (Camel Pose)
- Madhyadeha Parivrttana (Torso Twist)
- Natarajanasa (Dancer Pose)

Saturn Asanas

Asanas that focus on foundational structure and the first chakra activate and balance the energy of Saturn. A few examples include:
- Paschimottanasana (Seated forward bend)
- Tadasana (Mountain Pose)
- Tada Mudra (Body drops)

Rahu and Ketu Asanas

Asanas done in symmetrical pairs or movements activate and balance the energies of Rahu and Ketu. A few examples include:
- Matsyendrasana (Twisting Poses)
- Serabandana Kriya (Upward Dog – Downward Dog sequence)
- Parivrtta Trikonasana (Revolved Triangle)

Therapeutic and Practice Applications of Astrological Asanas

A person's approach to the practice of asana can be seen by the condition of the planets in an individual's birth chart. A strong Mars and Mercury, for example that are not supported by Jupiter and Saturn can create a gymnastic or competitive approach to asanas. A strong Saturn with a weak Moon and Venus may make it possible for a person to hold a meditative posture for extended periods but at the expense of mental suffering and ignoring the body's limitations.

By determining the dominant or controlling planets in an individual's birth chart, one can gain insight into the type of asanas that may prove most rewarding and how to design a successful practice. Consequently, planets that are challenged or weak may be aided by an asana practice that strengthens their qualities.

A specific posture may be used to activate, balance, or remediate the planet, sign or astrological energy associated with it. When using a single asana therapeutically, it is beneficial to hold the posture for three minutes or more.

Sequences of postures may be developed to work on one or more planetary energies according to the specific needs of the individual or what the birth chart may indicate. If a birth chart for example shows challenges with the Moon being in Scorpio, then a practice can be developed to strengthen the Moon or to balance Mars which rules the Moon in Scorpio.

Sequencing is vitally important in any asana practice, unless you are practicing established kriyas, or processes that use specific asana sequences. Simply performing all the postures related to Mars, for example, will not necessarily make for a satisfying or safe practice, and you may feel like going out and destroying a few countries after you are done. Postures must be sequenced to create a balanced and integrated effect in the body and in accordance of the astrological profile of the individual. This is where the skill of an experienced yoga teacher and astrologer is helpful.

If you are uncertain about how to put the asanas together, you can follow the established patterns of asana sequencing that are inherently present in traditional kriyas, according to the style you are practicing.

Asanas may also be performed during the day in which a specific planetary energy may be dominant or challenged. For example, Tuesday, which is ruled by Mars, might be a good day to work with the Martian postures or the signs ruled by Mars (Aries and Scorpio).

Example of Asana Sequence to Balance All the Planets

The following sequence of nine Hatha postures balances all the nine planets. While this is primarily a sequence built around standing postures, there are limitless asana sequences that can be devised to work on all or a subset of the planets.

- Tadasana (Mountain Pose) – Saturn
- Natarajanasa (Dancer Pose) – Venus
- Virabhadrasana I and II or only III (Warrior Pose) – Mars
- Trikonasana (Triangle) - Mercury
- Parivrtta Trikonasana (Revolved Triangle) – Rahu/Ketu
- Hasta Utthanasana (Raised arm pose) - Sun
- Padahastasana (Hand to foot pose) – Moon
- Serabandana Kriya (Downward Dog-Upward Dog) – Rahu/Ketu
- Guru Pranam (Extended Child Pose) - Jupiter

Performing Asanas to Balance the Planets

In addition to the specific asanas we choose to work with for the various planets, we can also take almost any asana sequence or yoga class and give it a planetary flavor by performing the asanas in a way that recognizes and incorporates a planet's basic energy in the following ways:

Sun Class – The asanas are done in a steady and firm manner and with a pacing that creates heat, exertion and circulation.

Moon Class – The asanas are done in soft and yielding manner with time for rest and pauses.

Mars Class – The asanas are down vigorously and with focus.

Mercury Class – The asanas are done with moderately fast movements.

Jupiter Class – The asanas are done slowly and meditatively.

Saturn Class – The asanas are done slowly and held for longer times.

Rahu Class – The asanas are done with a desire for accomplishment.

Ketu Class – The asanas are done with the eyes closed.

Planetary Pranayamas: Breathwork and the Planets

Pranayama, the regulation and control of the breath (or more exactly, the cultivation and utilization of prana), is often done with asanas, meditation, and in conjunction with the other yogic techniques of mudras and bandhas. Pranayama is the bridge between the physical body and the energetic body, between the world of matter and the world of spirit. As such, it plays a vital role in regulating and balancing the energies of the planets.

In the practice of Astrology Yoga the ability to perform pranayama effectively is dependent upon two planets, Mercury and Saturn. If both planets are strong or significant in the birth chart, practicing pranayama is easier and brings rapid rewards. If either or both of these planets are weak or challenged in a birth chart, the initial practice of pranayama will require extra effort but the rewards will be significant as it eventually strengthens both the functionality of Mercury and Saturn in an individual's life.

Mercury is the most important planet in the practice of pranayama because of its ability to connect our mind consciously to the flow of prana and regulate the breath. It is through Mercury that we develop the discerning mind that allows us to correctly control the breath. Without the mentality provided by Mercury, there can be no conscious relationship between the body and breath and therefore no pranayama. Mercury allows us to bring the unconscious movement of the breath into our mental realm and hold the focus.

Saturn provides the ability to engage in the basic pranayama practices of breath retention and breath suspension. While Mercury allows the breath to move consciously, Saturn allows us to halt that movement in a disciplined manner. If we use the definition of pranayama as given in the Yoga Sutras, that pranayama naturally follows with a cessation of the movements of inspiration and expiration, then the controlling ability of Saturn to retain the breath between the inhale and the exhale (antar kumbhaka) as well as to suspend the breath out between the exhale and the inhale (bahir kumbhaka), means that Saturn plays a vital role in achieving one of the ultimate purposes of pranayama, to quiet the mind and enter into meditation.

Another name for Saturn is Yama, the god that controls the length of the life or the length of the breath (prana) with its measuring and cutting process, another apt description for pranayama.

Sun and Moon Breath

While Mercury and Saturn play a vital role in the ability to practice pranayama, the Sun and Moon are the planets that fundamentally differentiate the practices of pranayama.

This is due to the association in yoga of the Sun energy with the right nostril breath and the Moon energy with the left nostril breath. This sun-moon, right-left, and male-female polarity in the body is an essential teaching of tantra and hatha yoga.

Breathing through the right nostril activates the sun energy channel know as the Pingala nadi and breathing through the left nostril activates the moon energy channel known as the Ida nadi. In fact, breathing only through the right nostril for a length of time subtly raises body temperature, makes the mind more analytical, and disposes one to projective action, much like the nature of the sun. On the other hand (or nostril!), breathing only through the left nostril subtly cools the body, makes the mind more intuitive, and disposes one to receptive experiences, much like the nature of the moon.

The natural breathing pattern is for one nostril to be dominant for one to two hours and then switch to the other side, with short periods where the breath flows through both nostrils equally.

In this way, we go back and forth between our sun and moon energy throughout the day. The different patterns of the breath either in right, left, or both nostrils influence our health, consciousness and our worldly activities.

The yogis extensively analyzed the effects of the Sun breath (right nostril) and Moon breath (left nostril) through the science and practice of Swara Yoga. Literally translated as "flow," Swara Yoga observed how different pranic rhythms through the right and left nostrils profoundly influenced the body and mind. In the 1970s, researchers in the western world began developing their own body of scientific literature on the different effects of right and left nostril breathing. One study demonstrated that when students practiced the Sun breath (right nostril breathing) for 10 minutes before a math exam, their scores improved significantly, thus validating the observations by yogis that the Sun breath makes the mind more analytical and activates the left hemisphere of the brain.

The following table shows some of the properties and concepts associated with the Sun and Moon breath.

MOON BREATH	SUN BREATH	EQUAL BREATH
Left Nostril	Right Nostril	Both Nostrils
Right Brain	Left Brain	Whole Brain
Ida Nadi	Pingala Nadi	Sushumna Nadi
Negative	Positive	Neutral/Balanced
Chandra Swara	Surya Swara	Shunia Swara
Chitta Shakti	Prana Shakti	Kundalini Shakti
Apana Vayu	Prana Vayu	All Vayus
Mental Activities	Physical Activities	Spiritual Activities
Female	Male	Beyond Polarity
Cold	Hot	Temperate
Parasympathetic System	Sympathetic System	Central Nervous System
Night	Day	Dusk/Dawn
Internal	External	Centered
Passive	Dynamic	Balanced
Intuition	Logic	Wisdom
Desire	Action	Knowledge
Subconscious	Conscious	Supraconscious
Subjectivity	Objectivity	Awareness
Blue	Red	Yellow

Table 4-4: Attributes of the Moon and Sun Breath

Sun and Moon Qualities of the Major Pranayamas

As with the asanas, the fundamental principles of Brimhana, Langhana, and Samana can also be applied to the practices of pranayama to determine which are Sun Pranayamas and which are the Moon Pranayamas. Brihmana is expanding, projective, and heating, like the Sun. Langhana is lightening, calming and cooling, like the Moon. Samana is a balance between these two planetary energies.

So a brihmana pranayama (or Sun practice) would be heating and projective (masculine) and a langhana pranayama (or Moon practice) would be cooling and receptive (feminine). A pranayam in which the Sun and Moon energies were balanced would be a Samana pranayama.

PRANAYAMA	QUALITY	EFFECT	SUN-MOON BALANCE
Sitali or Sitkari	Langhana	Tranquilizing	All Moon energy
Chandra Anga	Langhana	Tranquilizing.	All Moon energy
Chandra Bheda	Langhana	Tranquilizing	All Moon energy
Anuloma Krama	Langhana	Tranquilizing	Mostly Moon
Bhramari	Langhana	Tranquilizing	Mostly Moon
Anuloma Ujjayi	Langhana	Balancing	More Moon than Sun
Kapalabhati	Langhana	Vitalizing	More Moon than Sun
Nadi Shodhana	Samana	Balancing	Equal Moon and Sun
Agni Pran *	Samana	Balancing	Equal Moon and Sun
Ujjayi	Brimhana	Balancing	More Sun than Moon
Viloma Ujjayi	Brimhana	Balancing	More Sun than Moon
Viloma Krama	Brimhana	Vitalizing	Mostly Sun
Surya Bheda	Brimhana	Vitalizing	All Sun energy
Surya Anga	Brimhana	Vitalizing	All Sun energy
Bhastrika	Brimhana	Vitalizing	All Sun energy

* Breath of Fire

Table 4-5: Moon and Sun Qualities of the Major Pranayamas

Sun and Moon Pranayama Practices

The following breath series balances the Sun and Moon energy, as well as the emotions. It is an excellent daily practice to set your energy for the day.

The first four pranayamas in the series are done an equal length of time, 1 to 3 minutes each. The last pranayama is done 3 to 7 minutes:

1. Chandra Anga Pranayama (inhale left nostril, exhale left)
2. Surya Anga Pranayama (inhale right nostril exhale right)
3. Chandra Bheda Pranayama (inhale left, exhale right)
4. Surya Bheda Pranayama (inhale right, exhale left)
5. Agni Pran (breath of fire) or Nadi Shodhana (alternate nostril)

The energetic difference between the Anga and Bheda pranayamas is that the Bheda practices create a stronger energy and are best done after the Anga practices. These pranayamas may also be combined to create different Sun and Moon energetic effects as follows:

To quickly increase Sun energy:
- Surya Anga Pranayama with Agni Pran (Breath of Fire)

To quickly increase Moon energy:
- Chandra Anga Pranayama with Agni Pran (Breath of Fire)

To create cooling and relaxing Moon energy:
- Sitali or Sitkari (inhale mouth) and Chandra Anga (exhale left)

Other Planetary Pranayama Practices

The following pranayama practices can be used to balance and activate the other planetary energies. They may be done separately for 5 to 15 minutes or as part of a yoga class or meditation practice.

Mars Pranayama Practices

Breathing techniques that focus on the navel point and abdominal area activate and balance the planetary energy of Mars. These are three Mars pranayamas:
- Bhastrika (Bellows Breath)
- Kapalabhati (Shinning Forehead Breath)
- Agni Pran (Breath of Fire)

Mercury Pranayama Practices
Breathing techniques that focus on the throat area, as well as those that move the breath quickly, activate and balance the planetary energy of Mercury. These are three Mercury pranayamas:
- Ujjayi (Victorious Breath)
- Agni Pran (Breath of Fire)
- Bhramari (Humming Bee Breath)

Jupiter Pranayama Practices
Breathing techniques that focus on expanding the breath capacity and retaining the breath after inhalation activate and balance the planetary energy of Jupiter. These are three Jupiter pranayamas:
- Antara Kumbhaka (Breath Retention After Inhale)
- Anuloma Viloma (Alternate Nostril with Retention)
- Whistle Breath (Inhale/exhale with a light whistle)

Venus Pranayama Practices
Breathing techniques that focus on the heart center and create emotional balancing activate the planetary energy of Venus. These are three Venus pranayamas:
- Sama Vritti Pranayama (Equal Breathing Inhale and Exhale)
- Nadi Shodhana Pranayama (Alternate Nostril without Retention)
- Three Part Segmented Breath (Inhale 3 segments, exhale 3 segments)

Saturn Pranayama Practices
Breathing techniques that focus on suspending the breath out and working with the bandhas (locks) activate and balance the planetary energy of Saturn. These are three Saturn pranayamas:
- Bahya Kumbhaka Pranayama (Breath Retention After Exhale)
- Anuloma Viloma (Four part ratio, 4:1:2:4)
- Dirga Pranayama (Three part breath with Maha Bandha after exhale)

Rahu and Ketu Pranayama Practices
Breathing techniques that focus on the two major energy channels of the body (nadis), called the Ida and the Pignala, activate and balance the planetary energies of Ketu and Rahu. These are three Rahu/Ketu pranayamas:
- Nadi Shodhana Pranayama (Alternate Nostril breathing)
- Surya Bheda Pranayama (inhale right, exhale left)
- Chandra Bheda Pranayama (inhale left, exhale right)

Planetary Mudras: Astrology Yoga in Your Hands

One of the more powerful yet neglected yoga techniques is the use of mudras, or hand positions, as an aid for meditation, pranayama, and healing. The practice of mudras is also an important connection to working and managing the energies of the planets.

A mudra, literally translated as a "seal", is a psycho-neural lock formed with a hand position (hasta mudra), muscular lock (bandha), gaze (dristi), head position (mana mudra), or a body posture (kaya mudra) that directs the flow of prana through the subtle body to enhance breathing, focus, healing and meditation. For the purposes of Astrology Yoga, we will focus on the hasta mudras as they offer the most versatility.

There are thousands of hasta mudras, or hand and finger positions, available to yoga practitioners that make important connections in the nervous system to stimulate specific energy channels (nadis) while also increasing energy and blood circulation to different parts of the brain as well as important nerve areas and the glands.

For example, certain mudras (including the classical gyan mudra in which the index finger tip touches the thumb tip) help control the involuntary physiological functions of breathing. The mudras achieve this by controlling the mind-brain processes and the functions within the nervous system by uniting various nerve terminals of the sympathetic and parasympathetic nervous systems.

These connections between the fingers (mudras) and the brain are hard-wired before birth. During an early stage of fetal development the fingers are intimately connected to the developing brain area. Hand and finger positions thus become a keyboard to access different areas of the brain. By touching fingers to other fingers and different areas of the hand, we send messages to the mind and body energy system to alter consciousness.

The early yogis mapped out the mudras and their associated reflexes that related to various areas of the body and brain as well as to different emotions or behaviors. Among these mudras is an important subset that relates to working with and managing the energies of the planets.

These planetary mudras were used in Ayurveda, the healing system of ancient India, as well as in the temple dances and by yogis in advanced meditation. In many ways, mudras are the easiest yoga practices to tap into a planet's energy and are accessible to everyone.

Planetary Mudras

We know from astrology that the planets themselves represent different energies, psychological states, physical body areas, and states of mind.

All thoughts, all actions, all elements of the material world, all parts of the body, all have a connection with one or more of the major planetary energies. It should be no surprise that the different areas of the hands and fingers also have a connection with the various planets.

This planetary connection with the area of the hand was well known by ancient astrologers. Indeed, before the age of easily generated computer birth charts, Eastern astrologers learned to discern the planetary make up of an individual through the examination of the hands. This branch of astrology, or Hast Jyotish, later became known as Palmistry in the Western world. Unlike Western palmistry, however, which became primarily a predictive tool, the Eastern astrologers used Hast Jyotish as a way to gauge the relative strength of the planets in the birth chart and to help rectify an uncertain time of birth.

This relationship between the planets and the fingers makes it possible to work with planetary energies through yogic mudras that use the fingers in various hand positions. To balance and activate the flow of the energy of Jupiter, for example, a hand mudra would be formed that uses the finger associated with Jupiter.

Planetary Fingers

Hast Jyotish associates the two luminaries (Sun and Moon), the five visible planets (Sun, Moon, Mars, Mercury, Jupiter, Venus and Saturn), and the two shadow planets (Rahu and Ketu) with the various fingers and areas of the hand, both right and left, as follows:

Sun - Ring finger and below base of that finger

Moon - Outside mound below little finger and above base of palm

Mars - Thumb and below base of thumb

Mercury - Little finger and below base of that finger

Jupiter - Index finger and below base of that finger

Venus - Outside mound below thumb and above base of palm

Saturn - Middle finger and below base of that finger

Rahu - Between Mars, Venus, Moon areas, below base of middle finger

Ketu - Above the wrist between the Moon and Venus areas

The Seven Planetary Mudras

The seven planetary mudras of the visible planets are formed by touching the thumb and fingers together as well as to different areas of the hand. The thumb in Vedic thought and Ayurveda is linked to the element of fire, the element that brings the transformative energy of action to whatever it touches. As such, the thumb is often used to activate the other four fingers and their associated planetary energies.

Each mudra is named after the Sanskrit name of the planet associated with the finger, or area of hand, as follows:

Surya Mudra (Sun)

Technique: Touch the thumb to the ring finger.

Named after the Sun (Surya), this mudra is also called Ravi Mudra (another name for the Sun) and is formed by bringing the thumb tip to the ring finger tip. Like the Sun, this mudra gives revitalizing strength, excellent health, immunity, nerve strength, stability and outwardly directed energy. It is also used to strengthen potency and efficacy.

Chandra Mudra (Moon)

Technique: Join the outside of the hands together below the little finger to the base of the palms.

Named after the Moon (Chandra), this mudra is formed by bringing the two Moon mounds (along the outside of the hands) together with the palms facing up. Like the Moon, this mudra enhances our receptivity and intuition and helps to bring a balance between our emotions and our thoughts as well as between our fantasies and our plans.

Mangala Mudra (Mars)

Technique: Make a fist of the hand with the thumb extended or curled inside.

Named after Mars (Mangala), this mudra is formed by curling the fingers into the palm and bringing the thumb outside the fist or extended up. Bringing the thumb to the base of the ring finger and making a fist around the thumb can also form it. This mudra increases courage, vitality, strength, assertion, and ability to overcome obstacles.

Buddhi Mudra (Mercury)

Technique: Touch the thumb to the little finger.

Named after Mercury (Buddhi), this mudra is formed by bringing the thumb tip to the little fingertip. This mudra, like Mercury the messenger of the gods, enhances all areas of communication. It gives quickness to the mental processes, increases analytical ability, and develops intuition and psychic faculties. It is also beneficial for commerce and prosperity.

Gyan Mudra (Jupiter)

Technique: Touch the thumb to the index finger.

Named for the wisdom (gyan) of Jupiter, this mudra is also called Chin Mudra or Jnana Mudra and is the most practiced of the planetary mudras. It is formed by bringing the thumb tip to the index fingertip. This mudra receives and integrates knowledge and brings calmness, expansion, and understanding. Since the dispelling of ignorance (avidya) is the first step toward enlightenment, this mudra is often used in meditation and pranayama practices. It is also associated with opportunity and good fortune.

Shukra Mudra (Venus)

Technique: Interlace the hands with thumbs resting side by side and not crossing.

Named after Venus (Shukra), this mudra is formed by interlacing the fingers of both hands with the thumbs resting side by side and the outer thumb pressing on the mound above base of palm and below thumb side (Venus Mound). Fingers are interlaced so men press the right thumb on the mound and left little finger is on bottom. Women press the left thumb on the mound with right little finger on the bottom. This mudra channels sexual energy into love and compassion and balances our sensuality.

Shani Mudra (Saturn)

Technique: Touch the thumb to the middle finger.

Named after Saturn (Shani), the lord of Karma, this mudra is formed by bringing the thumb tip to the middle finger tip. Saturn represents discipline, hard work, holding to the task, duty, responsibility, and selfless service. The mudra is used to give patience and perseverance so we can understand the lessons of time. It produces calmness, purity and humility.

BASIC PLANETARY MUDRAS

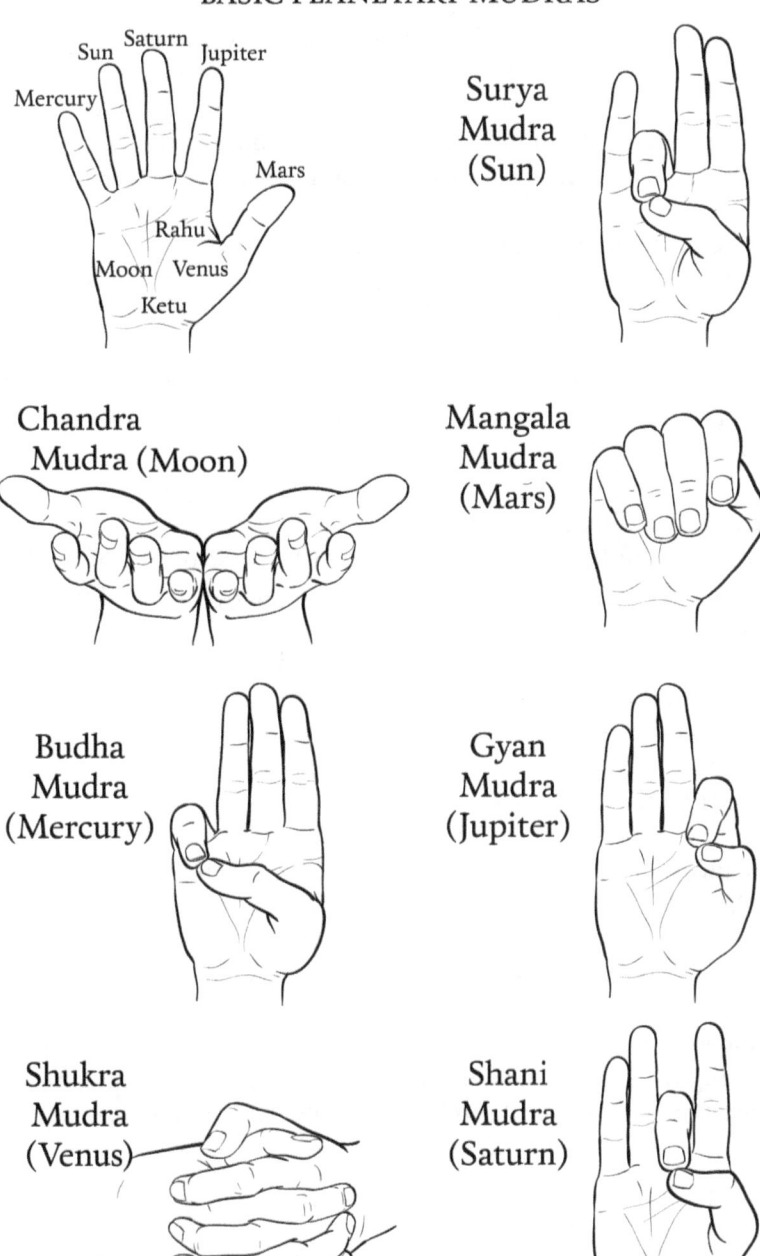

ASTROLOGY YOGA: COSMIC CYCLES OF TRANSFORMATION

Using the Mudras

Mudras are typically used to balance or receive the energy of a planet, but they can also be used to increase or strengthen that energy as well as to diminish the energy if it is an overactive and challenging planet.

The mode or method of operation of the mudras is determined by the relationship between the thumb and the four fingers as described here:

Receptive or Balancing Mode

This is the most often used method in which the tip of the thumb touches the tip of one of the fingers. This brings in the planetary energy of the finger that is touched in a balanced way.

The Receptive Mode allows the planetary energies to be received and integrated. In general, the Receptive Mode is preferably used to cultivate and optimize needed energies.

Active or Strengthening Mode

This occurs when the thumb tip touches to the base of one of the fingers. This strengthens and tonifies the planetary energy of the finger that is touched at the base.

The Active Mode of the mudra is used for more strenuous yoga practices and meditations where the energies of a planet need to be vigorously harnessed and used.

Sedated or Diminishing Mode

This occurs when the thumb holds one of the fingers down or covers it. This reduces the planetary energy of the finger that is held down or covered.

The Sedated Mode of the mudra allows the planetary energies to be diminished or sedated to lessen the energies of a challenging planet.

The following illustrations show the three different modes of the mudra for working with Saturn (Shani Mudra), but the process is the same for the other three fingers for Jupiter (Gyan), Sun (Surya), and Mercury (Buddhi) Mudra.

MUDRA MODES

Receptive or Balancing Mode

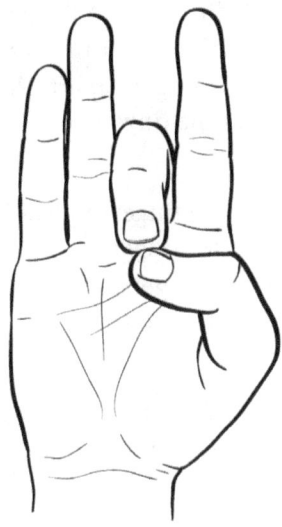

Active or Strengthening Mode

Sedated or Diminishing Mode

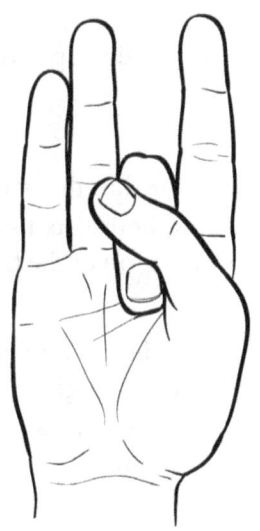

The Navagraha Mudras

The navagraha mudras are from the classical Indian dance traditions. These mudras require both hands be held in front of the body. The nine mudras were described in the ancient text Abhinaya Darpana, as follows:

Surya (Sun) Mudra

Right Hand: Press the middle, ring and little fingers into the palm. Extend the thumb up and touch the first pad of the index finger to the thumb tip.

Left Hand: Turn the palm up and stretch the fingers apart. Pull the little finger toward the palm and fan out the rest of the fingers.

Chandra (Moon) Mudra

Right Hand: Face the palm forward, extend the fingers upward, and bend the thumb to touch the outside base of the index finger.

Left Hand: Turn the palm up and stretch the fingers apart. Pull the little finger toward the palm and fan out the rest of the fingers.

Angaraka (Mars) Mudra

Right Hand: Make a fist with the thumb extended or curled inside.

Left Hand: Extend the index finger straight up with the other fingers held down by the thumbs.

Budha (Mercury) Mudra

Right Hand: Face the palm forward, extend the fingers upward, and bend the thumb to touch the outside base of the index finger.

Left Hand: Make a fist with the thumb extended upward.

Guru (Jupiter) Mudra

Right Hand: Make a fist with the thumb extended upward.

Left Hand: Same as the right hand.

Shukra (Venus) Mudra

Right Hand: Make a fist of the hand with the thumb resting on top.

Left Hand: Same as the right hand. Bring both fists together, knuckle to knuckle, with thumbs resting side by side on top of the fists.

Shani (Saturn) Mudra

Right Hand: Face the hand forward, hold the little finger down with the thumb and extend and separate the other three fingers.

Left Hand: Make a fist with the thumb extended upward.

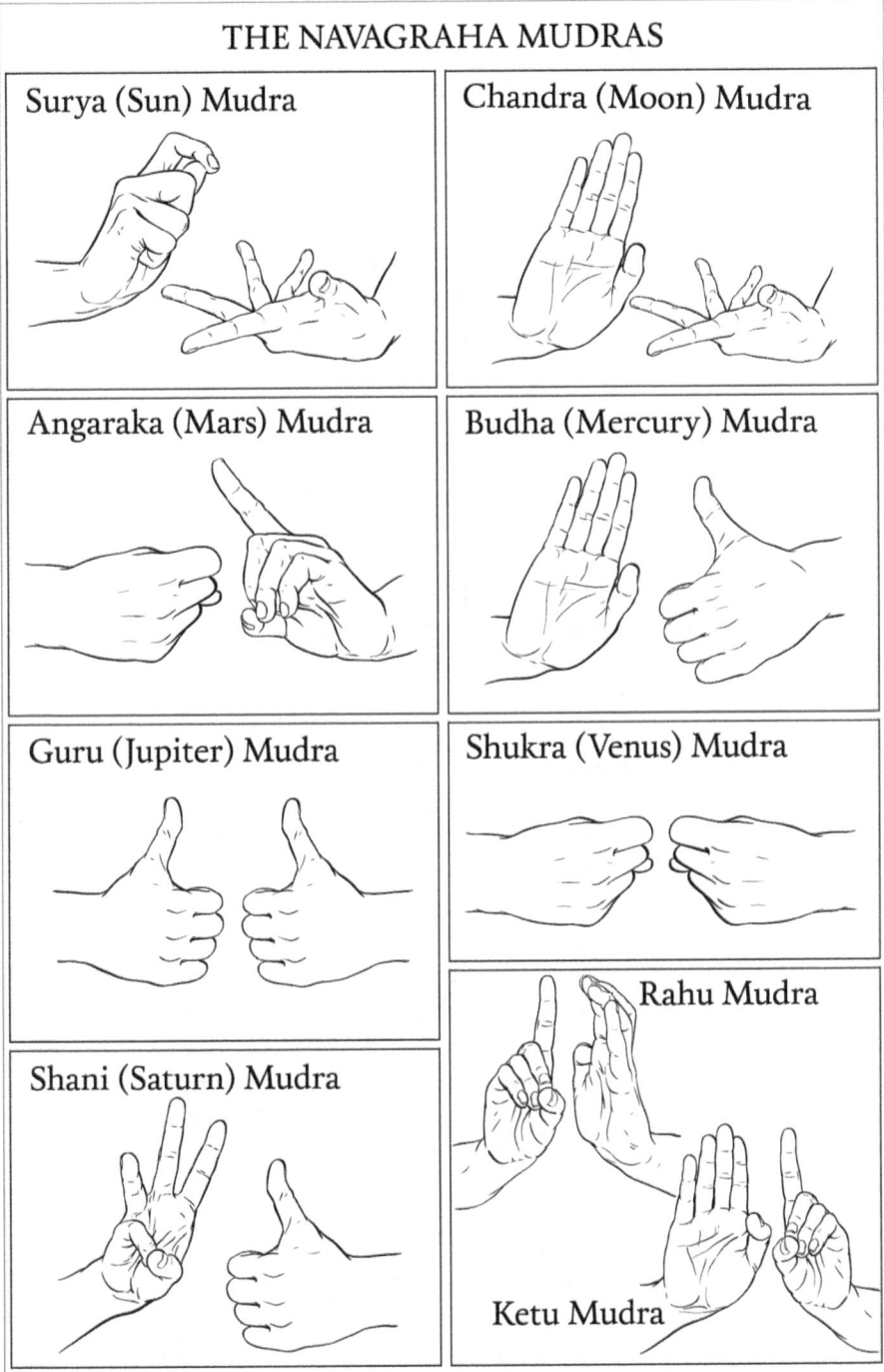

Rahu Mudra

Right Hand: Extend the index finger straight up with the other fingers held down by the thumbs.

Left Hand: Face the hand forward, extend the fingers and thumb together, and then round the fingers slightly to imitate the hood of a cobra snake.

Ketu Mudra

Right Hand: Face the palm forward, extend the fingers upward, and bend the thumb to touch the outside base of the index finger.

Left Hand: Extend the index finger straight up with the other fingers held down by the thumbs.

Advanced and Combined Planetary Mudras

A distinction about mudras is that the right hand is projective energy (solar) and the left hand is receptive energy (lunar). In this case, a Jupiter mudra using the right hand would project Jupiter energy out into the world while the left hand would bring that energy into our inner self.

Often the same mudra is used on both hands to balance the projective and receptive energies of a planet. However, on occasions only one hand may form the mudra to create a particular shift in consciousness or actions.

Both hands can form different planetary mudras simultaneously to create a synthesis of energy. Forming a Saturn mudra with the left hand and a Sun mudra with the right hand, for example, allows us to project solar vitality and leadership qualities while receiving the saturnine qualities of patience and perseverance.

Another synthesized mudra, called Narayan Mudra in one tradition, joins the two hands from the tips of the little fingers down to the base of the palm and the hands are slightly cupped with the fingers together. The sides of the little fingers touching invoke Mercury energy while the base of the palms touching at the mounds of the little fingers activates Moon energy. The two index fingers then curl and touch the thumb tips to form Gyan Mudra for Jupiter energy. This mudra would be comparable to an astrological occurrence of Moon, Mercury and Jupiter in conjunction or aspect and synthesizes the energies of all three planets.

The hand mudras may be used to represent planetary energies in many different ways. Fingers may be crossed, extended without touching, or joined in an array of complexities to spell out almost any astrological combination or state of the planets.

Mudras are indeed the yogic sign language of astrology and a major therapeutic tool for the astrologer and yoga practitioner.

Planetary Mantras: Celestial Sounds of Power

The most powerful way to work with the planets is through mantra and sound. Mantra was the first yoga technique described in the Vedas and the original method used to propitiate the planetary energies.

To work with a particular planetary energy, the mantra for that planet is chanted for a length of time or number of repetitions (usually 108 times) over a period of time (for example, 40 days) or until a certain number of total repetitions is reached (for example, 84,000). A mala may be used to count the repetitions, and the mantra may also be repeated silently.

There are many mantras associated with the planets, and we will look at the three major categories of the name mantras (nama), the seed mantras (bija), and the power mantras (shakti).

Planetary Name Mantras

The following are the name (nama) mantras for the planets to balance their influences and to use for propitiation and rituals.

PLANET	NAME MANTRA
SUN	OM SURYAYA NAMAHA (Om Soor-yah-yah Nahm-ah-ah)
MOON	OM CHANDRAYA NAMAH (Om Chahn-drah-yah Nahm-ah-ah)
MARS	OM MANGALA NAMAH (Om man-gah-la Nahm-ah-ah)
MERCURY	OM BUDHAYA NAMAH (Om Bood-hah-yah Nahm-ah-ah)
JUPITER	OM GURAVE NAMAH (Om Goo-rah-vey Nahm-ah-ah)
VENUS	OM SHUKRAYA NAMAH (Om Shoo-krah-va Nahm-ah-ah)
SATURN	OM SHANAYE NAMAH (Om Shah-na-yee Nahm-ah-ah)
RAHU	OM RAHAVE NAMAH (Om Rah-hoo-vey Nahm-ah-ah)
KETU	OM KETAVE NAMAH (Om Key-too-vey Nahm-ah-ah)

Table 4-6: Planetary Name Mantras

Planetary Bija (Seed) Mantras

The following are the various seed (bija) mantras for the planets to balance their influences and to use for propitiation and rituals. You can select any one of these powerful one-word sounds to use by themselves.

They carry the essence of the planetary energies into the subconscious. They can also be chanted in the form of: OM (Bija Mantra) NAMAH, such as OM RAM NAMAH for the Sun.

PLANET	BIJA MANTRAS
SUN	RAM (Rahm), SUM (Soom), HRIM (Hreem)
MOON	CHAM (Chahm), SOM (Soom), SHRIM (Shreem)
MARS	AM (Ung), KUM (Kum short "u" like "put"), RUM (Room)
MERCURY	BUM (Bum short "u" like "put"), AIM (Aym), DHIM (Dheem)
JUPITER	GAM (Gum short "u"), BRIM - (Brim "i" like "it"), KRIM (Kreem)
VENUS	SHUM (Shum "u" like "put"), HRIM (Hreem), SHRIM (Shreem)
SATURN	SHAM (Shahm), KLIM (Kleem)
RAHU	RAM (Rahm), DUM (Doom like "room"), HUM (Hum short "u")
KETU	KEM (Kame), HUM (Hum short "u" like "put"), RUM (Room)

Table 4-7: Planetary Bija (Seed) Mantras

Planetary Shakti Mantras

The Shakti mantras are used to energize the higher powers of the planets.

PLANET	SHAKTI (POWER) MANTRAS
SUN	OM HRIM SUM SURYAYA NAMAHA HRIM (Hreem) - the power of attraction and fascination
MOON	OM SHRIM SOM SOMAYA NAMAH SHRIM (Shreem) - the power of peace and letting go
MARS	OM KRIM KUM KUJAYA NAMAH KRIM (Kreem) - the power of courage and change
MERCURY	OM AIM BUM BUDHAYA NAMAH AIM (Aym) - the power of guidance and teaching
JUPITER	OM STRIM BRAHM BRIHASPATAYE NAMAH STRIM (Streem) - the power of expansion and evolution
VENUS	OM KLIM SHUM SHUKRAYA NAMAH KLIM (Kleem) - the power of love and contentment
SATURN	OM HLIM SHAM SHANAYE NAMAH HLIM (Hleem) - the power of controlling and halting
RAHU	OM DHUM RAM RAHAVE NAMAH DHUM (short "u") - the power of hiding and deceiving
KETU	OM HUM KEM KETAVE NAMAH HUM (short "u") - the power of destruction and transformation

Table 4-8: Planetary Shakti (Power) Mantras

How to Use the Planetary Mantras

Setting an intention and connecting to the energy of the planet magnifies the effects of the mantra. Mantras are repeated a set number of times during a practice. The common number of repetitions is 108 times, a sacred number in both Vedic astrology and Yoga. Variations on the number of repetitions can range from as low as 3 to 11 repetitions and up to 125,000 repetitions, called a "purascharana." Mantras can also be chanted for a length of time as well, for 40 days, 120 days or 1000 days.

Mantras can be chanted on the day of the week associated with that planet, or other auspicious times. Here are opportune times to chant a specific planetary mantra or to start an extended practice for that planet.

PLANET	DAYS AND TIMES FOR USING THE MANTRAS
SUN	Sunday during the day. Also dawn, noon, sunset.
MOON	Monday. Evening. Before Full Moon and at Half Moon.
MARS	Tuesday
MERCURY	Wednesday
JUPITER	Thursday
VENUS	Friday
SATURN	Saturday
RAHU	Saturday, or the day of the planet ruling Rahu at birth
KETU	Saturday, Tuesday, or the day of the planet ruling Ketu at birth.

Table 4-9: Days and Times for Planetary Mantras

Using A Mala With Your Planetary Mantras

The planetary energies can be enhanced by using a mala made from gems associated with a planet. The malas have 108 beads to keep track of the repetitions. When using a mala for the first time, begin on the weekday associated with the planet and use the Shakti mantra for that planet to initiate and set the energy for the mala.

The following table is not exhaustive. You can also use beads of the same color as the ones given for the planets as well.

PLANET	MALA GEMS OR BEADS
SUN	Ruby, spinel, garnet, sunstone, red zircon, red tourmaline
MOON	Pearl, cultured pearl, moonstone
MARS	Red coral, carnelian, red jasper
MERCURY	Emerald, aquamarine, peridot, jade, green tourmaline
JUPITER	Yellow sapphire, topaz, citrine, yellow zircon, yellow tourmaline
VENUS	Diamond, white sapphire, clear zircon, clear quartz, white coral
SATURN	Blue sapphire, Lapis lazuli, amethyst, turquoise, blue tourmaline
RAHU	Hessonite garnet, golden grossularite garnet
KETU	Chrysoberyl, other cat's eye (mainly quartz)

Table 4-10: Mala Gems and Stones to Use With Planetary Mantras

Using Planetary Mantras with Asanas

You can chant the planetary mantras with an asana practice, chanting each mantra before the posture or during the posture on the natural exhalation. You can pick a planetary mantra based on the day of the week you are practicing or for the posture that is associated with a planet.

One traditional way is to chant the Sun mantras for the Sun salutations and the Moon mantras for the Moon salutations as described here.

Surya Namaskara Mantras

Each of the twelve postures in the Sun salutation (see the section on the Planetary Postures) is accompanied by a mantra. The mantras are the names, or meanings, of the Sun. These twelve mantras are chanted on both sides to complete one round of Surya Namaskara:

1. OM Mitraya Namaha (Friendly One)
2. OM Ravaye Namaha (Shining One)
3. OM Suryaya Namaha (Active One)
4. OM Bhanave Namaha (Illumined One)
5. OM Khagaya Namaha (Moving One)
6. OM Pushne Namaha (Strong One)
7. OM Hiranya Garbhaya Namaha (Golden Cosmic One)
8. OM Marichaye Namaha (Lord of Dawn)
9. OM Adityaya Namaha (Son of the Cosmic Mother)
10. OM Savitre Namaha (Creative One)
11. OM Arkaya Namaha (Praiseworthy One)
12. OM Bhaskaraya (Enlightened One)

Each mantra can be chanted before or while moving into each posture.

Bija (Seed) Mantras for Sun Salutations

You can use seed (bija) mantras for sun salutations, especially if the sequence moves too quickly for longer mantras. There are six seed mantras for the Sun Salutation. A mantra is chanted for each posture so the six sounds are repeated twice for one side of the body and twice for the other side for a total of four repetitions in one round. The six seed mantras are:

1. OM Hraam
2. OM Hreem
3. OM Hroom
4. OM Hraim
5. OM Hraum
6. OM Hraha

Chandra Namaskara Mantras

Each of the 14 postures in the Moon Salutation series (see the section on the Planetary Postures) is accompanied by a mantra for each position. The mantras are the 12 different names, or meanings, of the Moon. The names are chanted when the postures are done on both sides to complete one round of Chandra Namaskara.

The 14 mantras are:

1. OM Kamesvaryai Namaha (She who fulfills desires)
2. OM Bhagamalinyai (She who brings prosperity)
3. OM Nityaklinnayai Namaha (She who is ever compassionate)
4. OM Bherundayai Namaha (She who is fierce)
5. OM Vahnivasinyai Namaha (She who resides in fire)
6. OM Vajreshvaryai (She who is thunderous)
7. OM Dutyai Namaha (She who delivers)
8. OM Tvaritayai Namaha (She who is swift)
9. OM Kulasundaryai (She who is virtuous)
10. OM Nityayai Namaha (She who is eternal)
11. OM Nilapatakinyai Namaha (She who is adorned)
12. OM Vijayayai Namaha (She who is victorious)
13. OM Sarvamangalayai Namaha (She who brings good fortune)
14. OM Jvalamalinyai Namaha (She who is surrounded by light)

Each mantra can be chanted before or while moving into each posture.

Bija (Seed) Mantras for Moon Salutations

You can also use seed (bija) mantras for the moon salutations, especially when the sequence moves too quickly to accommodate the longer mantras. There are seven seed mantras for the Moon Salutation.

A seed mantra is chanted for each posture so the seven sounds are repeated twice for one side of the body and twice again for the other side of the body for a total of four complete repetitions in one round. The seven seed mantras are:

1. OM Saum
2. OM Cham
3. OM Shrim
4. OM Hrim
5. OM Klim
6. OM Krim
7. OM Maa

Using Chakra Mantras to Balance All the Planetary Energies

Traditionally there are five seed (bija) mantras for the first five chakras that are used to balance these energy centers and their corresponding elements. These five mantras may also be used to work with the various planetary energies as well. In addition there are seed mantras for the upper two chakras that also strengthen and balance the planets.

Note that the "a" in the mantras are pronounced with a short "a" sound that is slightly extended.

CHAKRA	MANTRA	ELEMENT	PLANETS STRENGTHENED
FIRST Muladhara	LAM	EARTH	MOON, VENUS
SECOND Svadhisthana	VAM	WATER	JUPITER, VENUS, MOON
THIRD Manipura	RAM	FIRE	SUN, MARS, KETU
FOURTH Anahata	YAM	AIR	MERCURY
FIFTH Vishuddha	HAM	ETHER	MERCURY, JUPITER
SIXTH Ajna	(K)SHAM	LIGHT	MOON, MERCURY
SEVENTH Sahasrara	OM	THOUGHT	SUN, SATURN

Table 4-11: Chakra Bij Mantras and Planetary Energies

The mantras may be chanted from first to seventh chakra, placing an image of one of the planets at that chakra, and then repeating the entire sequence as many times as desired. Alternatively, one mantra may be chanted repeatedly for 108 times to energize a specific chakra and its corresponding planet(s).

Planetary Meditations: Mastering Time and Space

All the planets in Vedic astrology support the practice of meditation, even the ones that seem very physical (Mars) or materialistic (Rahu).

Each planet is associated with different meditation techniques and provides specific benefits from working with its energies during meditation. There is truly a meditation planet and approach for everyone. Here's an overview of techniques and benefits associated with the nine planets of Vedic Astrology.

Sun Meditations

Sun meditations focus on light and visualizations. They include gazing (tratakam) at the sun, a candle flame or a fire, meditating on the inner light in the body or on the light in the heart, as well as mediations employing mandalas and yantras. Using the Sun mudra and mantras are helpful, as is meditating at sunrise, sunset and noon. Hatha yoga practices are an excellent preparation for Sun meditations.

Meditation on the Sun produces self-confidence and self-belief.

Suggested Sun Meditation – The Inner Sun of the Heart

1. Sit in a meditative posture.
2. Chant OM SURYAYA NAMAHA (Om Soor-yah-yah Nahm-ah-ah) 3 or more times.
3. Touch the right thumb to the right ring finger.
4. Bring the right hand up by the shoulder, palm facing forward.
5. Block the left nostril with the left index finger.
6. Breathe slowly through the right nostril for 26 times.
7. Release the hands and rub the palms together hard, 2 to 3 minutes.
8. Hold the right palm over the left palm, 4 to 6 inches apart.
9. Cup the palms in front of the heart as if holding a miniature sun.
10. Breathe into the sun between the palms, growing brighter with each breath, for 3 to 7 minutes.
11. Visualize the sun in front of the heart illuminating the heart center.
12. Chant OM SURYAYA NAMAHA (Om Soor-yah-yah Nahm-ah-ah) 3 or more times.

Suggested Sun Meditation
The Inner Sun of the Heart

Moon Meditations

Moon meditations focus on the element of water and feminine figures. Meditations around water, hearing the sound of running water or waves, meditations on peace and serenity, and meditations on the universal Mother Goddess or feminine deities are all effective Moon meditations. Meditating on the days of the Full and New Moon are especially beneficial, as well as meditating in the moonlight (but not gazing directly at the moon itself which is said to unbalance the emotions). Bhakti yoga practices are an excellent preparation for Moon meditations.

Meditation on the Moon produces serenity, security and happiness.

Suggested Moon Meditation – The Creative Mother

1. Sit in a meditative posture. Bring the hands with palms facing upward in front of the heart and then join the two sides of the hands together, from the base of the little finger to the bottom of the hand. Visualize a miniature moon held in the hands.
2. Chant OM CHANDRAYA NAMAH (Om Chahn-drah-yah Nahm-ah-ah) for 3 or more times.
3. Make fists of both hands at the heart level, left palm facing up and right palm down. Hook the little finger of the left hand around the thumb of the right hand and pull for slight tension. Close the eyes and focus at the third eye.
4. Chant the mantra AIMA with a long extended sound (AHHH EEEE MAAH) for 11 minutes.
5. Then relax and bring the back of the hands on the knees, arms fairly straight, and touch the index finger tips to the thumb tips.
6. Inhale fully and chant the long sound of MAAAAA for 8 times on one breath.
7. Repeat the breath and the eight repetitions of the chant for 3 to 11 minutes, meditating on the mother and moon energy.
8. To finish, sit quietly and visualize a brightly shining full moon at the heart center. Let the light expand and remember the first four years of your life in detail.
9. End by chanting OM CHANDRAYA NAMAH (Om Chahn-drah-yah Nahm-ah-ah) for 3 or more times.

Suggested Moon Meditation
The Creative Mother

Mars Meditations

Mars meditations focus on activity, movement, and have a physical component. Moving meditations, meditations that develop focus and will power, martial art meditations, meditations that are asana-based, such as holding postures for an extended period of time, and all meditations that increase tapas, the inner heat of the body, are effective Mars meditations. Hatha yoga practices are an excellent preparation for Mars meditations.

Meditation on Mars produces strength, courage and stamina.

Suggested Mars Meditation – Transcendental Meditation for Mars

1. Sit in a meditative posture. Bring the palms together at the heart center.
2. Chant ONG NAMO GURU DEV NAMO (Ong Na-mo Goo-roo Dave Na-mo) 3 times.
3. Touch the middle finger tip to the thumb tip of both hands.
4. Raise both arms out to the sides, with the elbows bent so the upper arms are parallel to the ground and the forearms are perpendicular, palms facing forward.
5. Inhale through the mouth with a whistle. Exhale through the nose, for 3 to 11 minutes.
6. Inhale; focus strongly inside the center of the head.
7. Chant the mantra SAT NAAM in a forceful quick way for 3 to 11 minutes.
8. Relax the arms. Interlock the two index fingers around the middle joint at the heart center. Arms are parallel and pull consistently on the finger lock.
9. Close the eyes and chant the long sound of LAAAAAAAAAH for 5 minutes.
10. Then inhale through the rounded lips and exhale through the nose twice.
11. Chant the mantra OM MANGALA NAMAH (Om man-gah-la Nahm-ah-ah) for 3 or more times.

Suggested Mars Meditation
Transcendental Meditation for Mars

Mercury Meditations

Mercury meditations focus on breath, sound and intuitive discernment. All pranayama meditations, meditations that focus on mudras, meditations that use sound and mantra, and working on asanas that increase flexibility are effective Mercury meditations. Reading sacred texts out loud in their original language, such as chanting the Yoga Sutras of Patanjali in Sanskrit or reading the Sri Guru Granth Sahib of the Sikhs in Gurmukhi, are examples of powerful Mercury meditations. Jnana yoga practices, as well as chanting and breath work, are an excellent preparation for Mercury meditations.

Meditation on Mercury produces good communication skills and improved memory.

Suggested Mercury Meditation – Controlling the Mercury Projection

1. Sitting in a meditative posture, bring the palms together at the heart center.
2. Chant ONG NAMO GURU DEV NAMO (Ong Na-mo Goo-roo Dave Na-mo) for 3 times.
3. Bring the palms up in front of the heart, fingers pointing up, spread apart. Stretch the thumbs back toward the heart. Touch the tips of the thumbs, index fingers, and middle fingers together to form an open triangle.
4. Keep the ring and little fingers spread and separated from each other and also keep the palms stretched apart as well. Keep the thumbs, index fingers, and middle fingers always touching throughout.
5. Now bring the tips of the little fingers together, while keeping the ring fingers apart. Chant the mantra WHAA-HAY GU-ROO in distinct syllables in a monotone (about 1 ½ seconds).
6. Now bring the tips of the little fingers apart so that both the ring fingers and little fingers are apart and the other fingers and thumbs still stay connected. Again chant the mantra WHAA-HAY GU-ROO in distinct syllables in a monotone (about 1 ½ seconds).
7. Continue alternating between touching little fingertips together and pulling them apart, repeating the mantra each time, for 3 to 11 minutes.
8. Finish in silence and then chant the mantra OM BUDHAYA NAMAH (Om Bood-hah-yah Nahm-ah-ah) for 3 or more times.

Suggested Mercury Meditation
Controlling the Mercury Projection

Jupiter Meditations

Jupiter meditations focus on rituals, offerings, and ceremonies, as well as on the divine teacher. Sacred pujas, creating an altar, installing sacred scriptures, meditating upon the image of a teacher, and dana (charitable giving) are all effective Jupiter meditations. Teaching can also be done as an act of meditation, as well as discourse on the sacred texts. Raja yoga practices are an excellent preparation for Jupiter meditations.

Meditation on Jupiter produces prosperity and expansion of potentials.

Suggested Jupiter Meditation – To Experience Your Expansive Nature

1. Sit in a meditative posture. Bring the palms together at the heart center.
2. Chant ONG NAMO GURU DEV NAMO (Ong Na-mo Goo-roo Dave Na-mo) 3 times.
3. Cross the middle finger (Saturn) of the left hand over the back of the index (Jupiter) finger. Hold the two small fingers down with the thumb. Rest the back of the left hand on the left knee.
4. Extend the right index (Jupiter) finger straight up in the air with the other fingers held down by the right thumb. The right hand is held about chin level with the elbow bent.
5. Close the eyes, and quickly move the right index finger in a circle, spinning in a fast tight orbit.
6. Move only the index finger, keeping it slightly tight, and concentrate on the moving finger.
7. Silently chant the mantra WHAHE GURU (Wha-hey Goo-roo) throughout the meditation, focusing at the third eye.
8. Continue for 11 minutes. Then inhale and tighten all the muscles of the body tightly for 10 seconds. Exhale powerfully and repeat twice more.
9. Chant OM GURAVE NAMAH (Om Goo-rah-vey Nahm-ah-ah) for 3 or more times to finish.

Suggested Jupiter Meditation
To Experience Your Expansive Nature

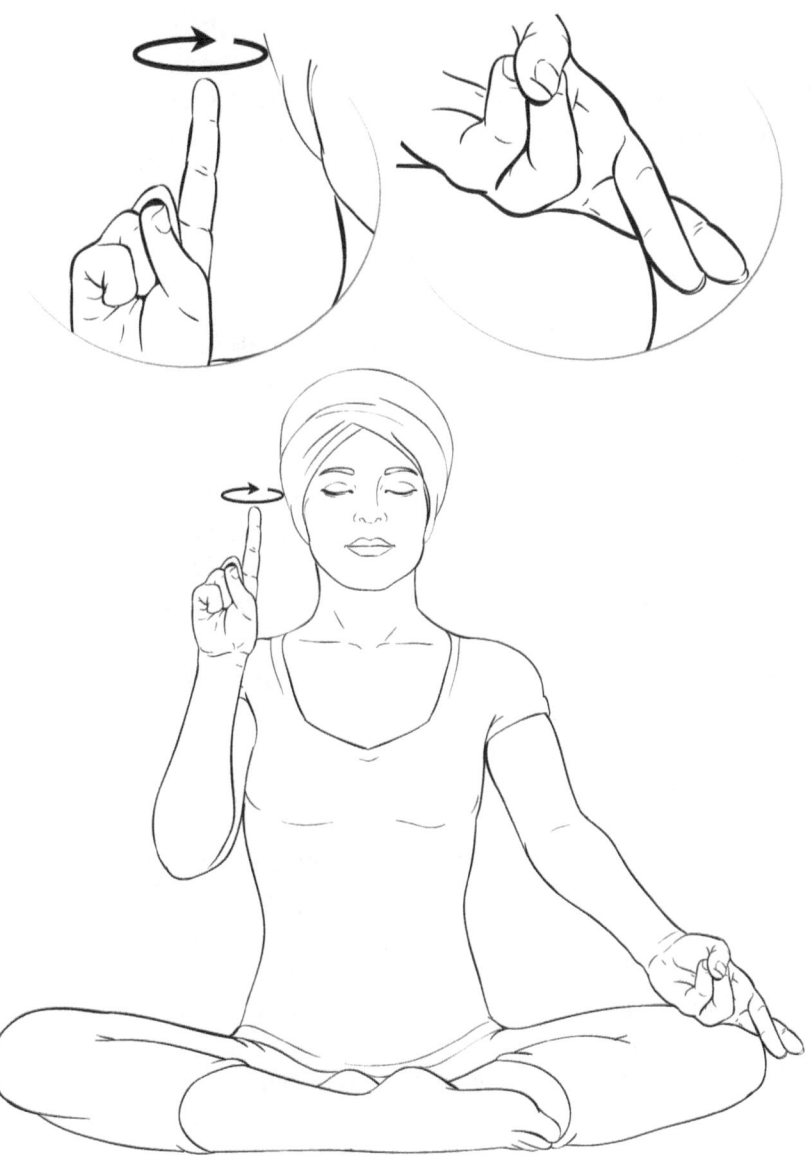

Venus Meditations

Venus meditations focus on devotional practices, partner meditations, compassion-centered meditations and meditations involving the heart chakra. Tantric practices, as well as using art, music, and other creative expressions, can be effective Venus meditations. Meditations that work on balancing male and female polarities and creating loving relationships are also good Venus meditations. Bhakti yoga practices are an excellent preparation for Venus meditations.

Meditation on Venus produces better relationships and self-compassion.

Suggested Venus Meditation – Blessing for Self-Love

1. Sit in a meditative posture. Interlace the hands in the lap in Venus mudra. Women with left index on top, men with right index finger on top. Thumbs rest side by side against the mount of Venus.
2. Chant OM SHUKRAYA NAMAH (Om Shoo-krah-ya Nahm-ah-ah) 3 or more times.
3. Bring the right palm 6 to 9 inches above the top center of the head, palm down as if to bless yourself. Bend the left elbow and raise the left palm forward as if to bless the world. Breathe very slowly with an attitude of deep affection. Hold the position for 11 minutes.
4. Inhale deeply and immediately extend your arms straight out in front of you, palms down and parallel to the earth. Stretch the arms and focus the closed eyes toward the tip of the chin. Breathe slowly for 3 minutes. Move directly into the next posture.
5. Stretch both arms up with the palms facing forward, straight and stretching up. Focus the closed eyes toward the tip of the chin. Breathe slowly for 3 minutes.
6. Inhale and retain the breath 10 seconds and stretch the arms even more and tighten the whole body. Exhale powerfully. Repeat this two more times. Relax the hands back into the lap in Venus mudra as you began.
7. Chant OM SHUKRAYA NAMAH (Om Shoo-krah-ya Nahm-ah-ah) 3 or more times.

Suggested Venus Meditation Blessing for Self-Love

Saturn Meditations

Saturn meditations include those that focus on seva (selfless service), breath retention and the bandhas, as well as any meditation that requires patience to complete. Austerities, silence, and fasting are also effective Saturn meditations, particularly when performed on Saturday. Karma yoga practices are an excellent preparation for Saturn meditations.

Meditation on Saturn brings discipline, patience, and humility.

Suggested Saturn Meditation – To Reverse Saturn Difficulties

1. Sit in a meditative posture.
2. Chant ONG NAMO GURU DEV NAMO (Ong Na-mo Goo-roo Dave Na-mo) for 3 times.
3. With the palms facing down, interlace the fingers in front of the body and release the middle fingers (this is the Saturn finger) so you can bend them downward under the palms, pointing toward the earth. Press the tips of the middle fingers together and join them at the first joint.
4. Bend the elbows and raise the arms so the hands are held in front of the shoulders, right below chin level, and the forearms are parallel to the floor.
5. Thumb tips touch together and slightly angle down so they point back to the heart center. Focus the eyes on tip of nose.
6. Inhale completely and repeat the following mantra twice (2x) on one breath in a powerful monotone from the navel center. Accentuate the HAR sound each time:
7. HARI, HARI, HARI, HARI, HARI, HARI, HARI, HAR
8. Chanting the mantra twice should take about 12 seconds, including inhale.
9. Recommended practice time is 31 minutes. Minimum time 3 to 11 minutes.
10. Chant the mantra OM SHANAYE NAMAH (Om Shah-na-yee Nahm-ah-ah) for 3 or more times.
11. This practice will bring extra benefits when done on Saturday, the day of Saturn and is especially helpful when Saturn is in retrograde motion.

Suggested Saturn Meditation To Reverse Saturn Difficulties

Rahu Meditations

Rahu meditations focus on alternative approaches to meditation, as well as meditations involving technology. Biofeedback, video meditations, and meditations done to attract attention or make a statement (such as public meditation events) are all Rahu meditations. Meditations on the chakras are also Rahu meditations, and Kundalini yoga practices are an excellent preparation for these meditations.

Meditation on Rahu can bring temporal fame and fortune and increase ambition.

Suggested Rahu Meditation – The Power to Manifest

1. Sit in a meditative posture. Bring the palms together at the heart center. Chant OM RAHAVE NAMAH (Om Rah-hoo-vey Nahm-ah-ah) 3 or more times.
2. Fold the thumbs across the palms of the hand and touch them directly below the base of the middle finger and draw them down a little.
3. Keeping the thumbs tucked, slide both hands palm down under the buttocks and sit on the hands.
4. Use this mantra: Hum Dum Har Har, Har Har Hum Dum. (Hum is pronounced with a short "u" and Dum rhymes with "room." Har is pronounced with the tip of the tongue striking behind the front teeth on the "R".)
5. Turn the head side to side as you chant each sound powerfully. Begin to the right. (Hum – turn right. Dum – turn left. Har – turn right. Har – turn left. Har – turn right. Har- turn left. Hum – turn right. Dum – turn left.)
6. Continue for 5 minutes.
7. Inhale to center. Exhale release the hands.
8. Bring the palms together at the heart center. Chant OM RAHAVE NAMAH (Om Rah-hoo-vey Nahm-ah-ah) 3 or more times.

Suggested Rahu Meditation
The Power to Manifest

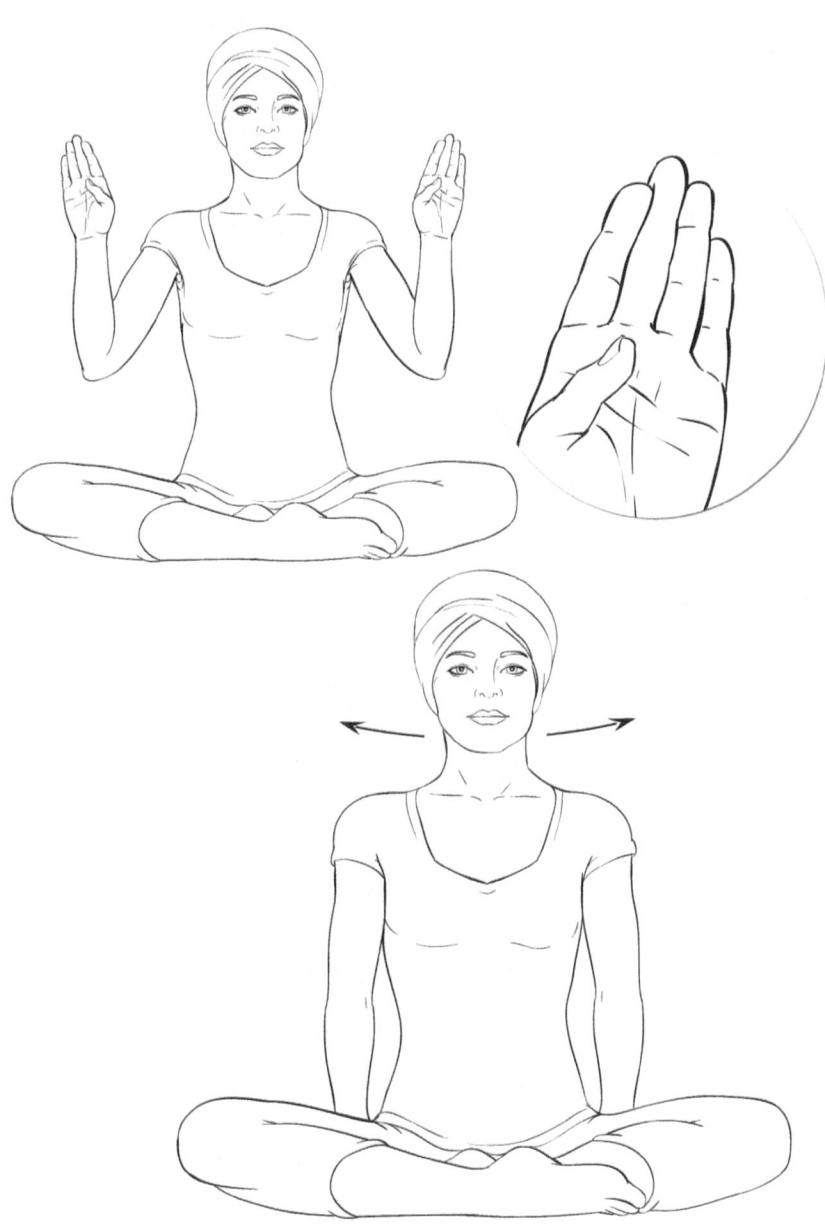

Ketu Meditations

Ketu meditations are minimalist in nature and do not focus on a specific technique. Mindful meditations, watching the breath, as well as Buddhist and Zen meditations are all Ketu meditations. Ancient meditations from old cultures are also Ketu meditations, as well as all forms of renunciation practices and withdrawal from the world. Kundalini yoga practices are an excellent preparation for Ketu meditations.

Meditation on Ketu can bring spiritual liberation and transcendence of the material world.

Suggested Ketu Meditation – Yoni Mudra Kriya

1. Sit in a meditative posture with spine aligned. Bring both hands in front of the face, palms turned inward and fingers slightly spread.
2. Close the eyes and gently place the index fingers on the closed eyes. Do not press hard.
3. Place the middle fingers on the side of the nose so you will be able to press both nostrils gently closed.
4. Place the tips of the ring fingers over the closed lips.
5. Place the little fingertips on the front of the chin.
6. Place the thumb tips to close the ears.
7. Bring your concentration to the center of the skull.
8. Inhale completely.
9. Roll the tongue up to press against the roof of the mouth. You can press the top of the tongue or roll the tongue back and press the bottom of the tongue against the palate.
10. Now exhale completely and close all the openings of the head with the fingertips, including the nose.
11. Suspend the breath out as long as possible. Become very still.
12. Release the nostrils to inhale and keep the other fingers and tongue in place.
13. Then exhale again and repeat, closing the nostrils.
14. Complete 11 cycles total.
15. Chant the mantra OM KETAVE NAMAH (Om Key-too-vey Nahm-ah-ah) three or more times.
16. Relax in a dark room or place an eye pillow over the eyes.

Suggested Ketu Meditation
Yoni Mudra

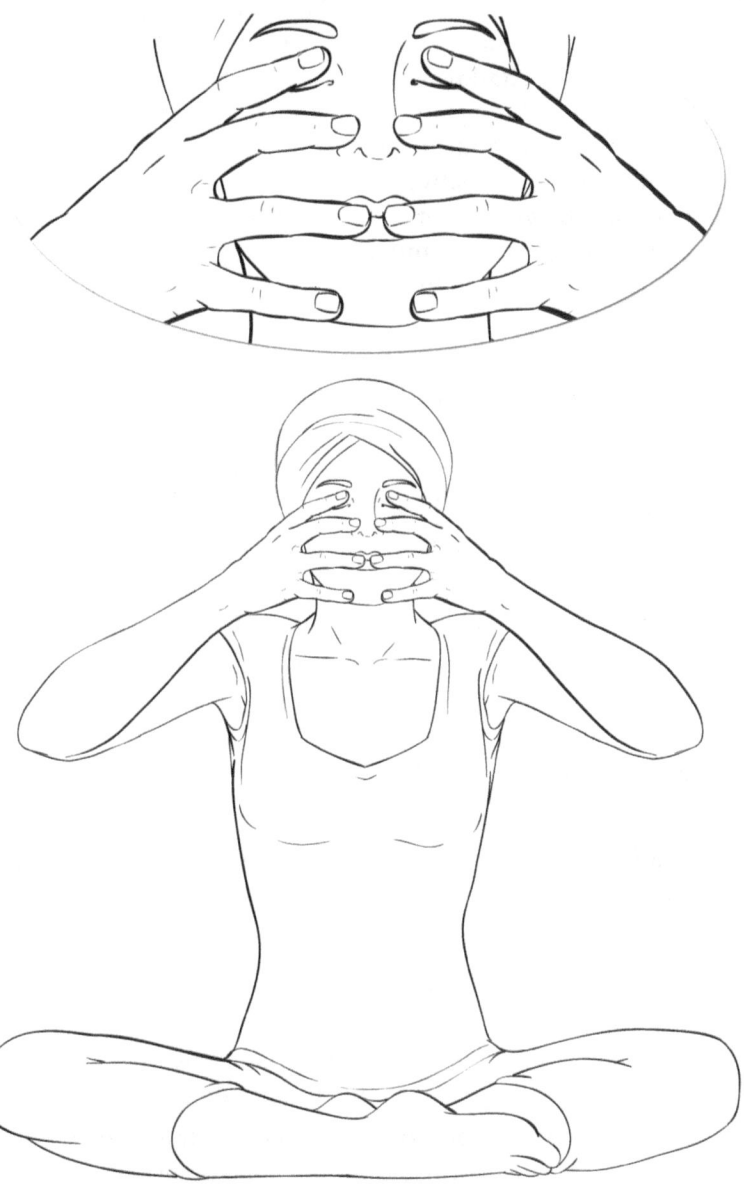

Meditation for All the Planets

All meditations balance and correct our planetary energies. Through meditation, we alter the patterns imprinted into the right hemisphere of the brain from the earth's magnetic field at the time of birth. This imprint corresponds to the planetary pattern of the zodiac in the birth chart.

The following meditation has been said to alter the pattern we carry with us from birth and is not related to a single specific planet.

The mantra chanted at the end of the meditation, Narayan Hari Narayan, calls upon the creative sustaining energy of the universe. Hari is the creative flow of the universe while Narayan is its sustaining energy, similar to the energy of Vishnu in the trinity of Brahma, Vishnu and Shiva. Narayan is related to the element of water that composes most of the human brain.

Meditation to Correct the Pattern of the Birth Chart

1. Sit in a meditative posture with spine aligned. Chant ONG NAMO GURU DEV NAMO (Ong Na-mo Goo-roo Dave Na-mo) 3 times.
2. Extend the right arm to the side of the body and raise 60 degrees angle with the elbow locked, no bend, and palm faces downward.
3. Keep all the fingers of the right hand joined and in line with arm.
4. Bend the left arm so the forearm is parallel to the ground and bring the left hand in front of the heart with the palm facing down, the elbow out to the side.
5. Spread the fingers and thumb of the left hand far apart.
6. Focus the eyes on the tip of the nose (eyes may be almost closed).
7. Breathe consciously. Each inhale and exhale is under your will. Focus on controlling the breath at all times.
8. Continue the conscious breath and hold steady for 10 ½ minutes.
9. For the next 30 seconds deeply inhale and exhale powerfully and continuously (about 12 times).
10. Then relax the breath, bring the hands down into a meditative position and go into a deep meditation for 2 minutes.
11. Inhale completely and exhale as you chant the following mantra six (6) times on one breath and for only one time:

    NARAYAN HARI NARAYAN
    (Naa-raaa-yan Haree Naa-raaa-yan)

Meditation to Correct the Pattern of the Birth Chart

Meditation to Balance the Seven Planetary Energies

1. Sit in a meditative posture with spine aligned. Perform the following planetary mudras and chant the accompanying mantras in succession one at a time, starting slowly and then going faster, repeating the sequence.
2. Perform Sun mudra. Chant OM SURYA NAMAHA.
3. Perform Moon mudra. Chant OM CHANDRA NAMAHA.
4. Perform Mars mudra. Chant OM MANGALA NAMAHA.
5. Perform Mercury mudra. Chant OM BUDAHA NAMAHA.
6. Perform Jupiter mudra. Chant OM GURU NAMAHA.
7. Perform Venus mudra. Chant OM SHUKRA NAMAHA.
8. Perform Saturn mudra. Chant OM SHANI NAMAHA.
9. Repeat the sequence 26 times or 108 times or as long as desired.
10. To end, inhale deeply, retain the breath. Perform the sequence again while holding the breath and silently chanting the mantras. Exhale. Inhale. Exhale.
11. Relax and meditate. Intuitively select one of the planetary mudras to hold and repeat its mantra silently for as long as desired.

This is an excellent practice for working with the seven visible planets. The meditation follows the sequence of mudras and mantras that correspond with the planetary weekday sequence (Sun, Moon, Mars, Mercury, Jupiter, Venus and Saturn).

> "Through the practice of concentration, meditation
> and Samadhi on the Pole Star,
> from that contemplation,
> all knowledge of the movements
> of the stars is given."
>
> Yoga Sutras (III, 29)

Meditation to Balance the Sun and Moon

1. Sit in a meditative posture with spine aligned.
2. Bring the right and left palms together in front of the heart, fingers pointing up and thumbs touching the chest in prayer pose.
3. Inhale fully and on one breath chant the following mantra:

    RA RA RA RA
    MA MA MA MA
    RAMA RAMA RAMA RAMA
    SA TA NA MA

4. The sound is rhythmic and harmonious. The "A" sound is like "ah." The third line is chanted almost the same length of time as each of the first two lines. The last line is chanted a little slower than the rest.
5. Repeat the chant for 11 to 31 minutes.
6. To end, inhale deeply, retain the breath and press the palms together so strongly that the spine is squeezed. Apply root lock or mulabandha with the breath retained. Exhale completely. Repeat the sequence twice more.
7. Relax and meditate.

This is an excellent practice for balancing the two major planetary energies, as well as working with our polarities and two sides of the brain. The RA sound is for the sun and the MA sound for the moon. They are chanted separately and then brought together with RAMA. The finishing line of SA TA NA MA completes the cycle of birth, life, death and rebirth.

This is an especially effective meditation when the sun and moon are in conjunction (New Moon), opposition (Full Moon), or during a solar or lunar eclipse, as well as around the equinoxes. On a weekly basis, this meditation is helpful when there is a transition from the solar energy to the lunar energy that occurs at sunrise and sunset, and particularly at sunset on Sunday when the day of the moon, Monday, officially begins.

Meditation for Your Rising Sign

You can also select a meditation based on your rising sign at the time of your birth. The rising sign is the sign associated with the first house in your birth chart. Your meditation practices are associated with the twelfth house in your birth chart, and the sign associated with that house is the sign immediately preceding your rising sign. The meditation planet is the planet that rules or is associated with the sign of the twelfth house.

If Your Rising Sign is:	Your Meditation Planet is:	Meditation Techniques and Types of Yoga Practices
ARIES	JUPITER	Extended meditations that require an application of will; teaching yoga
TAURUS	MARS	Physical practices that produce meditative states; Hatha Yoga
GEMINI	VENUS	Meditating on the truth revealed in spiritual literature; devotional mantra
CANCER	MERCURY	Pranayama practices that balance the emotions and focus the mind
LEO	MOON	Receptive, feminine practices that submerge the ego in service and caring
VIRGO	SUN	Practices that develop steadiness, focus, and strong sense of self
LIBRA	MERCURY	Practices that develop the discerning intelligence and physical flexibility
SCORPIO	VENUS	Practices that focus on devotion and turning passion into compassion
SAGITTARIUS	MARS	Physical practices that produce meditative states; Kundalini yoga
CAPRICORN	JUPITER	Goal-oriented meditations and working with teachers
AQUARIUS	SATURN	Karma yoga, meditation through service, and meditation in isolated locales
PISCES	SATURN	Meditations that require constant and steady discipline

Table 4-12: Meditation Planets and Practices for the Rising Sign

Your Astrological Life Cycles and Periods

While the birth chart is fixed at the time of birth, the cycles of the planets as they move through our life provide new insights and opportunities to work with our karmas, gifts and challenges.

Understanding the cyclical nature of the planets allows us to plan and take advantage of various periods in our lives by adapting our yoga practices to the time at hand.

Your Planetary Periods (Dasas)

Throughout your life, periods, or "dasas," occur which are associated with one of the nine planets. The planet that is associated with your current planetary period plays a major role in your life and yoga practice.

The planetary periods last from 6 to 20 years, depending upon which planet is in effect. At the time of birth, a specific planetary period (dasa) begins, depending upon the location of the Moon at the time of birth. Some people begin their life with the period of the Sun, some with Saturn, and so on.

Consequently, everyone experiences these planetary periods at different times. It is equally likely that a six-year old could be experiencing their period of Jupiter (Jupiter Dasa) as could be an eighty-six year old.

The planetary periods, or dasas, follow a set sequence. For example, the Saturn period in a person's life always follows their Jupiter period, and the period of Mercury always follows their Saturn period and so on. The order and length of the periods are in the following table. Remember that the period you start with in your life can be any one of these nine planetary periods, and a Vedic astrologer can tell you which period you are in.

PLANETARY PERIOD	LENGTH	AREAS AFFECTED
Sun	6 years	Accomplishments; career
Moon	10 years	Feelings; sensitivity
Mars	7 years	Actions; physicality
Rahu	18 years	Ambitions; materialism
Jupiter	16 years	Expansion; knowledge
Saturn	19 years	Service; discipline
Mercury	17 years	Learning; mentality
Ketu	7 years	Renunciation; spirituality
Venus	20 years	Relationships; pleasure

Table 5-1: Length and Sequence of the Planetary Periods (Dasas) and Major Effect

When a dasa or planetary period begins, that planet becomes prominent in your life and your yoga practice. For example, a Mars period might focus on the practices of asana (or engaging in sports) while the Mercury period may inspire you to practice pranayama (or study and write).

Sun Dasa (6 years)

During the period of the Sun, activities in the outer world and career increase. This outward directed energy could take you away from the inner meditation practices and inspire you to work on the physically vitalizing practices of yoga, including the shatkarmas or cleansing techniques. If you teach yoga, this period brings your teaching authority into prominence. You may desire more education, as well as an inclination to travel and study. You may also make progress toward self-mastery during the Sun Dasa but need to keep the spiritual ego in check.

Moon Dasa (10 years)

During the period of the Moon, there is a focus on sensitivity, nurturing, reflective self-study, meditation, yogic diet and food, and getting in touch with your feminine polarity. The softer practices of yoga, such as restorative yoga, hold special attraction. Gardening and preparing food can become a meditation and you may eat more intuitively. This is an excellent period to use yoga to create emotional balance in your life.

Mars Dasa (7 years)

During the period of Mars, the practice of asana becomes important to you. You'll derive pleasure in working with the Warrior poses and other martially inspired yoga practices. Watch for a tendency to become competitive in your yoga practices. You will enjoy challenging yoga poses that build strength and this is an excellent time to work on the core strengthening exercises of yoga. Your willpower may increase and you can develop a regular yoga practice, or sadhana. Be aware of being impatient in your yoga practices or pushing too hard. Focus on the physical body as a vehicle for your consciousness and the Mars Dasa can bring great rewards in your yoga practice.

Rahu Dasa (18 years)

During the period of Rahu in your life, you may be attracted to technological approaches to your yoga practice, such as on-line classes or using the Internet to learn about yoga. There will be an increase in the material affairs of life, and sometimes the yoga practice can become subordinated to your desires to be successful in the outer world. If you teach yoga, this may be a period in which you become well known. Be careful with chasing after popular yoga teachers or becoming involved in unhealthy cult-like followings. There may be feelings of discontent with your yoga practice, regardless of how much you advance, for you always feel you could accomplish more. During this period, it is important to live a sattvic yogic lifestyle and resist temptation to use drugs or self-poison. If you can harness your ambitious nature during this period and create balance between your material and spiritual pursuits, this can be a rewarding period for you.

Jupiter Dasa (16 years)

During the period of Jupiter, you will meet wise teachers or become a teacher yourself. Fascination with higher knowledge, philosophy, and foreign culture increases, and travel of a spiritual nature is likely. There may be an attraction toward using rituals in your yoga practice and the creation of a home altar. Much progress can be made on the spiritual path during this period, and meditation proves profitable. There is a sense of expansion of both the mind and the purview of your consciousness, but do monitor a tendency to go overboard and move too far too fast. You may be recognized during this period for your spiritual wisdom and your ability to give wise counsel and advice is appreciated.

Saturn Dasa (19 years)

During the period of Saturn, you will be drawn toward karma yoga and the path of service. This is the time to learn discipline, patience, and perseverance regarding your yoga practice. One step at a time, one day at a time, a slow but consistent practice will give great rewards during the Saturn dasa. You may face obstacles in your yoga practice but hold to a steady course. You may encounter yoga teachers with roots in past lives. Saturn may feel heavy or overly serious at this time but in reality, Saturn can be the most spiritualizing planet by revealing to us what is important and what can be released. The yoga practices of pranayama, particularly with breath retention, and the conscious use of the bandhas (muscular locks) will bring great benefits during the period of Saturn.

Mercury Dasa (17 years)

During the period of Mercury, the yoga practices of mantra and pranayama gain prominence in your life. The fascination with yogic literature and scriptures increases and you may read or write about yoga. Develop your flexibility in your asanas during this period for Mercury can bring youthful suppleness regardless of chronological age. You may practice with or teach yoga to people younger than yourself. Yoga may become part of your professional or business life and you could enter the marketplace or commerce of yoga. The thirst for knowledge of all types increases, and keeping your focus on your yoga practice will be important.

Ketu Dasa (7 years)

During the period of Ketu, you may have intense spiritual experiences. If you are not awakened to yourself, this period will bring circumstances to turn you deeply within. Meditation becomes a consistent and constant part of your life. Your desire for solitude will increase and you may live in retreat-like environments or wander in foreign lands as you embrace your spiritual searching. Often we give up things from the past during this period, including negative personality traits and unhealthy attachments. It can be a time of consciously letting go and divesting ourselves of many material and emotional encumbrances that have held us back. About half way through this period, there will likely be a year when you have the opportunity to put the past in its place and understand your future. Ketu is the planet of liberation and much can be accomplished with your yoga practice and meditation during these seven years.

Venus Dasa (20 years)

During the period of Venus, you leave the austerities of the previous Ketu period and see the world of the senses, and sensuality, as part of the divine play to be enjoyed. There will be an attraction to beauty, art, and music, and creativity itself may become part of your spiritual path and yoga practice during this time. Even your asana practice may be more flow-like or dance-inspired in nature, and music complements your yoga. The need for a spiritual partner asserts itself during the period of Venus, and relationships and partnerships need to be consciously created. Meditating with your partner, or exploring couple's yoga practices, are especially satisfying during this time, as is discovering the mysteries of tantra.

Planetary Maturity

The complete expression of a planet comes to maturity at a specific age in our lives as shown in the following table. For example, the full effects of Mercury are not experienced until after 32. This is why the spiritual stage in our life, indicated by Ketu, may not fully manifest until the age of 48.

PLANET	MATURES	AREAS AFFECTED
Jupiter	16 years old	Expansion; knowledge
Sun	22 years old	Accomplishments; career
Moon	24 years old	Feelings; sensitivity
Venus	25 years old	Relationships; pleasure
Mars	28 years old	Actions; physicality
Mercury	32 years old	Learning; mentality
Saturn	36 years old	Service; discipline
Ketu	48 years old	Renunciation; spirituality
Rahu	48 years old	Ambitions; materialism

Table 5-2: Planetary Maturity and the Age It Begins

Look back or anticipate these times of planetary maturity in your life and see how the planets begin to exhibit their energy. For example, some astrologers say that after the maturity of Mars, which represents the passion in your life, married life is easier, and difficult marriage dynamics may improve by delaying marriage until after you are 28 years old.

Your Planetary Cycles

Whereas the planetary periods ("dasas") and planetary maturities occur only once during your life, the planetary cycles are repetitive and are based on the movements of the planets on a recurring basis as they move through the zodiac. These movements are described as transits (or Gorchara) as they travel, or transit, through the signs of the zodiac.

Your Sun Cycle

One of the most significant recurring cycles in our lives is when the Sun returns to the exact position in the zodiac that it occupied at the time of birth. This happens within several hours of the actual birth time, often on the same day as the birthday, but sometimes the day before or the day after.

This annual solar return in Vedic Astrology is called Varshaphala, or the "fruits of the year." A separate birth chart is made based on the time when the sun transits or returns to its original natal position. The Varshaphala chart is read similar to the birth chart and indicates where the main activities of your life will occur in the year ahead, as well as opportunities and challenges over the next 12 months.

While you need a Vedic astrologer to construct and interpret the Varshaphala or solar return chart, you can take advantage of your Sun cycle and solar return through self-study and meditation on your birthday.

Beginning 12 hours before and 12 hours after your birthday, be aware of what activities you find yourself doing and situations that arise. This day can be a microcosm of the year ahead, and you can influence the upcoming year by consciously engaging yourself. Developing healthy habits, meditating, putting yourself in positive environments, meeting your teacher, performing charities, and practicing gratitude and contentment help set the energies for the year ahead. The people you spend time with, the conversations you have, and even chance encounters can all be omens for the year to come.

Life literally changes on this day when the Sun completes its cycle and returns to its natal position, and marks the start of your true new year.

Your Jupiter Cycle

Jupiter takes twelve years to move through the twelve signs of the zodiac, spending about one year in each sign. Wherever Jupiter is in a birth chart, that area of life usually benefits from opportunities, gifts, and expansion. This beneficial effect lasts for one year, and can affect career, relationships, spirituality, travel, and so forth.

The yearly effects of Jupiter begin when it enters a new sign of the zodiac, and an astrologer can tell you which area of your life would be most affected as it depends on the location of your moon at your birth time.

The largest spiritual celebration on earth, Kumbha Mela festival in India, is celebrated when Jupiter enters the sign of Aquarius (Kumbha), after leaving its debilitated sign of Capricorn that inhibits its natural beneficence.

For everyone, the return of Jupiter to its original position in the birth chart happens every twelve years. The Jupiter return occurs at the ages of 12, 24, 36, 48, 60, 72, 84, 96, 108 and 120. The Jupiter return is usually beneficial and brings about a positive experience, expansive opportunities, and a new cycle of spirituality.

Ideally a human would experience ten Jupiter returns in what was originally considered to be a natural lifespan of 120 years. The tenth return would bring merger with universal consciousness and the attainment of the guru's grace.

At the beginning of each of these 12-year cycles, it is a good idea to examine your relationship to your teachers and your dharma. A correction made during these times can accelerate your spiritual development.

The Jupiter returns also bring opportunities to assume your role as a teacher, particularly at the later ages of 48, 60, 72 and 84, as well as the likelihood of meeting new teachers. The first three Jupiter returns at the ages of 12, 24 and 36 bring you significant teachers. The first significant teacher at 12 years helps you learn about the physical world. The second teacher at 24 years helps you learn about the mental realm, and the third teacher at 36 years can guide you through the spiritual realm.

Another way to work with the Jupiter cycle is to look back upon your previous 12 years (or even previous 24, 36, or 48 years!) and see what opportunities and issues were prominent at those times. This can give you beneficial direction for your current situation.

Your Saturn Cycle

Saturn is the slowest moving planet in Vedic Astrology and takes approximately 29 ½ years to transit through the 12 signs of the zodiac, spending about 2 ½ years in each sign. As a result, its astrological effects and influence on the life and yoga practices are long lasting when compared to the monthly cycles of the Sun or the daily cycles of the Moon.

Saturn is one of the most spiritualizing planets as it teaches us patience, discipline, perseverance, humility and service. The presence of Saturn is like a firm and unyielding teacher, determined to have you face your issues and overcome your obstacles on the journey toward self-realization.

Special attention should be given whenever Saturn enters a new sign of the zodiac (approximately every 2 ½ years) as it signals a new focus in everyone's life. These 2 ½ years cycles of Saturn through each of the zodiac signs affects each person differently, according to their moon sign and rising sign and can be best explained by an astrologer.

The other major Saturn cycles are when Saturn returns to its original position in your birth chart (Saturn Return) and when it moves into the opposite location from its original position in your birth chart (Saturn Opposition).

Saturn Return

A major Saturn cycle in every person's life is the Saturn Return that occurs every 29-½ years when Saturn returns to the place where it was at the time you were born. Your first Saturn return occurs between your 29th and 30th birthdays, the second Saturn return after your 59th birthday, and the third return around your 89th birthday. A Saturn return is a maturing influence that brings responsibility to your life and your spiritual journey.

The first Saturn return brings us the maturity of adulthood as we begin to make our mark on the world. The second return marks the culmination of our work in the outer world. The third return signals our preparation for the next world. It is important at these stages to see the truth of your life and make conscious changes rather than going the way of least resistance.

There is a focus on discipline and responsibility, and it is not uncommon that a major supporting influence in your life is removed during a Saturn return so you can learn these qualities. The Saturn return is an opportunity to re-evaluate your commitment and dedication to your yoga and spiritual practice, and to make the adjustments required to travel this path of mortality to infinity.

Saturn Opposition

Saturn moves opposite its original position in your birth chart between your 14th and 15th birthday, again between your 44th and 45th birthday, and for the third time between your 73rd and 74th birthday.

The Saturn opposition is a completion of the work over the previous 14 years. It can be a time of rewards coming through for you, if you learned the saturnine lessons of discipline, patience, humility and service.

The first Saturn opposition represents the manifestation of our childhood struggle to establish an identity. Hopefully during this 14 to 15 year period we are exposed to a spiritual path and learn the value of a disciplined life. If not, we tend to experience the difficulties that such a missed opportunity provides us by the time of our first Saturn return between 29 and 30 years old.

The second Saturn opposition in the mid-forties can be an early mid-life crisis if we did not learn the lessons of Saturn between 29 and 44 years. For some, it can herald an opportunity or painful need for a spiritual awakening. This second opposition can bring a sense of career fulfillment.

The third Saturn opposition marks the ending or peak of our career endeavors and can bring accomplishment and satisfaction if we did the work following the second Saturn return. This is also a time to immerse ourselves into our spiritual journey as we withdraw from the mundane activities of the world.

The Shining of Saturn: Sade Sati

The most significant and transformational cycle of Saturn in Vedic Astrology is called Sade Sati, or the Shining of Saturn. This is an approximate 7 ½ year period where Saturn is near the place of the Moon when you were born (natal moon). Saturn is "shining" on your Moon when it transits or moves into the zodiac sign before your natal moon, then the sign of your natal moon, and finally through the sign after your natal moon, for a total of three signs or 7 ½ years.

For example, if the Moon was in the sign of Taurus at the time of your birth, your Sade Sati period would begin when Saturn moves into the sign of Aries, then into Taurus, and finally into Gemini. Saturn spends 2 ½ years in each of these three signs and so creates the 7-½ year Sade Sati cycle.

The Sade Sati cycle is a time of change and transformation, and it can occur two to three times in your life. Some people may have their first Sade Sati period when they are very young, while others may not have it until they are 23 years old. You need to know the sign of your birth Moon to know when your Sade Sati period begins and ends.

All that one can say with certainty about a Sade Sati period is that it brings life-altering changes. You may find you must give up something – a place, a person, a career, or a way of seeing yourself. We face our fears, overcome them, and then move toward realizing our life's purpose.

The best way to meet this time is by practicing yoga, the technology of change. Daily meditation is an absolute requirement during this 7 ½ year period. Without a baseline and benchmark of a daily spiritual practice, the changes of Sade Sati may outstrip your ability to successfully integrate them into your life. Yoga is the technology of change and the best way to make this time of your life positively transformational.

While some astrologers see only the negative side of Sade Sati, it can be a most rewarding time of your life as it re-orients you in a beneficial way if you learn the lessons of Saturn: patience, service, discipline, humility and perseverance. Otherwise, Saturn will find a way for you to learn these lessons anyway and perhaps not on your terms.

Upcoming Schedule for Sade Sati

If you know the Vedic sign that your Moon occupies at your birth, you can determine when your Sade Sati begins and ends.

Moon in:	Sade Sati starts:	Sade Sati ends:	Moon in:	Sade Sati starts:	Sade Sati ends:
Libra	9/9/2009	10/26/2017	Aries	3/29/2025	5/30/2032
Scorpio	8/4/2012	1/24/2020	Taurus	10/22/2027	7/12/2034
Sagittarius	11/2/2014	1/17/2023	Gemini	4/17/2030	8/27/2036
Capricorn	10/26/2017	3/29/2025	Cancer	5/30/2032	10/22/2038
Aquarius	1/24/2020	10/22/2027	Leo	7/12/2034	1/27/2041
Pisces	1/17/2023	4/17/2030	Virgo	8/27/2036	12/12/2043

Table 5-3: Sade Sati Periods for the Natal Moon Sign

Your Cycles of Karma: Rahu and Ketu

The karmic planets of Rahu and Ketu travel together in opposite signs and take approximately 18 years to return to their location in the zodiac at the time of your birth.

This means that at the ages of 18, 36, 54, 72, 90 and 108, you come to a karmic reckoning that signals new growth and a need to re-evaluate how you want to live over the next 18 years. During these times, you become aware if you are meeting the expectations you have for this life or if you need to move in another direction. It is also a time when you have to examine the purpose of your life and live in balance with your past and future karmas

As the physical body is the karmic vehicle for this incarnation, these 18-year cycles also signal a new way we need to relate to the body, particularly in the areas of exercise, sexuality, and diet. A 54-year old should not eat like a 36-year old and a 72-year old should not emulate the sexuality of an 18-year old. In all things physical, we must become age appropriate. This is most often seen in the amount and types of food we eat. It's been observed that we usually need to eat less food with each passing cycle so that in our later years we are eating about $1/4^{th}$ the amount of food we ate at the age of 18 years.

There is also a cycle that occurs when Rahu and Ketu are in the opposite signs that they occupied at your birth, or in other words, at the ages of 9, 27, 45, 63, 81, and 99. Often these ages signal a development of latent potentials and fructification of hidden talents. It's a good time to tap into and discover our hidden inner resources as we work on our karmic issues.

> "Do your work in the peace of Yoga,
> Free from selfish desires,
> And be not moved in success or failure.
> For Yoga is evenness of mind –
> A peace that is ever the same."
>
> Bhagavad Gita (2,48)

Cosmic Cycles for Everyone

While the movements of the planets create different effects for individuals depending upon the nature of their birth chart, there are universal cosmic cycles that affect everyone. For example, as the Moon moves into a different nakshatra each day, the energy of that day has a similar effect on everyone, regardless of when they were born.

Similarly as the planets enter different signs of the zodiac, their energy is expressed differently. Venus in Pisces for example brings a sensual and loving nature to our relationships while Venus in Aries can bring a sense of urgency and impulsiveness into our personal interactions.

These cycles occur on a yearly, monthly, weekly, daily and even hourly basis with the movements of the planets through the zodiac. These cycles create a masterful and intricate cosmic clock so that we know when to perform the necessary material and spiritual actions to achieve the optimal outcome.

This was originally the main impetus for the study and development of astrology: to anticipate when the time was most propitious to perform our spiritual practices in order to gain the best results.

As we pay attention to these recurring cycles, we can adapt and select our yoga practices that are most suitable for each moment in time. Understanding these cycles give yoga teachers a set of tools to plan classes and to direct their students' progress.

Wise astrologers know that the cosmic cycles do not foretell the future. Astrology is not a predictive science. But it is an indicative method that allows us to see the possible outcomes that are present in each moment of time and how we can exercise our awareness to affect the outcome.

The majority of human activity is based upon a daily rhythm. Yoga itself is also best experienced as a daily practice, an activity incorporated into our mundane existence to remind us of our eternal spiritual nature.

We'll begin the study of the universal cosmic cycles that affect our yoga practices and our lives by looking at the repeating cycle of the seven days of the week.

> "All actions take place in the cycles of time,
> By the interweaving forces of the Divine;
> But persons lost in selfish delusion
> Believe they are the actor."
>
> Bhagavad Gita (3, 27)

Planetary Practices for the Days of the Week

The traditional seven-day week has its origins in ancient astrological traditions and was later modified by different cultures to reflect their dominant religious traditions.

The Sun, Moon and the five planets visible to the naked eye (Mars, Mercury, Jupiter, Venus, and Saturn) were each associated with a day of the week that was named accordingly.

This naming convention of the weekdays after the seven luminaries or "planets" was universally true for the far eastern cultures, the ancient Sumerian and Babylonian cultures, the Vedic, Greek and Roman cultures, and later the Germanic cultures (which gave us some of our modern names for the days).

You can see these astrological influences directly in our English names, Sunday (Sun), Monday (Moon) and Saturday (Saturn).

The names for Tuesday, Wednesday, Thursday, and Friday come from the Germanic names for the gods (and originally from the Greeks and Romans) that are associated with the same planets, such as Tyr (or Tiu) for Tuesday (god of war and the sky, like Mars), Wodan (chief Anglo-Saxon god of the hunt and cunning, like Mercury) for Wednesday, Thor (Norse god of thunder like Jupiter) for Thursday, and Freyja (or Fria, the Teutonic goddess of love and beauty, like Venus) for Friday.

In summary, each day of the week, or "vara" as it is called in Vedic astrology, is named after the seven visible planets in Vedic astrology:

WEEKDAY	PLANET	VARA NAME
Sunday	Sun	Ravi-Vara
Monday	Moon	Soma-Vara
Tuesday	Mars	Mangala-Vara
Wednesday	Mercury	Budha-Vara
Thursday	Jupiter	Guru-Vara
Friday	Venus	Shukra-Vara
Saturday	Saturn	Shani-Vara

Table 5-4: Planets Associated with the Days of the Week

Each day of the week exerts an influence based upon the planet that is associated with that day, and we see mundane examples of this occurring in our culture. For example, Sunday is a typical day for worship. In Vedic astrology, one of the Sun significations is the temple or place of worship. Monday is the day of the Moon, or mother and the home. In the western world, Monday was a traditional washday or a day for the domestic chores associated with the Moon. Tuesday, being ruled by Mars, the planet of war, would be a good day to start a battle (but not a good one to get married!).

Interestingly enough, most marriages in the West take place on Saturday, or the day of Saturn, which for many (but not all) couples would be a challenging time to get married. Friday, the day of Venus, would be best suited since it rules love and relationships. Saturday, however, can be a good day for long-lasting things, so if you were married on that day, you can have a stable and steady marriage if you learn patience, humility and service, the keywords of Saturn.

Astrological Influences and the Day of the Week

The days of the week were originally associated with the celestial body that was most prominent on that day, or which was in strongest force at the time of sunrise.

For example, on Saturday the energy of Saturn would be the strongest of all the planets, with Saturn's day lasting from sunrise on Saturday to sunrise on Sunday. (In Vedic Astrology the day always begins at sunrise – not midnight. So Tuesday 3 AM would still be considered Monday.) The strongest planetary effects of a planet are felt before noon.

From this understanding of a planetary ruler for each day of the week, the qualities of the day can be better understood, as well as the types of activities that are in harmony with the dominant planetary energy.

Traditionally, certain activities were considered to be more appropriate for each day of the week, as follows:

Sunday

The day of the Sun, as the beginning of the astrological week, is considered to be a good time to make plans and set the intentions for the week ahead but not necessarily favorable for beginning to implement them. As the ruler of temples, it is traditionally a day of worship, particularly of the Divine Father figure and a good time to respect all traditions.

As a day of tradition, Sunday was an excellent day to respect those who represent traditions and traditional values, such as parents and teachers. Not only parental and spiritual authority, but also authority figures of all types, include governmental officials, are best interacted with on Sunday.

As the Sun is the most self-centered and independent of all the planets, Sunday is an appropriate day for self-related activities as meditation (self-study), receiving personal honors, and realizing gains in one's career and status.

On the other hand, the egocentric nature of the Sun inhibits such relationship activities as marriage, sexual intercourse and conception, and even business partnerships and cooperative ventures.

Monday

The day of the Moon highlights the Mother, home, emotions and nurturing. All activities involving women and children are favorable on Monday, especially those relating to child rearing, education, and all household affairs. Whereas Sunday is about worship of the Divine Father, Monday is for acknowledgement of the Divine Mother, as well as all devotional rituals. All contemplation and meditation practices are favored on Monday.

The home environment is prominent on Monday: cooking, cleaning, laundry, family time, and educating and playing with children.

The Moon is considered to be the most sociable of all the planets (visiting each planet every month) and so all social activities, friendships, and interactions with the general public are highly favorable. Business affairs, particularly those conducted through family and friends, are auspicious on Mondays and social networking is favored.

Marriage, sexual activity, conception and childbirth are all good on Monday.

Medical treatments are favored (the Moon rules the nursing profession), and herbs and earth related cures are especially effective.

All activities connected to the water – play, business and travel – are generally more auspicious on a Monday.

Tuesday

The day of Mars highlights physical activity, competition, strategy, sports and high-energy ventures. All activities involving mechanical work, combat, eradication of one's enemies (even insects and weeds!), and overcoming obstacles are favored on Tuesdays.

In general, Tuesday is a favorable day for repair work of all kinds, including both mechanical and physical (such as dental work). Surgery is also favored as are all invasive healing modalities (including acupuncture).

Tuesday is also auspicious for research work, detection, mathematical and analytical studies, all scientific work, and applications of logical thinking.

It is not a good day to sit still as energy is restless and can become impulsive if not positively channeled. However, travel is usually not favored.

Tuesday is typically an inauspicious day for social and relationship interactions (including sexual activities and marriage) or any matters that require subtlety and concern for feelings.

Wednesday

The day of Mercury highlights all communications, travel, learning, education, and business affairs. Wednesday is an excellent day for commerce of all kinds, including trading and interacting with people from diverse backgrounds.

Talking, writing, teaching, and studying are successful on Wednesday as well as all mental activity. This is an excellent day to plan and theorize instead of putting something in actual practice.

Finances, making money, doing business deals, having meetings, making schedules, drawing up contracts are all done well on Wednesday.

In the area of spirituality, this is a good day for meditative practices particularly those that develop intuition and discernment (the buddhi mind in yoga). Wednesday is also beneficial for the creation of healing potions, herbal preparations, and healing work, specifically psychological healing and therapy. Marriage and sexual activity are also suitable on this day.

Activities with young people are favored on Wednesdays.

Thursday

The day of Jupiter highlights beneficial and good activities and is the most favorable day of the week according to astrologers.

Thursday favors all spiritual and religious activities, rituals, meditation, study of scriptures, and worship of the Divine in all its forms, interacting with spiritual teachers, and embarking on pilgrimages.

This is also an excellent day for legal affairs, dealing with lawyers, business matters (particularly expansive and speculative ventures), charity and foundation work, and career advancement.

Thursday is auspicious for all social affairs, including sexual activity, marriage and the conception of children. This is a good day to exchange gifts and favors, practice diplomacy, mediations, and reconciliations, as well as engaging in outdoor activities, working and playing with children, and performing healing practices and regimens.

Friday

The day of Venus brings good energy to activities involving relationships, beauty, art and pleasures. It is usually considered to be the most beneficial day for forming partnerships, getting married, and making love.

Friday is excellent for partner yoga, devotional chanting and kirtan, tantric exercises, bhakti yoga, and using music, art and creativity as part of your meditation practices.

The day of Venus is also favorable for buying beautiful (not necessarily functional) clothes, jewelry, and works of art. Marriage counseling, and indeed all forms of counseling, go well on this day.

Friday is auspicious for diplomacy, wearing new clothing and jewelry for the first time, all self-adornment and beauty techniques and all artistic expression and appreciation.

Saturday

The day of Saturn is about discipline, austerity, service and hard work. It is usually considered to be the best day to fast or practice silence and perform acts of karma yoga. When you need to stay on task and get it done, Saturday is an excellent day.

Spiritual practices favored on the day of Saturn are pranayama exercises, particularly those that involve retention and suspension of the breath, cleansing and purification practices such as the shatkarmas, as well as holding postures for a lengthy time and meditating in insolated locales.

Saturday is good for activities involving the land, such as farming or real estate, taking care of the elderly, dealing with matters of death, and aiding the poor or doing charity work.

This day is auspicious for all practices that develop self-discipline, dealing with things that are old or in need of repair, and making purchases that are useful and at bargain prices.

Yoga Practices for Each Weekday

It is a good idea to do a yoga practice that is associated with a planet on its day of the week. For example on Wednesday, the day of Mercury, our practices may involve the Mercurial traits of flexibility, pranayama, mantra, scriptures, and self-study. Here are guidelines for yoga practices for the days of the week:

Sunday (Sun Day)
Enjoy the energy of your self. Shine your soul. Deep inner spiritual connection through your practice. High vitality and a chance to purify. Sun salutations and using yantras in meditation.

Monday (Moon Day)
Good day to work with the emotions and the mind during your practice. Some gentleness and a more feminine practice. Moon salutations and pranayama. Bhakti and Restorative Yoga,

Tuesday (Mars Day)
High energy, strong physical activity. Masculine and fiery practice; be careful of pushing, however, and avoid accidents. Challenging asana work. Hatha and Kundalini Yoga.

Wednesday (Mercury Day)
Good time to work with mantra and sound. A quick paced practice that keeps the mind engaged is also enjoyed. Reading yogic texts. Mantra and Jnana Yoga.

Thursday (Jupiter Day)
An expansive practice, exploring the teachings behind yoga. Opening into meditation, seeking inner wisdom. Meeting and studying with teachers. Guru Yoga (tratakam meditation on a spiritual teacher or deity).

Friday (Venus Day)
Enjoy the senses and pleasure of a yoga practice. Opening to heart and compassion. Beautiful movement and flow, like a dance. Vinyaysa, Bhakti, and Tantric Yoga.

Saturday (Saturn Day)
Challenge yourself and work hard. Pranayama practices with breath retention and suspension, using the bandhas and locks. A great day to develop your discipline!

Planetary Practices for the Hours of the Day

As each day has a primary planetary energy, each hour of the day, or in Sanskrit the "hora," also has a planetary energy associated with it.

The first hour of the day, which is defined as the first hour after sunrise, is associated with the same planet that influences that day. For example, the first hour of Wednesday, a day associated with Mercury, is also associated with Mercury. The second hour of Wednesday, however, is associated with another planet, and the third hour with yet another planet, and so on. In this manner, all the planets bring their energies into each day, according to the hour.

During each day, the planets rule the hour (hora) in a specific sequence, as follows:

1. Saturn
2. Jupiter
3. Mars
4. Sun
5. Venus
6. Mercury
7. Moon

So if Saturn is ruling the hour, then Jupiter rules the next hour, followed by Mars and so on. After each of the seven planets has ruled its hour, the sequence begins again.

This sequence of planetary rulerships over the hours of the day is a universal astrological principle both in Vedic Astrology and in Western Astrology that is based on the Ptolemaic system of the same planetary sequence. The major difference is that in the Vedic system the hourly sequence begins at sunrise while in the Greek or Babylonian system, it begins at sunset.

The hourly sequence begins at sunrise with the planetary ruler for that day. So on Sunday, the first hour after sunrise is ruled by the Sun, the second hour by Venus, the third hour by Mercury, the fourth hour by the Moon, the fifth hour by Saturn, the sixth hour by Jupiter, the seventh hour by Mars, and then repeating again with the eighth hour by the Sun and so on.

On Friday, the first hour after sunrise is ruled by Venus and then, according to the planetary sequence, Mercury the second hour of the day, Moon the third hour, Saturn the fourth hour, and so on.

TABLE OF PLANETARY HOURS
Each day lasts from sunrise to sunrise

HOUR	SUN	MON	TUE	WED	THU	FRI	SAT
Sunrise	Sun	Moon	Mars	Mercury	Jupiter	Venus	Saturn
2nd Hour	Venus	Saturn	Sun	Moon	Mars	Mercury	Jupiter
3rd Hour	Mercury	Jupiter	Venus	Saturn	Sun	Moon	Mars
4th Hour	Moon	Mars	Mercury	Jupiter	Venus	Saturn	Sun
5th Hour	Saturn	Sun	Moon	Mars	Mercury	Jupiter	Venus
6th Hour	Jupiter	Venus	Saturn	Sun	Moon	Mars	Mercury
7th Hour	Mars	Mercury	Jupiter	Venus	Saturn	Sun	Moon
8th Hour	Sun	Moon	Mars	Mercury	Jupiter	Venus	Saturn
9th Hour	Venus	Saturn	Sun	Moon	Mars	Mercury	Jupiter
10th Hour	Mercury	Jupiter	Venus	Saturn	Sun	Moon	Mars
11th hour	Moon	Mars	Mercury	Jupiter	Venus	Saturn	Sun
12th Hour	Saturn	Sun	Moon	Mars	Mercury	Jupiter	Venus
13th Hour	Jupiter	Venus	Saturn	Sun	Moon	Mars	Mercury
14th Hour	Mars	Mercury	Jupiter	Venus	Saturn	Sun	Moon
15th Hour	Sun	Moon	Mars	Mercury	Jupiter	Venus	Saturn
16th Hour	Venus	Saturn	Sun	Moon	Mars	Mercury	Jupiter
17th Hour	Mercury	Jupiter	Venus	Saturn	Sun	Moon	Mars
18th Hour	Moon	Mars	Mercury	Jupiter	Venus	Saturn	Sun
19th Hour	Saturn	Sun	Moon	Mars	Mercury	Jupiter	Venus
20th Hour	Jupiter	Venus	Saturn	Sun	Moon	Mars	Mercury
21st Hour	Mars	Mercury	Jupiter	Venus	Saturn	Sun	Moon
22nd Hour	Sun	Moon	Mars	Mercury	Jupiter	Venus	Saturn
23rd Hour	Venus	Saturn	Sun	Moon	Mars	Mercury	Jupiter
24th Hour	Mercury	Jupiter	Venus	Saturn	Sun	Moon	Mars

Table 5-5: Planets Associated with Each Hour of the Day

The hours are adjusted for sunrise each day. For example, if sunrise is at 5:42 AM Tuesday, then 5:42 AM to 6:42 AM is associated with Mars, and 6:42 AM to 7:42 AM is associated with the Sun, and so on until the last hour of Tuesday (before sunrise on Wednesday) is associated with Venus.

This is helpful for understanding the secondary energy of the day if you are teaching or doing a yoga practice. For example, for a 4:30 PM yoga class on a Thursday in which sunrise occurred at 6:30 AM, you are practicing during the 11th hour after sunrise which is associated with Venus. At this time, take into consideration that the dominant energy of Thursday (Jupiter day) is expansive and meditational and the energy of a Venus hour is associated with the heart and compassion; therefore, this is a good time for opening the heart chakra through meditation.

Another example would be a 9:00 AM yoga practice done on a Tuesday with the sunrise occurring at 6:00 AM. Mars rules the first hour of the day from sunrise (6-7 AM in this case), the Sun rules the second hour (7-8 AM), Venus the third hour (8-9 AM), and so Mercury rules the fourth hour (9-10 AM) at the time of the yoga practice. In this case, we have a class on a Mars day (Tuesday) done during an hour ruled by Mercury.

The primary influence of Mars dictates a strong physical practice that is modified by Mercury. This could be a good time to work on flexibility and strength or to use focused pranayama or mantra practices (Mercury) in the physical practice.

Many serious yoga practitioners practice around the same time each day, usually in the early morning hours. By doing so, we systematically connect to all the planetary energies throughout the week. For example, a morning practice at sunrise each day connects to the dominant planetary energy of that day. If you have a practice that begins before sunrise, then ending at sunrise with a meditation for that planetary hour of the day sets the energy in harmony for the rest of that day since the planet for the sunrise hour is the same as the planet for that entire day.

One benefit of a consistent yoga practice done at the same time each day, and specifically at sunrise every day, is that over a week you will have practiced in each of the seven planetary hours and thereby created an overall balance of your energies.

> 'The breeze at dawn has secrets to tell you.
> Don't go back to sleep."
>
> Rumi

Planetary Practices for the Moon Cycle

The monthly practices of yoga are dictated by the Moon phases, or the synodic cycle from New Moon to Full Moon and back to New Moon. The synodic Moon cycle, or lunar month, is approximately 29 ½ days.

Astrology Yoga, or Vedic Astrology, is primarily a lunar-based system, whereas Western Astrology is solar-based. The moon cycles play an important role not only in yoga practices but also in how we experience the daily energies of our lives and in determining which activities, both worldly and spiritual, are the most auspicious or favorable to undertake.

The monthly moon cycle, from New Moon to Full Moon and back to New Moon, is divided into two major parts, the approximate two weeks of increasing, or waxing, light (New Moon to Full Moon) called Shukla Paksha and the approximate two weeks of decreasing, or waning, light (Full Moon to New Moon) called Krishna Paksha.

In general, a waxing moon is considered a good time for action, expansion and starting new projects, whereas a waning moon is good for completing work and resting. Outward directed activities are typical for the waxing moon period (Shukla Paksha) and inward directed activities for the waning moon (Krishna Paksha). Starting an active yoga practice during the waxing moon is favorable while eliminating bad habits and engaging in meditation practices are favored during the waning moon.

Days of the Month: Tithis of the Moon

The monthly moon cycle in Vedic Astrology is divided into 30 parts called Tithis, or lunar days, which begin at varying times of the solar day and also vary in length from 19 hours to 26 hours. The 30 tithis consist of the New Moon day, the 14 lunar days after the New Moon, the Full Moon day, and the 14 lunar days after the Full Moon

The day, or tithi, of the New Moon is called Amavasya while the day of the Full Moon is called Prunima. These are two important days in the astrological month and are discussed in the next two sections.

The remaining 28 tithis are divided into two groups, the 14 tithis after the New Moon and the 14 tithis following the Full Moon. The first tithi after the New Moon and the first tithi after the Full Moon have the same name and meaning, as does the second tithi after the New Moon and Full Moon, and so forth.

Each of these 14 tithis has a specific energy associated with it and appropriate yoga practices as well.

Shukla Paksha Waxing Moon	Tithi Name	Krishna Paksha Waning Moon	Yoga Practices
1st Tithi	Pratipat	1st Tithi	Good for all practices
2nd Tithi	Dvitiya	2nd Tithi	Creating lasting practices
3rd Tithi	Tritiya	3rd Tithi	Ending negative practices
4th Tithi	Chaturthi	4th Tithi	Removing obstacles
5th Tithi	Panchami	5th Tithi	Therapeutic practices
6th Tithi	Shashti	6th Tithi	Group yoga practices
7th Tithi	Saptami	7th Tithi	Spiritual journeys
8th Tithi	Ashtami	8th Tithi	Strengthening practices
9th Tithi	Navami	9th Tithi	Destruction of bad habits
10th Tithi	Dasami	10th Tithi	Good for all practices
11th Tithi	Ekadasi	11th Tithi	Fasting, healing, prayers
12th Tithi	Dvadasi	12th Tithi	Light meditations; sacred fires
13th Tithi	Trayodasi	13th Tithi	Celebrations, sexual tantra
14th Tithi	Chaturdasi	14th Tithi	Spiritual guidance
15th Tithi **New Moon** Amavasya	Amavasya Purnima	15th Tithi **Full Moon** Purnima	Meditation and healing

Table 5-6: The 30 Tithis of the Moon Cycle

To find out which tithi is in effect, you can refer to an Indian astrology almanac called a Panchanga or look on-line for the current moon tithi. Alternatively, you can simply approximate a tithi as lasting one day. In this way, you would do healing and fasting during the tithi knows as Ekadasi on the 11th day after the New Moon or 11th day after the Full Moon.

New Moon and Full Moon Days

The New Moon and Full Moon days are important in the practice of Astrology Yoga and are excellent for meditation and healing. Spiritual aspirants often fasted and observed silence on these days. The New Moon is favorable to begin a meditation or yoga practice while the Full Moon allows us to reap the rewards of such a practice.

The day of the new moon is contractive and tends to make one disinclined towards the physical exertion of a strong asana practice and is better suited for meditation, or working with apana and the cleansing practices of the shatkarmas.

The expansive full moon energy, in contrast, can cause one to overreach in an asana practice and thereby create injuries, or can bring too much emotionality into a practice.

If the yoga practitioner is non-celibate, full moon days are favored for sexual activity as this is when vitality is highest and any resulting birth will be strong. Tantric yoga practices are auspicious at this time. According to Ayurvedic thought, women ideally ovulate on Full Moon when sexual energy is at a peak and begin menstruation on New Moon, which is best suited for rest and cleansing rather than strong yoga practices.

In general, women are advised to forgo intense yoga practices on the first three days of their moon cycle and focus on pranayama or breath work that aids emotional balancing (such as alternate nostril breathing) and using mantras and meditation to set the energy for the new cycle.

The Moon is considered relatively strong in its astrological actions during the period extending from the fifth day after the New Moon until the tenth day after the Full Moon. These days are the high energy and productive days for practicing yoga.

Another yoga practice connected with the New and Full Moon days is to begin a meditation or yoga practice on the New Moon or Full Moon and finish it when the Moon has completed 1-½ cycles. In other words, start on a New Moon and end on the second Full Moon following, or start on a Full Moon and end on the second New Moon following.

This 1 ½ lunar cycle takes about six weeks, or the traditional 40-day period of fasting and meditation, which is observed by spiritual practitioners from many cultures and traditions. Psychologists have also discovered that a six-week, or 40-day, period is also the length of time it takes to establish a habit and create a lasting behavioral change.

Beginning a 40-day practice on the New Moon is most useful for creating a new habit or yoga and meditation routine, while beginning a 40-day practice on the Full Moon supports the removal of destructive habits that prevent success in yoga.

The Moon Nakshatras: The Secrets of Vedic Astrology

Before the twelve zodiac signs, the ancient Indian astronomers divided the cosmos into 27 divisions called *nakshatras*. While the 12 zodiac signs are based on the movement of the Sun each month, the 27 nakshatras are based on the movement of the Moon during each month.

Approximately over a 24-hour period, the moon enters a new nakshatra or moon sign and moves through all 27 nakshatras over the period of a month. This means that unlike the Sun, which changes its zodiac sign once a month, the moon changes its nakshatra sign daily. This daily movement of the moon through a nakshatra determines the quality of energy of that day and which activities are likely to bring success or difficulties.

The primary purpose of the nakshatras in ancient Indian culture was to determine when religious rituals were to be performed. The position of the Moon was critical to the successful outcome of any ritual or undertaking, including major life events such as marriage or significant journeys. Later, the nakshatras become important in determining which mundane or daily activities were likely to be successful when the Moon was in a certain nakshatra and which activities were best avoided during that time.

For example, there are excellent nakshatras for travel, for marriage, for making love, performing harsh actions, and so on. All important actions are best done when the moon is in a favorable nakshatra for that activity.

Since the Moon moves through one nakshatra on the average every 24 hours, each day also has its appropriate yoga practices to do, as well as ones that are best avoided. A new nakshatra may begin in the morning or evening and often two nakshatras are affecting the energy on any particular day.

You can find out the nakshatra for the moon each day by using an Indian almanac called a Panchanga, which is now commonly available as a software application, or by looking up the nakshatra for the day by using an on-line nakshatra calculator.

The following section gives the nakshatras in their traditional order, beginning with the first degree of Aries, and the suggested yoga and spiritual practices for the day of that nakshatra.

> "To every thing there is a season,
> And a time to every purpose under heaven."
>
> Ecclesiastes 3:1

ASHWINI

When the moon is in the nakshatra of Ashwini, it is a great day to begin a yoga practice or learn new yogic techniques. All self-improvement activities are favored this day, as well as learning the spiritual sciences of yoga, astrology and Ayurveda. Adopting a spiritual name is also auspicious on this day. This is one of the best times of the month to create an altar and engage in all practices of yoga, including healing meditations, and taking special herbs and elixirs.

BHARANI

When the moon is in the nakshatra of Bharani, it is an excellent day to perform the shatkarmas, or the cleansing practices of yoga, and to fast by eating a restricted or mono-diet. Sexual yoga practices are also highlighted this day, as are all creative activities, including gardening and taking care of children, create a flowing meditative experience. If you have postponed a yoga practice, this a good time to revisit and recommit. Do be aware that slow and gentle yoga practices may be more challenging on this day and you may need to work with your breath to create calm energy in your practice.

KRITTIKA

When the moon is in the nakshatra of Krittika, get rid of your self-limiting habits and make changes you need to get on your spiritual path. You can make important decisions today, and it's generally favorable for taking on new activities and yoga practices. There is a discerning critical nature to this day so be aware of any tendency to critique yourself in your yoga practices or being overly critical of your yoga students. Instead of criticizing, nurture. It may be difficult to practice extended relaxation on this day, so you may want to employ active relaxation techniques in your classes and practices, using breath, mudras, or mantra instead of lengthy periods of rest. If you use the gong, or drums, in your yoga class on this day, it will be well received.

ROHINI

When the moon is in the nakshatra of Rohini, the yoga practices should acknowledge the role of the senses by incorporating beautiful music, fragrant smells, flowers and greenery, and even pleasant tactile sensations, such as a meditation shawl or comfortable cushion. All self-improvement practices are favored this day, and it is a good time to start a spiritual practice or create a healthy habit. Take time to meditate or be outside with yourself and connect to the earth by doing yoga barefoot. If you've desired a meditation mala, this is a good day to obtain one. Couples can use yoga as preparation for love making today.

MRIGASHIRSHA

Make your yoga practice light and fun. You will feel lightness in your activities and it's a good time to drop an overly serious approach to your spiritual path. Socializing with friends goes well today, and all communications are favored. In your yoga practices, both as a teacher and a student, it is important to avoid any type of confrontations, even obliquely. An excellent day to practice healing meditations and doing the rejuvenation practices of yoga, such as pranayama and guided relaxation.

ARDRA

The best activity for this day is to identify your most self-limiting and destructive habit and then destroy it. This is the time to do the hard work and in your meditation you may discover a lurking problem that you need to confront. Your teacher, or your higher self, may challenge you to release your resistance to change. This is not the day for auspicious beginnings or spiritual ceremonies. It is time instead to end, let go, and release all the old and useless things you no longer need to carry with you. So if your yoga mats, yoga clothes or any other material or non-material things are getting worn out or outdated, toss them out this day!

PUNARVASU

When the moon is in the nakshatra of Punarvasu, it is an excellent day for meditation, self-reflection, and all spiritual activities. This is a good time to restart a neglected meditation or yoga practice. If you teach yoga or are learning yoga, this day will be full of ease as all teaching and educational activities are favored, including learning new subjects, new yoga poses, and so on. This will also be a good time for healing activities and using yoga therapeutically. Remember that yoga can be practiced in many ways, and today you can do it through renewing your relationships with close family and starting projects that benefit others. If you enjoy gardening and nurturing, make those activities your meditation as well. If you are a parent, your children will teach you some important spiritual lessons. Connecting to mother earth and the mother energy is a favored part of our higher practices today, including the acknowledgement of the Mother Goddess energy, what the yogis call Maha Shakti, and will bring you favorable results.

PUSHYA

When the moon is in the most auspicious nakshatra of Pushya, we can do anything today for good results as long as we refrain from harsh and negative actions. It is one of the best times during the month to start a yoga practice or spiritual activity. We can be creative, even artistic, in our approach to our yoga practice. Bring music or even dancing into your class or practice. Your relationship with food and diet can be profound this day. Absolutely and positively, prepare at least one meal today for yourself and someone you love. Teaching yoga to children (or creating a fun celebration for them) and doing yoga with your mother (or simply spending time with her) will bring happiness.

> "Enthusiasm, perseverance, discrimination,
> Unshakeable faith, and courage are the ways
> To bring success to Yoga."
>
> Hatha Yoga Pradipika (1, 16)

ASHLESHA

When the moon is in the nakshatra of Ashlesha, we must choose our activities wisely. This is a secretive and mysterious time where the hidden areas of life assert themselves in both positive and possibly destructive ways. This is a time to do battle with the enemies of your spiritual progress, your negative personality traits and habits, and to take what may even seem to be harsh but necessary actions to overcome the obstacles to your growth and well-being. It is a wonderful time to explore the mysteries of the chakras, plumb the unconscious mind, and enjoy sexuality as a way to understand your eternal self. If you practice Kundalini Yoga, this nakshatra can be one of the most favorable times to do so.

MAGHA

When the moon is in the nakshatra of Magha, it is an excellent day to study ancient knowledge, including astrology and yoga. All ritual and spiritual ceremonies are favored today, as well as all types of performances and public celebrations. Yoga teachers can take center stage in the class today with an element of theater to communicate the practice of yoga but watch for tendencies to take on a regal or superior approach. This will be a good time to approach people in authority, such as asking for help or favors from your teachers. Sun salutations, and all yogic practices relating to the sun, may be undertaken with success.

PURVA PHALGUNI

When the moon is in the nakshatra of Purva Phalguni, rest and relaxation are beneficial and time spent in savasana can be extended in your practices and yoga classes. Bring joy and enjoyment into your yoga today. It is a time to be in the emotional realm rather than in the mind, so the practice of jnana or gyan yoga is not optimal today. Creating art as meditation is favored today, as are all creative activities. This is not the best time to start new yoga practices but find the pleasure in the ones you already do. The therapeutic practices of yoga, including Ayurveda, are best postponed and simply enjoy a time of easy rest and rejuvenation.

UTTARA PHALGUNI

When the moon is in the nakshatra of Uttara Phalguni, it is a favorable time to start things of a lasting nature, which can be anything from a relationship to a business to a yoga practice or meditation. Beginning or opening ceremonies are very auspicious, and this would be an excellent time to create a new yoga space. This is also an enjoyable day to practice yoga with your partner to build intimacy on all levels. If you have been waiting for a good time to wear new yoga clothing or jewelry, such as a meditation mala, this is the day for it. If you were planning to bring a yoga practice, or any other ongoing activity, to an end on this day, it will be much better if you can wait.

HASTA

When the moon is in the nakshatra of Hasta, this is an excellent time to study astrology, yoga, Ayurveda, and all the Vedic sciences. You will also have success working with Sanskrit and learning languages today. This is a superb time to practice yoga mudras, or the hand positions, for meditation and healing. Hasta literally means 'hand" and working with mudras will come easily today, as will all types of skills involving the hands. Consequently, you will find this to be a good day for handstands in your yoga practice, as well as asanas that feature the use of the hands prominently. Children's yoga is highlighted today, and playing yoga games will be well received. If possible, do your yoga during the daytime, as this is not a favorable time for most nighttime activities, except for crafts, arts, and hobbies.

CHITRA

When the moon is in the nakshatra of Chitra, health improvement activities go well, including yoga and healing. Using yogic herbs and preparing herbal mixtures or teas get excellent results, and this would be a good time to investigate using herbs such as turmeric and ginger to support a yoga practice. This is a good day for creating a wardrobe that reflects your natural and yogic lifestyle, and for using gemstones for healing. All spiritual practices are favored today, and can be done with elegance and grace. This would be an excellent day to offer or attend a yoga workshop as all creative and non-confrontational actions go well today.

SWATI

When the moon is in the nakshatra of Swati, this is a time to go with the flow and forgo all aggressive behavior. You will enjoy doing yoga in a class or a social situation today, but it's best to stay local and avoid long distant travel. You will love to learn during this time, so a great day to read and study yoga as well as attend lectures. All educational and public events are well received today, as are pursuing the arts and sciences. If you are a yoga teacher, this is a good time to work with the general public and offer an introductory class or talk about yoga. It is a good day to conduct the business of yoga and take care of financial transactions.

VISHAKHA

When the moon is in the nakshatra of Vishakha, it is a perfect day to develop the sixth yogic limb of dharana, or concentration. You can create a strong mental focus during this time, and it would be a good time to investigate the yogic practice of tratakam, or fixing the gaze and attention one-pointedly. You can engage in a stronger physical yoga practice today, testing your limits with a focused effort. If you are considering making a resolution about your practice or your lifestyle habits, this is a good time to set an intention and make long-lasting decisions. On the softer side, this day favors ceremonies, ornamentation, dressing up and romantic activity.

ANURADHA

When the moon is in the nakshatra of Anuradha, this is an excellent time for meditation, particularly in a natural setting or outdoors. Group related yoga activities go well today, and a good opportunity to spend time with your yoga friends. This would also be a good day for yogic healing or cleansing practices. Research, self-study, and time spent in beneficial isolation can support your meditational activities. Foreign travel and financial activities are also favored today, as well as things that must be done secretly or in private. This is not a good time to start significant new activities or engage in confrontation.

JYESHTHA

When the moon is in the nakshatra of Jyeshtha, it is a good time for the hidden practices of yoga, working with the subtle energy body, balancing the chakras, and exploring the kundalini. Investigating what lies beneath the surface of your yoga practices and your mind will meet with success today. All occult activities are auspicious today. This is the time to be firm with yourself, set a strict discipline, and hold yourself to your grand plans. This is the day for mystical transformation with no room for resentment, depression, or selfishness. Time spent with the elderly today, and especially teaching them yoga or other spiritual techniques, will bring untold benefits.

MULA

When the moon is in the nakshatra of Mula, it is a favorable time to go to the root of the matter, as if it were research, be it in your yoga practice or your life. This is an excellent day to gather higher knowledge and spend time in contemplation. Using mantras, especially with music or singing, as in kirtan, is especially beneficial. Yogic healing, using herbs and natural medicines, is effective. In general, this is a good day to have adventures, explore, and study the transformational practices of yoga and meditation.

PURVA ASHADHA

When the moon is in the nakshatra of Purva Ashadha, it is a time for self-forgiveness and settling with others. This will be an excellent day to renew your goals for yoga and your life and for meditating around water. Visiting ancient sites and holy places is favorable at this time. This is an excellent time for practices involving the feminine energy principles, such as using the Adi Shakti mantra in the Kundalini Yoga tradition or visualizing the powerful feminine deities in your belief system. This is also a good day for yoga practices involving the moon and feminine lunar energy. Walking, swimming, sailing, gardening, exploring nature, and even horseback riding can all take on a spiritual significance today.

UTTARA ASHADHA

When the moon is in the nakshatra of Uttara Ashadha, all religious and spiritual activities are favored. It is a wonderful time to begin new practices and spiritual sadhanas, and make your plans for the future. You may find creative activities, including sex, take on a meditative quality today. The key for this day is to do new things, make plans, initiate actions and routines, start habits that support you and do not try to end anything today. It's a time for beginning and bringing the new into your life and your yoga practices.

SHRAVANA

When the moon is in the nakshatra of Shravana, all spiritual rituals are favored. Learning yoga and studying sacred language and literature is recommended today, as are all forms of reading and writing, especially spiritual journaling. This is another good day for beginning new ventures, entering new places, and buying new items. Social interaction is highlighted, as is the study of philosophy and music. Meditation will be easier today, and it's a great time to start a new 40-day meditation practice. Healing, taking herbs and doing yoga therapeutically will bring good results when the moon is in Shravana.

DHANISHTHA

When the moon is in the nakshatra of Dhanishtha, it is a good day for spiritual observances, rituals, and creating alters. Music as meditation and worship is highly favorable during this time. This is one of the best times of the month for using the gong for yoga and meditation, as one of the symbols for this nakshatra is the metal drum. All percussive instruments may be used at this time and this is a great day for concerts, celebrations, and yoga festivals. Healing with gemstones and herbs gives good results. Not the best time for forming partnerships or practicing tantric yoga but a good time for deep meditation by yourself.

SHATABHISHA

When the moon is in the nakshatra of Shatabhisha, all meditation and yoga practices are highly favorable. This is an excellent time to study and read about yoga as all educational activities go well. The ancient texts also indicate that this is a good day to study the "cosmos," or learn astrology. Therapeutic yoga practices get good results during this time, as does taking Ayurvedic formulas and medicines. This would be a great day to travel and practice yoga by the ocean, or even begin an ocean cruise.

PURVA BHADRAPADA

When the moon is in the nakshatra of Purva Bhadrapada, it is a good time to confront one's mortality and explore issues around death. The old tantric practices recommended meditating at a gravesite on this day as well as honoring teachers who have left this material plane. Most activities do not get favorable results now and it is not a good time to begin new practices or activities.

UTTARA BHADRAPADA

When the moon is in the nakshatra of Uttara Bhadrapada, meditation is highly favorable, particularly those that work with the sixth chakra and develop the psychic powers, or siddhis. Health treatments of all types work well. It is also a good time to make promises or take vows (including marriage). It is not a good day to push your yoga practice or attempt strong physical activities. A softer asana practice will get good results, and one can take time to enjoy the sexual practices of yoga as well.

REVATI

When the moon is in the nakshatra of Revati, it is favorable for learning and healing. Relax, rest and rejuvenate with an inspiring book or creative activities. This is a good day to put the final touch on projects, perhaps finishing a meditation practice or yoga series. This is not a good time to engage in strenuous activities, so back away from strong asana practices and try restorative yoga or yoga nidra. Forget about solving problems or dealing with difficulties on this day as it is best spent on leisure pursuits.

Planetary Practices for the Sun Cycle

The astrological year cycle is determined by the Sun as it moves through the twelve signs during the year. In Vedic Astrology, the sun enters a new zodiac sign approximately at the middle of each month (between the 13th and 17th day).

MID-MONTH	SUN SIGN
January to February	Capricorn
February to March	Aquarius
March to April	Pisces
April to May	Aries
May to June	Taurus
June to July	Gemini
July to August	Cancer
August to September	Leo
September to October	Virgo
October to November	Libra
November to December	Scorpio
December to January	Sagittarius

Table 5-7: Monthly Sun Cycles and Signs of the Zodiac

During the transition from sign to sign around the middle of each month, the Sun is said to be in "sandhi" or in-between signs. As a result, the energy may be weakened or ill defined on this day and it is not a good time to make decisions about a yoga practice (or many other things!) as life is in flux. It is a good time, however, to meditate, reflect, and set an intention for the upcoming month.

Remember that each sign consists of 30 degrees and the Sun travels approximately one degree each day. The Sun tends to express the greatest characteristics of a sign when it is at the mid-point, or 15 degrees or 15 days into the sign. Another piece of information about the Sun sign is that the New Moon also occurs in the same sign that the sun occupies and the Full Moon occurs in the opposite (180 degrees) sign from the Sun.

If we look at the meanings of the signs themselves, we can gain additional insights into how a particular monthly period (for example, mid-May to mid-June) is conducive to different yoga practices or provide a specific spiritual focus.

MID-MONTH	VEDIC NAME	SPIRITUAL AND YOGA PRACTICES
January to February	Magha	Creating structure for yoga practices and adhering to discipline.
February to March	Phalguna	Karma yoga, practicing the yoga of service and helping others.
March to April	Caitra	Yoga Nidra, other realms of consciousness, group practices.
April to May	Vaisakha	Beginning a deeper practice of the asanas. Strengthening will power, concentration
May to June	Jyaishta	Adhering to a fixed routine, becoming unshakable in our practice.
June to July	Asadha	Reading, studying the yogic texts. Learning mantra and sacred languages.
July to August	Sravana	Balancing the emotions with mantra and pranayama. Creating a home practice.
August to September	Bhadra	Establishing our self-identity through our yoga practices. Teaching others.
September to October	Asvina	Creating healthy habits and routines. Fasting and improving diet and hygiene.
October to November	Kartika	Creating balance in our yoga practices. Meditating or practicing yoga with a partner.
November to December	Magasirsa	Transformational practices, including tantra. Working with the chakras.
December to January	Pausa	Spiritual journeys. Studying with teachers and exploring philosophy.

Table 5-8: Monthly Sun Cycles and Yoga Practices

Solstices and Equinoxes

Since ancient times, in all cultures, and before all religions, the day of Solstice (both Summer and Winter) was the turning point of the year, the time when the Sun "stood still" (the literal translation of the word solstice) and a time for ritual, celebration, and spiritual connectivity.

Many communities centered their holy and sacred buildings such as tombs and temples upon the direct alignment with the solstices. And there is speculation that astronomy was developed to observe these powerful days.

The Solstices were long considered to be the premium times for meditation and spiritual practices. They were the original holy days or holidays when we celebrated the return of the Sun at Winter Solstice as the days started to lengthen and the culmination of the Sun energy at Summer Solstice, the longest day of the year. The days of the Summer and Winter Solstices are sacred in the yoga tradition and are known as punya kala, or times of great merit.

The Equinoxes were similarly celebrated because they heralded the balance and equalization of the Sun and Moon energies as day and night became equal in length and the two major luminaries were in balance, at the traditional times of Spring and Fall.

The two Solstices and two Equinoxes provide unique opportunities for the practice of yoga.

Summer Solstice

On Summer Solstice, the solar energy is at its highest, the soul's light at its brightest, and our ability to connect to this light during the longest day of the year the most opportune. If there is a single "high holy day" in Astrology Yoga, it is the day of Summer Solstice. This day marks the beginning of Dakshinayana, the six-month period when the Sun begins its apparent southward journey through the sky.

The Sun in both yoga and astrology represents the energy of the Soul. Many practices in yoga are based on working with the body's internal solar energies, with sun salutations, surya bheda (right nostril breathing), and some of the oldest mantras, such as RAM or RAMA, or the ancient Sun mantra, OM SURAYA NAMAH.

All yoga practices connected with the Sun are powerful on Summer Solstice, and it is the most powerful day of the year to connect to your soul's inner sun and meditate, meditate, meditate. While the energy is high around the Solstice, it is also a good time to fast and perform austerities such as late evening meditations while the sunlight still lasts.

While Summer Solstice is the peak of this experience, it is the 10 days leading up to Solstice that give us a powerful opportunity to heal and to strengthen the glandular system. These 10 days are the perfect time of the year for a yoga summer vacation or retreat where we can leave our usual responsibilities and eat a pure diet in a highly energy charged environment such as the mountains or by the ocean.

Time spent in healing and meditation at the time of Summer Solstice carries us through to the Winter Solstice.

Winter Solstice

On the longest night of the year and the shortest day, the day of Winter Solstice, we celebrate the return of the Sun as the days start to lengthen and the darkness recedes. Winter Solstice portends the return of the light of the soul, the Sun, and we see our journey moving from darkness to ever increasing light. It is the time of Guru, a word that literally means "dark" (Gu) and "light" (Ru) and Winter Solstice signals the transition from darkness to enlightenment. This day marks the beginning of Uttarayana, the six-month period when the Sun begins its apparent northward journey through the sky.

The energy of this day is the opposite of the Summer Solstice. Rather than high energy and solar practices, it is time for turning inward and the lunar practices. Left nostril breathing, the lunar postures, and meditating on the feminine energies is helpful on this day when the Moon rules.

In the days immediately before and after Winter Solstice, restorative yoga practices are best. Tratakam on a candle flame, meditating with the sound of water, and a traditional milk fast may be observed on these days.

This is also an optimum time to clear out the past and our clutter, literally and spiritually. At this turning point of the year, we reflect on where our journey has brought us from the previous Summer Solstice and what we may wish to divest ourselves of over the next six moths. Winter Solstice is truly the "new year" for resolutions, new beginnings and leaving the past behind.

Spring and Fall Equinoxes

On the days of the Spring and Fall Equinoxes, the length of days and nights are nearly equal and the sun and moon energies are in balance. These are ideal days to balance our inner sun and inner moon to bring harmony to our lives and yoga practices.

On the equinoxes, balancing postures are highlighted, such as Tree Pose, Dancer Pose, Arm Balances, and Headstand. Finding a balance between heating (Sun) postures and cooling (Moon) postures are effective this day, and Sun Salutations can be alternated with Moon Salutations.

The classic yoga practice for Equinox is alternate nostril breathing to balance the solar and lunar energies of the body. A 31-minute practice of alternate breathing, with or without retention, is a beautiful Equinox meditation. The mantra for Spring and Fall equinoxes is the sound of RAMA, which marries the energy of the Sun (Ra) with the Moon (Ma).

Eclipses

Eclipses occur when the light of the sun or moon is partially or fully obscured. Solar eclipses occur on a New Moon while lunar eclipses occur on a Full Moon. The day of an eclipse is powerful as new energies are created and released in the shadow of the luminaries.

If the eclipse occurs in your Sun sign or Moon sign, it will tend to have a greater effect on you, especially if it is within 2 degrees of your birth Sun or Moon. Pay close attention as to what occurs on that day as it can give you deep insight into your consciousness and mind.

A solar eclipse is considered to be the most influential as it represents the transformation of consciousness (the Sun) and the effects of this day are usually felt over the following 6 months. A lunar eclipse is the darkening of the mind (the Moon) and it tends to be felt mostly during the month it occurs.

One way to understand the eclipses is that they take away light to create darkness. From this darkness, we discern a new light as the eclipse passes. We have the opportunity to re-illuminate the mind (Sun) and gain a fresh perspective on our emotional state (Moon). The energies this day are full of psychic impressions and are not conducive for making big decisions or taking new actions. Instead, it is a time to be meditative, reflective, and work on being centered and avoiding emotional dramas. Often old fears arise, as well as issues around the mother and father. This is a time to remember that it is in the darkness we can discover the light.

During the solar eclipse, increasing the Sun energy through yoga practices, mantras and meditations, such as breathing through the right nostril is preferred. The lunar eclipses lend themselves to strengthening and working with the moon energies, and left nostril pranayama is good for this day as it balances the lunar and emotional energy.

On eclipse days, it is advised to meditate near water, or submerge in water, and increase liquid intake. Heal, rest, and meditate and you will gain a new emotional perspective as the eclipse passes.

Practicing and Teaching Astrology Yoga

There are two main approaches to practicing and teaching Astrology Yoga: 1) Strengthen and balance the appropriate planetary energies by using the yoga techniques and styles of yoga associated with those planets, and 2) Select and practice the appropriate yoga practices for the current astrological cycle occurring in your life, as well as the current planetary positions that are affecting everyone.

To do this, you need to understand your inherently strong and weak planets, and the challenges and opportunities these planets bring. These can be determined from this book, as well as from your astrological birth chart.

You also need to know the current cycle of time, including the cycles that affect everyone, such as the day of week, moon cycles, and major astrological events, and the cycles of time that might be particular to your life or your students' lives, such as planetary periods, planetary returns, and planetary transits. Such cycles can be determined from regular calendars, astrological calendars (such as the Panchanga in India), and an ephemeris.

You can simplify these approaches by working with the planets individually on the day of the week they are most associated with. For example, practice the yoga techniques associated with the moon on Monday, Mars for Tuesday, Mercury for Wednesday, and so forth. This elementary approach brings good results to all the planets.

As your sophistication and learning deepens, you can expand this approach and refine your yoga practices to address long-term concerns, prepare for major life transitions, and improve specific areas of your life, such as career, relationships and health.

Working with the Planetary Energies

To begin working with your planetary energies, re-read the descriptions of the planets at the beginning of the book. Pay attention to the qualities of the planets that you need in your life, as well as the symptoms that manifest when these planets are weak. Over time, you can learn to see these qualities and symptoms in others as well, and this can guide you in selecting and working with the planets through yoga practices.

The next step is to re-read the information about your Vedic sun sign, the star sign (nakshatra) where your sun is located, the planet associated with the day of the week you were born, and the information connected with the signs occupied by the karmic planets, Rahu and Ketu. All this information can be determined by your birth date alone.

Then, if you have your Vedic astrology birth chart (or adjust the planetary positions in your Western birth chart back 23 degrees), you can read about your moon sign, your rising sign, the star signs (nakshatras) for all your planets, the zodiac signs and houses for all your planets, your planetary period and the strength of your planets.

You can also gain a good insight into your basic planetary energies by examining where your primary planets are located in your chart and their relative strengths and weaknesses.

Your Primary Planets

The three primary planets throughout your life are the Sun, the Moon, and the planet associated with your rising sign that is known as the ruling planet, or the ascendant lord (or lagnesha in Sanskrit).

These three planets are connected with the three bodies described in yoga: the physical body (represented by the planet associated with your rising sign, the ruling planet), the subtle or astral body (represented by the Moon), and the causal or soul body (represented by the Sun). These three planets are also associated in yoga philosophy with the ego, or ahangkar (represented by the ruling planet), the sensory mind, or manas (represented by the Moon), and the soul, or atma (represented by the Sun).

These three planets indicate our physical health, emotional well-being, and strength of the soul and they greatly affect your life and yoga practice. Using the techniques of yoga to strengthen and balance the sun, moon, and your rising sign planet is an excellent way to work with the planetary energies in your life.

Astrology Yoga and Therapeutics

Astrology gives the yoga teacher and practitioner a set of diagnostic tools to use yoga therapeutically. Through the birth chart we can see which areas of the body are susceptible to weakness or disease, what personality traits may create psychological blocks, and which planetary energies need balancing or strengthening.

While an advanced knowledge of astrology and yoga are needed to work at a deep therapeutic and counseling level, there are general astrological guidelines we can use to beneficially support others and ourselves on our healing and spiritual journey.

A simple approach is to read the descriptions of the various planets in their weakened states as given in the section on the planets (grahas). If you or your student identifies with the challenges of a weakened planet, that is a good place to begin strengthening and working with that planet's energies through the yoga practices associated with it.

If you know in which astrological signs your planets are located, you can use the following table to see if they may be challenged or weakened by being in that sign. Remember, this is for planets in signs according to Vedic or Yoga astrology – not Western. Be aware there can also be positive factors in a birth chart that negate these weakness and **the planet may not be compromised at all.**

Planet	Weak Sign	Challenged Signs
Sun	Libra	Capricorn, Aquarius, Taurus
Moon	Scorpio	None
Mars	Cancer	Gemini, Virgo
Mercury	Pisces	Cancer
Jupiter	Capricorn	Gemini, Virgo, Taurus, Libra
Venus	Virgo	Leo, Cancer
Saturn	Aries	Leo, Cancer, Scorpio

Table 6-1: Weak and Challenged Signs for the Planets

Notice that no planets are weak or challenged in Sagittarius, the positive sign associated with planet Jupiter, a naturally benefic planet.

Planetary Illnesses and Diseases

You can also use physical symptoms or a disease-based approach to diagnose a weak planet by understanding the common ailments associated with a dysfunctional planet. Again, this is an oversimplification as **there can be more underlying astrological causes than simply a single planet**. With that caution in mind, the following table shows typical illnesses associated with a weakened or unfavorable planet:

Planet	Physical Ailments and Symptoms of Weak Planets
Sun	Low vitality, coldness, headache, fevers, liver and gall bladder disorders related to bile, heart troubles, eye disease (particularly right eye), bone disorders, skin problems, circulation problems, epilepsy, irritability, difficult digestion
Moon	Phlegm and mucous disorders, anemia, jaundice, menstrual disorders, female reproduction problems, diseases of the breast, diarrhea, left eye, nervousness, sleepiness, fevers with chills, dyspepsia, water retention, weak lungs, obesity, bronchitis
Mars	Blood disorders, high blood pressure, biliary inflammations, fevers, gall stones, spleen disorders, itching, hemorrhoids, diseases above the neck, diseases of the uterus, ulcers, excessive bleeding, heat rashes, injuries, anemia, acne
Mercury	Nervousness and nerve disorders, vertigo, skin diseases, speech disorders, impotence, diseases of ear, nose and throat, deafness, tendency to fall, lung disorders, arms, hands and shoulder issues, illnesses caused by mental disorders and instability
Jupiter	Liver, gall bladder, spleen and pancreas disorders, obesity, anemia, fainting, diabetes, hypoglycemia, edema, ear troubles, diseases related to fatty tissues, gout, cholesterol
Venus	Sexually transmitted diseases, bladder infections, urinary disorders, pancreas, cataract, kidney stones, typhoid, menstrual disorders, appendicitis, diabetes, reproductive issues, eye diseases (particularly tear glands), tiredness, exhaustion
Saturn	All chronic illnesses, nerves, lymphatic system, colon, rectum, stomach troubles, paralysis, tumors and cancers, fatigue, glandular disorders, bone structure, arthritis, depression, constipation, amputations, stiffness, emaciation, deafness

Table 6-2: Illnesses and Conditions Associated with the Planets

Planetary Unfavorable Expressions

When a planet needs strengthening or propitiating in your life, you may exhibit the following expressions or disabilities. Again, this is an oversimplification as **there can be more underlying astrological causes than simply a single planet**. With that caution in mind, the following table shows expressions associated with a weakened or unfavorable planet:

Planet	Unfavorable Expressions of Weak Planets
Sun	Reluctant to be noticed, disinterested, unmotivated. Negative attitude about self-improvement. Lacking in will power, feels victimized and easily challenged. Lack of taking action, unable to advance in life, unable to turn aspirations into reality
Moon	Lack of empathy, out of touch with emotions. Difficulty in articulating feelings. Not interested in nurturing or getting involved in the lives of others. Weak connection with mother. Does not feel at home or comfortable. Moody and remote.
Mars	Unassertive, lack of energy and drive. Procrastinates, difficulty with long-term tasks. Poor planning, lack of priorities. Backs down, hesitant, avoids confrontations. Low passion, unreliable. Acts at last minute. Avoids challenges.
Mercury	Difficulty communicating, poor decision-making, lack of clarity.. Irrational, cannot adapt easily. Does not follow through on ideas. Intellectually defenseless, reluctant to learn new things or consider new ideas. Unable to see connections.
Jupiter	Ignores opportunities, unable to expand and grow. Unclear about ethics or values. Handicapped by limitations. Pessimistic, selfish, lacking in spirituality. Absence of generosity and sense of prosperity. Struggles to develop the higher mind.
Venus	Does not give importance to harmony in relationships. Poor taste, unrefined manners. Low attraction to beautiful things, detached from pleasures. Lacking warmth and friendliness. Absence of grace and diplomacy. Passive aggressive.
Saturn	Difficulty in setting boundaries. Lack of focus, consistency, commitment. Not a good listener. Little sense of long-term timing. Isolated from relationships. Hard to get to know. Impatient with traditions. Easily distracted.

Table 6-3: Unfavorable Expressions Associated with the Planets

Planetary Problems with People

When a planet needs strengthening or propitiating in your life, you may experience difficulties with the types of people represented by those planets. Again, this is an oversimplification as **there can be more underlying astrological causes than simply a single planet**. With that caution in mind, the following table shows the people problems associated with a weakened or unfavorable planet:

Planet	Difficult Relationships with These People
Sun	Father, boss, figures of authority, government officials.
Moon	Mother, caregivers, women in general.
Mars	Brothers, law enforcement officials, athletes, strong males.
Mercury	Sisters, younger siblings, business people, students, writers.
Jupiter	Teachers, lawyers, children, religious figures, husband.
Venus	Artists, musicians, women, wife, intimate relationships.
Saturn	Elderly, poor, servants, stern figures of authority.

Table 6-4: Difficult Relationships Associated with the Planets

> "He sees himself in the heart of all beings
> And he sees all beings in his heart.
> This is the vision of the Yogi of harmony,
> A vision which is ever one."
>
> Bhagavad Gita (6,29)

Working with the Daily Cycles

There are small and large cycles of time that permeate our lives, ranging from a day to a week to a month to a year to the longer planetary cycles of 1 to 2 ½ years, and then the planetary periods (dasas) that last from 6 to 20 years. Each of these cycles has optimal yoga practices.

For most yoga practitioners, the cycle of the day is the most important consideration since ideally we maintain a daily yoga practice. The moon is the planet that affects our daily life or mundane affairs, and so considering the moon's daily position and condition is one of the most important ways we work within the cycles of time.

Working with the Moon Cycle

The moon's daily energies affect us all, regardless of our personal astrological profile, and are most important not only for a personal practice but especially for public yoga classes since the moon represents the general public (as well as women). The two most important moon considerations are its nakshatra (or sign) and its phase (or tithi).

Nakshatra of the Moon

The Moon enters a new nakshatra, or star sign, on a daily basis and determines the mood and energy of the day. This is one of the more important daily considerations as it determines the most favorable yoga activities to do. Remember that the moon nakshatra may change during the day that you are teaching or practicing yoga. While it may be helpful to know the zodiac sign the moon occupies at the time of a yoga practice (such as Aries or Pisces), it is the nakshatra that provides the most information. There are online and computer applications that can easily calculate the nakshatra for your place and time, or you could refer to the traditional Indian almanac, the Panchanga.

Moon Tithi and Phase

The lunation cycle of the moon (tithi) and if the moon is increasing (waxing) or decreasing (waning) are important considerations for determining an optimal practice. Every two weeks we begin a moon cycle with the full and new moon. These powerful days are good for meditation and healing. Yoga practices will also change depending if the moon is increasing or decreasing, or which tithi it is in. Again, there are online and computer applications that can easily calculate the tithi for your place and time, or you can refer to a calendar for the current moon phase.

Other Daily Considerations

The other considerations to use when planning a daily practice or yoga class is the day of the week and the hour(s) of the day the practice occurs.

Day of the Week

Each day of the week is ruled by one of the seven visible planets. Consider the planet that is associated with the day and work with the techniques associated with that planet to align with the planetary energy of the day. A Friday practice, for example, will add a quality of Venus to the day, regardless of the nakshatra that the moon may be occupying. The weekday planet represents the outward actions while the moon nakshatra indicates the more subtle or inner energies.

Using only the day of the week, and the planetary energy associated with that day, is an easy and instructive way to begin to understand the daily cycles of time and your yoga practice. Perhaps you can also see how important it is that you practice yoga or meditate every day in order to fully balance and integrate the energies of the planets. If you only do yoga, for example, on Sunday and Tuesday, then you are only working with the fiery energies of the Sun and Mars and neglecting the more feminine and meditative energies of the other planets.

Hours of the Day

If you want to refine your yoga down to the hour, determine the planetary hour(s) in effect at the time of the class or practice, using the tables in the book. Alternatively, determine which planetary energy you wish to emphasize in your personal practice and do it during that hour.

Remember that at the hour of sunrise each day, the planet that rules that first hour of the day is the same as the planet that rules that day. At sunrise on Thursday, which is associated with Jupiter, the planetary energy is also in effect for the first hour of this day. When we have a consistent daily practice at sunrise every day, it is much easier to fully integrate all the planetary energies in our lives and be in alignment with that day.

This can also be helpful if you begin your daily yoga practice in the hour before sunrise as this marks the end of the energy of the previous day, and you can integrate the previous day's energy with the new energy that is emerging at sunrise.

Designing Yoga Classes and Practices

Astrology Yoga is especially useful in creating yoga classes, workshops, and trainings that take into consideration the dominant and current planetary energies in effect at that time. You can also select best dates and times to have a specific yoga class or personal yoga practice as well.

Example of Creating a Yoga Class Astrologically

Here are the astrological conditions surrounding a class taught on Friday April 26, 2013 from 7 to 9 PM in Memphis, Tennessee:

Day of the Week: Venus (Friday)

Hour of the Day: Mars (7:00 PM), Sun (7:18 PM), Venus (8:18 PM)

Moon Nakshatra: Vishakha

Moon Tithi and Phase: Dwitiya (day after full moon)

Special Considerations: There are seven planets total in both Aries (including the sun) and Libra (including the moon). Class occurs during sunset.

Friday is the day of Venus, so yoga practices that use music, flowing movements, and bhakti mantras and meditations are favored this day. In addition, the moon nakshatra Vishakha is excellent for creating a strong mental focus and concentration and for testing the physical limits of one's practice. The moon tithi Dwitiya is good for creating a lasting impression or yoga practice and its occurrence the day after the full moon provides high energy. The planetary alignment in Aries and Libra energizes relationships with the Aries nature of self and the Libra nature of the partner. Sunset during this time makes it an ideal time for meditation as the energies move into the Sushumna, the central nadi of the body, and creates a state conducive for meditation.

There was much Venus energy present due to the day of the week (Friday), the hour of the day (the workshop ends during the hour of Venus), and the moon in Libra, the sign of Venus. The decision was made to use the musical sound of the gong and to work on the heart chakra.

Since the class starts during the hour of Mars, followed by the Sun hour, this indicates the need for a strong physical practice. In addition, the moon nakshatra Vishakha also favors a challenging practice and there is high energy on this day, being the tithi after the full moon.

With all the planets in Aries and Libra, a partner meditation was used to take advantage of the meditative state at sunset, and the ending during the hour of Venus was relaxation to music.

Working with the Larger Cycles of Time

Beyond our daily practice, our yoga evolves throughout our lifetime, changing from month to month, year to year, and over the decades. In addition, there are recurring events that can override the daily practices.

Solstices

The summer and winter solstices, the major turning points of the sun, present the greatest opportunities for spiritual practice. To a lesser extent, spring and fall equinoxes are also significant. These special days take precedence over the usual normal daily considerations for a practice.

Eclipses

Both solar and lunar eclipses are major astrological events that affect our lives and yoga practices. On the average, there are two solar and two lunar eclipses each year for a total of four eclipse days (there can be 3 or 5 eclipses in a chronological year). Again, these days are special occasions that require planning to take full advantage of their energies.

New Sun Sign

The Sun enters a new sun sign each month and this provides opportunities to work with this new energy. Remember that around the middle of the month, the sun is transitioning between the signs and this is a good time for extended meditation rather than dramatic actions.

New Planetary Signs

When a planet enters a new sign of the zodiac, it brings changes to different areas of our lives. The moon changes signs every 2 ½ days, the sun enters a new sign every month, and Mars, Mercury and Venus change signs several times a year. The slower moving planets Jupiter, Saturn and Rahu and Ketu remain in signs for longer periods (Saturn for 2 ½ years, Rahu and Ketu for 1 ½ years, and Jupiter for 1 year), and bring longer lasting changes to our lives. On the day a planet moves into a new sign, consider the energies represented by the planet and the sign it is entering.

For example, when Saturn entered Virgo in September 2009, it marked a period of discipline (Saturn) in areas of diet and self-improvement (Virgo), as well as an indication for the need to be of service (Virgo) and do the work of karma yoga (Saturn). These areas would be highlighted in our yoga practices and life. Practicing the cleansing practices of the shatkarmas, for example, would be highly recommended during such a cycle.

Planets Returning to Natal Positions in the Birth Chart

Saturn, and to a lesser extent Jupiter, signal big changes in our yoga practices when they return to certain positions relative to our birth charts. The Saturn return (every 29 ½ years), the Jupiter return (every 12 years), and especially when Saturn returns to the sign preceding our natal moon position (Sade Sati) are full of opportunities for deep transformation and spiritual awakening. Also, when these planets transit the natal positions of other planets in our birth chart are significant times to work with the energy of those planets.

Planetary Periods

Some of the longest periods of time that affect our yoga practices are our planetary periods, or dasas, which run from 6 to 20 years. The time when one of these periods is ending, and before the next period begins (usually a 6 month to 3 year period), is an opportune time for spending more time in meditation to prepare for a change that usually only occurs 6 to 7 times during a normal life span.

Lifetimes and Lifetimes

Finally we should remember that the practices and rewards from both yoga and astrology are lifetimes in the making. By understanding the karmas of our past lives (as shown by the planet Ketu) and our present life (as shown by Rahu), we can discern the yoga practices and meditations that are most appropriate to us in this incarnation as we work with the samskaras of past lives and fulfill the promises of this life's journey.

The cycles of time are endless, yet they carry us inexorably forward to our final destination of liberation and merger with the infinite.

> "No step is lost on this path of Yoga,
> And no dangers are found.
> And even a little progress is freedom from fear."
>
> Bhagavad Gita (2,40)

The Future of Astrology Yoga

The future of Astrology Yoga lies in its past. The ancient sister sciences of yoga and astrology were originally taught, learned and employed together to cover all aspects of human life.

The care of the physical body and living a healthy lifestyle was accomplished through the dietary and hygienic guidelines given by yoga. Similarly, developing our potentials and accomplishing our life's purpose are also realized through the practices of yoga.

The development of the subtle, or astral, body and living in accordance with the laws of time was the purpose of astrology, or Jyotish. Recognizing and organizing our karmic potentials, as well as understanding the unfolding of our life's purpose, is accomplished through the study of astrology and our birth chart.

If we practice yoga without understanding the teachings of astrology, the timing and the types of our practices may not be appropriate or effective. And if we practice astrology without the support of yoga, we can remain trapped in the cycles of time. When understood and practiced together, yoga and astrology allow us to powerfully manifest proper vitality, right karmic actions, and spiritual intent.

The Vedic birth chart is likened to the DNA of the soul, and Yoga Astrology can help unlock your karmic code. As this code unfolds through life, astrology helps with the timing of events and the use of therapeutic measures to optimize your actions.

And ultimately the practice of yoga allows you to go beyond the influences of your karma. Sadhana, a daily spiritual yoga practice, changes everything – it can "re-write" your birth chart and take you to the destiny promised therein.

The future of Astrology Yoga is to reclaim and utilize both these powerful systems of knowledge and so achieve our highest potential as spiritual beings having a human experience.

"You are the master of your destiny.
You are the prediction of your horoscope.
You are the leader of your day.
You are the light of your life."

Yogi Bhajan

About the Author

Mehtab Benton is a certified Vedic astrologer and graduate of the American College of Vedic Astrology. He has mentored students in the practice of Vedic Astrology and has given astrological readings and consultations to individuals and yoga practitioners around the world. He has taught yoga since 1974 and has trained hundreds of yoga teachers in the Hatha and Kundalini Yoga traditions. Mehtab presented one of the first courses in the Western world on Vedic Astrology for yoga teachers and is the author of twelve books, including *Gong Yoga: Healing and Enlightenment through Sound*.

Astrology Yoga Personal Readings
Workshops and Trainings
www.astrologyteacher.com

Mehtab is available for one-on-one personal astrology readings and yoga consultations in person, by phone and through Skype.

Astrology Yoga workshops, trainings and certification programs are available at your location or by distance learning.

A free monthly newsletter is offered through the above website.

About Bookshelf Press

Bookshelf Press is a print and electronic publisher of books on yoga, health, Eastern astrology, and literary works of high imagination.

Bookshelf Press retains all subsidiary rights for its books. Rights are available through the publisher for foreign editions and other media adaptations.

Wholesale and retail orders are available directly from the publisher.

www.bookshelfpress.com

Undying Moon

The Adventures of Chandra Kane

A Yoga Fantasy for Children and Young Adults

Undying Moon is a novel with a 15-year old heroine who is an accomplished yogini with a mysterious past. Written for ages 11-17 as well as adults, the novel follows the fantastic adventures on Chandra Kane who sets out to solve the mystery of her past and her own identity.

Chandra Kane is a teenager who has a parrot that quotes Shakespeare, a living corpse that hides under her bed, and a pair of magical bracelets that belonged to her dead mother. Her evil clone is seducing her boyfriend and a murderous midget is stalking her girlfriends. Could life be any weirder for a fifteen year-old girl? Absolutely, because Chandra Kane is about to celebrate her one-hundredth birthday!

A fantasy adventure novel set in the present world, Undying Moon features an Indian-Asian girl as its heroine who must solve the mystery of her missing life in order to save the world. Her best friends are Di Valentine, a teen pageant queen and martial artist, and Nastia Hicks, an African-American girl and Junior Olympic gymnast.

The underlying themes of friendships, death, self-belief, and emerging sexuality take this debut novel by Raveyn Knight beyond an ordinary teen reading experience as it wrestles with the question what it means to be yourself, regardless of your age.

"It is fascinating to spend time with a character who keeps her inner calm in every situation, even when she has lost her family, her past, and even her identity. What yoga practice can apparently give you is a capacity to carry your truth and calm through any situation, be yourself, and be at home anywhere. FIVE STARS!"

Available from Bookshelf Press and all major booksellers.

www.bookshelfpress.com

Gong Yoga
Healing and Enlightenment Through Sound

Mehtab Benton
Author of Astrology Yoga

Gong Yoga is the first comprehensive book on practicing and teaching yoga with the sound of the gong. You will learn about the origin, history and use of the gong for yoga and meditation as well as its current therapeutic applications for healing and transformation.

The book contains a step-by-step training guide to teach you how to play the gong through a series of practice sessions. You will learn the basic techniques to play the gong as well as advanced techniques to create your own gong playing sessions. You will learn how to structure gong yoga classes and gong yoga therapy sessions for your students and clients.

A comprehensive chapter on Yoga and the Gong describes the chakras, the major energy channels of the body (the nadis), and the five sheaths of existence (the koshas), that are key to understanding how the gong integrates with the practice of yoga. Special sections explain the use of Kundalini Yoga mantras for playing the gong, how to select and care for your gong and additional resources to develop your skills.

Written by a long-time yoga teacher and international trainer of students and therapists in the art of playing the gong for meditation and healing.

"Information on how to play the gong and the spiritual aspects of the sound of the gong are difficult to find. **GONG YOGA** *is a wonderful introduction to all aspects of the gong and the yoga that is associated with it. The interesting history of the gong, its uses in Western and Eastern music, how to play it and the gong's effects on the body's energetic system are all discussed. FIVE STARS!"*

Available from Bookshelf Press and all major booksellers.

www.bookshelfpress.com

www.ingramcontent.com/pod-product-compliance
Lightning Source LLC
Chambersburg PA
CBHW052100280426
43673CB00070B/28